Constance Gale

San Diego Christian College
2100 Greenfield Drive
El Cajon, CA 92019

D0220401

Sound Ways of Knowing

780.712
B274s

Sound Ways of Knowing
Music in the Interdisciplinary Curriculum

JANET R. BARRETT
CLAIRE W. McCOY
KARI K. VEBLEN

SCHIRMER

THOMSON LEARNING

Australia • Canada • Mexico • Singapore • Spain • United Kingdom • United States

Copyright © 1997 by Janet R. Barrett, Claire W. McCoy, and Kari K. Veblen

All rights reserved. No part of this book may be reproduced or transmitted in any form or by any means, electronic or mechanical, including photocopying, recording, or by any information storage and retrieval system, without permission in writing from the Publisher.

**Schirmer is an imprint of Wadsworth, a division of Thomson Learning, Inc.
Thomson Learning™ is a trademark used herein under license.**

Library of Congress Catalog Number: 97-19813

Printed in the United States of America

Printing number

2   3   4   5   6   7   8   9   10

Copyright notices and permissions for reproduced material appear on pages 327–28

Library of Congress Cataloging-in-Publication Data

Barrett, Janet R.
    Sound ways of knowing : music in the interdisciplinary curriculum / Janet R. Barrett.
      p.   cm.
    Includes bibliographical references and index.
    ISBN: 0-534-25088-2
    1. School music—Instruction and study. 2. Interdisciplinary approach in education.
    I. McCoy, Claire W.   II. Veblen, Kari K.   III. Title.
    MT10.B3 1997
    780'.71'2—dc21   97-19813
                                                CIP
                                              MN

This paper meets the requirements of ANIS/NISO Z39.48–1992 (Permanence of Paper).

To my family, Mark, Alex, and Paige, with gratitude for their love and encouragement.

JRB

To Celia and David, with thanks for their patient and loving support.

CWM

To the memory of James Robert McKinty, who loved music and knowledge, and with appreciation to Brian Stuart Yandell for his encouragement and support.

KKV

TABLE OF CONTENTS

PREFACE

Sound Ways of Knowing: Music in the Interdisciplinary Curriculum presents a vision for teaching and learning in which the potent power of music is integrated throughout the curriculum. Through lessons that feature the study of music along with history, cultures, and the other arts, *Sound Ways of Knowing* shows how music specialists, classroom teachers, and other arts specialists collaborate to plan rich and multifaceted learning experiences for elementary and secondary students.

Sound Ways of Knowing is a word play on the double meaning of *sound.* The most obvious meaning, of course, is the musical one. We propose that music brings us to a fuller understanding of ourselves and the world in which we live. Music is a reflection of the expressive impulse; sound organized as music is a window to thought and feeling, history and culture, the individual and society. *Sound* also connotes strength, validity, and substance, as in *sound* judgment or *sound* reasoning. In this sense, we place music at the fundamental center of school programs, to be addressed by teachers and students as a curricular imperative for a comprehensive education.

In most schools, specialists provide instruction in the discipline of music based on a well-defined, sequential curriculum. Such instruction is essential to students' development of music concepts and skills. But, as the subtitle of this book, *Music in the Interdisciplinary Curriculum,* implies, there are also sound connections to be made between music and other disciplines within the curriculum. Because music is inextricably linked with artistic expression, history, and culture, other disciplines within the curriculum that are also concerned with these broad concepts—such as language, art, dance, theater, and social studies—may be the most logical areas with which to forge interdisciplinary connections. In this book we focus on ways that the study of music can enhance students' understanding of artistic expression, history, and culture, and, conversely, how the study of artistic expression, history, and culture can enhance understanding of music. While other connections are possible—the relationship of rhythmic concepts to mathematics, for example—we feel that the study of artistic expression, history, and culture afford the greatest potential for teachers and students to make meaningful, organic connections.

This book was written for anyone who might participate in making these connections for students, including music specialists, other arts specialists, and classroom teachers (both preservice and in-service); arts supervisors; curriculum coordinators; and principals. The ideas and materials in this book have been field-tested in several college courses and in-service workshops.

Interactive Exercises

Exercises and activities appear throughout the text to help you engage with and make sense of the ideas we present. Your responses to these exercises and activities are critical to the development of your own ideas and practices for interdisciplinary teaching. Exercises encourage you to apply the central ideas introduced in the chapters to your own experience.

Classroom Focus

Throughout the book you will hear the voices of teachers: preservice teachers, music specialists, other arts specialists, and classroom teachers. Often, these voices are those of real people, but sometimes they reflect composites of teachers with whom we have worked. You will consider how ideas for interdisciplinary teaching are born, how they grow and evolve as a result of collaboration, and how they influence the intellectual and social climate of a school. You will see illustrations of the complementary roles that music specialists and classroom teachers play in planning and teaching interdisciplinary lessons. **Scenarios** use classroom situations to introduce, connect, or illustrate discussions of important concepts and issues in the chapter.

Relationships between Theory and Practice

Some of the chapters in this book provide an overview of general principles that serve as a foundation for developing interdisciplinary curricula, especially as they relate to artistic expression, history, and culture. Lesson plans in Chapter 7 explore connections between music and poetry, literature, art, and movement. Three chapters provide in-depth examinations of interdisciplinary approaches to specific topics, including the study of the Renaissance (Chapter 9), the American Civil War (Chapter 10), and the music and culture of Mexico (Chapter 12).

Fully scripted **lesson plans** are included in these chapters as models for classroom use. One such lesson features a side-by-side commentary on the rationale for each step of the lesson plan, and another contrasts a basic version of a lesson with a version that is enhanced by more careful attention to cultural authenticity. Sections within the lesson plans titled **Enhancing the Understanding of Context** provide descriptions of historical background and cultural practices for teachers' reference; information in these sections can also be provided to students as appropriate to their level of comprehension. Please note that while the term "lesson" may imply to some an educational experience limited to a single block of time, our lessons sometimes extend over a period of days or weeks.

Although the lessons in this book can be taught as presented, we include them primarily as models and illustrations of interdisciplinary planning. Because there are many paths that the pursuit of a particular idea could follow—more than can be explored within a single lesson—we also include ideas for extending the lessons that can serve as springboards for your own planning and development. Most of the lesson plans we present are designed for elementary and middle school students, but many could also be adapted for use with high school students.

Other features include **Strategies,** which provide guidelines and techniques for you to consider as you implement lessons or curricular projects of your own design. Sections titled **Controversy in the Curriculum** invite you to consider provocative issues in the selection of content that require the exercise of professional judgment.

Organization

If you read this book from start to finish, you will move from discussions of general principles to their applications in interdisciplinary planning. This approach might be most appropriate if you already have some experience with designing curricula or interdisciplinary lessons. If you have not, you may find it helpful to read some of the application chapters first to provide a context for the discussion of those general principles.

The first chapter, "Music in Our Lives," encourages you to examine the role of music in personal and communal experience, inviting your reactions and reflections in the form of a personal essay. The second chapter, "Music and the Interdisciplinary Curriculum," provides a more theoretical overview of the principles and practices of curriculum design, a discussion that is extended to issues of integrity in interdisciplinary work raised in Chapter 3. Chapter 4, "Getting to Know a Work of Art," describes the processes of learning new works before starting to design curriculum based on those works. Chapters 5 and 6 establish a foundation for interdisciplinary experiences in the arts by emphasizing the similarities and differences between and among art, music, theater, dance, and literature. The *facets model,* a planning tool for exploring artworks in depth, is introduced in these chapters and serves as the organizing structure for the remainder of the book.

The lessons in Chapter 7 show how you might use the facets model to expand germinal ideas into fully developed experiences. Chapters 8 and

11 raise issues and possibilities for exploring music's role in historical and cultural studies, which take curricular shape in Chapters 9, 10, and 12 through the study of the Renaissance, the American Civil War, and Mexico. These comprehensive chapters feature scenarios, discussions of instructional issues, and detailed lesson plans for interdisciplinary experiences. Finally, the last chapter portrays the creative intellectual engagement of teachers as they exercise curricular imagination.

ACKNOWLEDGMENTS

We wish to thank many individuals who contributed to this book and supported our work during its development and production. Colleagues who consulted with us and freely contributed their expertise include Daniel García Blanco, Karen Bradley, David J. Elliott, Paul Haack, James Hainlen, Lawrence Kaptain, William and Susan Kephart, Dane Kusic, Jesse and Sandra Lilligren, Scott Lowery, Ronald McCurdy, Fernando Meza, Pam Paulsen, Nancy Rasmussen, Roger Revell, Josh Ryan, Daniel Sheehy, Tom Solomon, David Tovey, and Brian Yandell. We are grateful to those who led us to helpful resources, including George Ferencz, Ramona Holmes, Geraldine Laudati, James McKinty, Brian Miller, Steven Sundell, and Ellen Zwilich. We would also like to acknowledge Lawrence Aynesmith, Steven Dast, Jon Lahann, Mitch Rosenfelt, Scott Ruffing, Erin Stapleton-Corcoran, and Diane Walder, who assisted in the production of materials used in the book.

For their useful and insightful reviews of the manuscript, we wish to thank Mary Hookey, Nipissing University; Jan McCrary, Ohio State University; Janice Smith, Asa Adams Elementary School; Judy Svengalis, Des Moines Public Schools; and Ellen McCullough-Brabson, University of New Mexico.

We are especially grateful to students in our undergraduate and graduate courses, whose enthusiasm for interdisciplinary work and thought-provoking questions have influenced and inspired our thinking. Special thanks to those students who have granted permission to use or describe class projects or journal entries as examples throughout the book: Kara Alt, Jeff Behling, Brett Brown, Joanna Cortright, Beth Herrendeen, Ruzica Jovanovic, Peter Kahl, Ellen Luchsinger, Kristin Martin, Jenine Meunier, Carla Moreña, and Donald Pochmara.

We express our appreciation to our photographer, Sandra Norstrom, and the teachers and children at three schools who graciously opened their classrooms to us: Tom Ryan of Purdy Elementary School in Fort Atkinson, Wis. (Rick Brietze, principal); Jane LeFevre of Milton West Elementary, Milton, Wis. (Carol Meland, principal); and Marilyn White and Vicki Samolyk of Elm Creative Arts School, Milwaukee, Wis. (Darrel Jacobs, principal). Thanks also to Shawn Kolles and Daniel Sheehy for photographs used in Chapter 12.

We extend our appreciation to Dean Karen Boubel of the College of Arts and Communication at the University of Wisconsin-Whitewater for well-timed research support for Janet Barrett in the fall semester of 1995.

We are grateful to our editor, Jill Lectka, of Schirmer Books, for her skill and expertise, and also to Andrew Libby, production supervisor, and to Andrew Ambraziejus, managing editor of Macmillan Library Reference, for guiding the manuscript to its final form.

chapter 1

MUSIC IN OUR LIVES

Imagine that a friend, who is taking a film class, needs a willing subject for a biographical documentary. Thinking that this is your only chance for stardom, you agree. Your friend asks you to assemble artifacts that will document who you are and the experiences that have shaped your life. In preparation for the filming, you gather scrapbooks of photographs and clippings, diaries, personal correspondence, diplomas, yearbooks, home movies and videos, treasured objects, and souvenirs. Your friend comes to your house, video camera in hand, and spends several hours filming as you tell your life story.

When you go to preview the film, you're curious and a bit apprehensive about the way the film will portray your life. As the film rolls, you realize that the music your friend has chosen for the soundtrack is all wrong—it has nothing to do with you. An important aspect of your identity, your music, is missing.

"Like your fingerprints, your signature, and your voice, your choices of music and the ways you relate to music are plural and interconnected in a pattern that is all yours, an 'idioculture' or idiosyncratic culture in sound" (Crafts, Cavicchi, & Keil, 1993, p. 2). The Greek word *idios* means "one's own." Your own musical world, or "idioculture," is like no one else's. Music is a constant presence in your life, although you may not be conscious of the depth and breadth of your musical experience. Most of us rarely take time to reflect on the array of music in our lives and the way our interactions with music shape our identity.

You may be wondering what a discussion of your own personal musical world has to do with the role of music in the interdisciplinary curriculum, the subject of this book. Have you thought about how your own music background, with its diversity of interests and experiences, can become a source of ideas for planning educational experiences for students? Have you considered that within a school community there are students and teachers whose musical worlds intersect in some way—through shared interests in a particular style of music, performer, or composer? There may be unique components of those musical worlds as well, as individuals hold special interests, knowledge, or expertise in a particular type of music. These interests, in all their richness, may be the starting points for planning imaginative lessons that link music with the study of culture, history, and expression. Sometimes individuals undervalue what their musical worlds have to offer to the classroom. As a first step toward recognizing the extent of your musical world, with its implications for connecting with the curriculum, we suggest you take time to engage in the following exercise.

Examining Personal Musical Experience

The Circles Exercise, Part 1

The purpose of this exercise is to think about your personal musical experiences and their impact in your life. On an unlined sheet of paper, draw circles to show different pools of musical activity in your personal history: your "music circles" diagram. The categories listed below may be helpful to get you started, but feel free to add additional categories to the list. Label each circle with the category title; inside each circle, jot down the titles or short descriptions of the music that fits within the category. Because some of these circles may be related in time or place, you may wish to make them appear close together or overlapping on your diagram. Others may stand alone as singular events.

- Early memories—songs you remember being sung to you as a child

- Songs you recall singing in school

- Musical works you have performed

- Songs you can sing or pieces you can play entirely from memory

- Recordings you would not want to live without

- Your least favorite music examples

- Music you have heard or performed in the past 24 hours

- Music you have taught (or love to teach) to others

- Music that puzzles, intrigues, or challenges you

- Hidden pleasures—what others might be surprised to know about your tastes

When you have completed drawing and labeling your circles, contemplate what they reveal about your music interests and involvement. In what ways do these circles reflect the influences of the time and place you were born, places you've lived, and significant people in your life?

Making Sense of Musical Experience

Three sets of circles representing the music idiocultures of three preservice teachers are provided to illustrate how music backgrounds can serve as a foundation for curriculum planning. In her circles (Figure 1.1), Kara, a preservice elementary teacher, recalls the influence of her family, school experience, and travel, and describes her current involvement with music. Another preservice elementary/middle school teacher, Brett, represents his personal history by drawing arrows to show the path of his music development and changes in taste from the songs his parents sang to him to his rediscovery of Native American music, a part of his cultural heritage (Figure 1.2). Don, a preservice music teacher (Figure 1.3), spends a great deal of time performing music as well as listening to it. Because music is both a personal source of satisfaction and the focus of his professional career, Don's circles show the intensity of his involvement with music.

What do these circles reveal? They suggest some of the various roles that music may play in one's life—for relaxation, for recreation, as a part of family and religious rituals, as a cultural expression, as a life's work. They may also reveal how one interacts with music through listening, performing, and valuing musical works. The circles can also show the breadth and variety of one's musical repertoire—children's songs, rock and roll, folk music of particular cultures, "classical" compositions, jazz, country music, reggae, music of the Renaissance, and Broadway tunes.

Figure 1.1
Kara's Music Circles

Figure 1.2
Brett's Music Circles

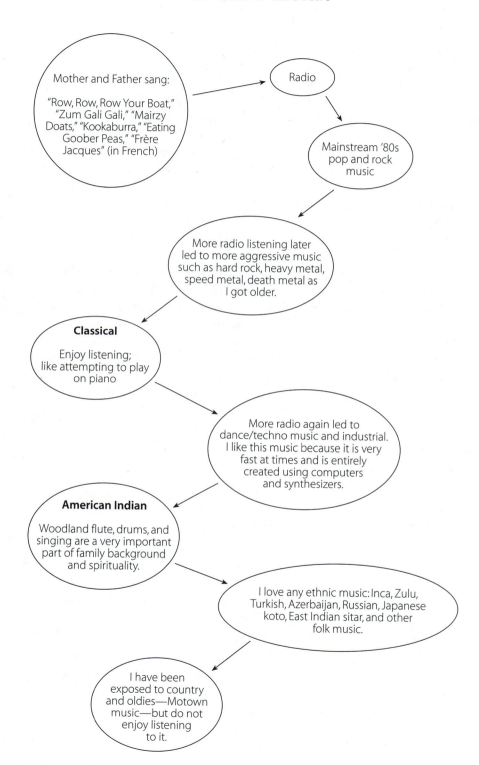

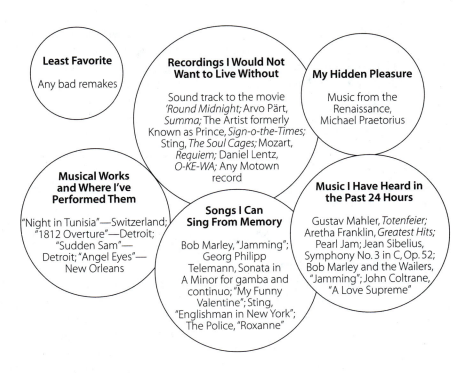

Figure 1.3
Don's Music Circles

Least Favorite

Any bad remakes

Recordings I Would Not Want to Live Without

Sound track to the movie *'Round Midnight;* Arvo Pärt, *Summa;* The Artist formerly Known as Prince, *Sign-o-the-Times;* Sting, *The Soul Cages;* Mozart, *Requiem;* Daniel Lentz, *O-KE-WA;* Any Motown record

My Hidden Pleasure

Music from the Renaissance, Michael Praetorius

Musical Works and Where I've Performed Them

"Night in Tunisia"—Switzerland; "1812 Overture"—Detroit; "Sudden Sam"— Detroit; "Angel Eyes"— New Orleans

Songs I Can Sing From Memory

Bob Marley, "Jamming"; Georg Philipp Telemann, Sonata in A Minor for gamba and continuo; "My Funny Valentine"; Sting, "Englishman in New York"; The Police, "Roxanne"

Music I Have Heard in the Past 24 Hours

Gustav Mahler, *Totenfeier;* Aretha Franklin, *Greatest Hits;* Pearl Jam; Jean Sibelius, Symphony No. 3 in C, Op. 52; Bob Marley and the Wailers, "Jamming"; John Coltrane, "A Love Supreme"

Even the least favorite styles and types of music are an indication of strongly held preferences and personal opinions.

Kara's early musical experiences may be an important source of insight into her work with elementary-aged students. She may remember the impact of her early musical experiences as she encourages the children in her classroom to develop their own music interests. The breadth of Brett's interest and participation in music may be expressed in many ways, as his eclectic tastes in contemporary popular music may intersect with the musical interests of his students. His wide-ranging involvement with the musics of many cultures, manifested in a listening repertoire that ranges from music of the Incas to the East Indian sitar, and his performance of Native American flute and drum music, may enable him to relate to students of diverse backgrounds. Brett may serve as a model of openness to many types of music expression for students whose music worlds are more limited than his. Don's intense engagement in music, which prompted him to become a music specialist, will be invaluable as he prepares to teach students of varied ages and levels of skill, and possibly even those with interest in music as a career. Don also enjoys listening to music of diverse styles and eras, spanning from 500 years ago to the present. The backgrounds, interests, and professional goals of Kara, Brett, and Don prepare them to bring music into students' lives in different and complementary ways.

As we have explored this idea of music idiocultures with students in our classes, we have been intrigued and informed by what we have discovered. Our students' ethnic and cultural heritages—Serbian, Hmong, Norwegian, Jamaican, Polish, Native American—have generated interest in music traditions new to us and to their classmates. Other students' circles revealed special areas of expertise, such as the music of the Civil War, the blues, and minimalism, which became the basis for creative lesson plans. We've also learned from students who have shared music examples drawn from extensive CD collections, performed a repertoire of folk dances from family traditions, or acquired an assortment of unusual instruments while traveling.

Examining the Musical Experience of Others

The Circles Exercise, Part 2

If you could look at the circles of experience that students in elementary, middle, or high school might draw, what would you learn about their idiocultures? Try the circles exercise with an entire class or with individual students. What do their circles reveal about the breadth and depth of their musical involvement? Compare your circles with theirs. Are there any commonalities? What realms of experience and types of music are different than your own? We know that personal interest plays an important role in learning. How could you use your understanding of students' musical worlds to make learning more meaningful for them?

As you conduct this exercise, you may change your expectations about the preferences of students. Young children are generally open to a range of musical styles and genres. As children approach adolescence, however, their tastes become more narrow and homogeneous (LeBlanc, Sims, Siivola, & Obert, 1996; May, 1985). But are those tastes really as homogeneous as adults perceive them to be? Adolescents' preferences tend to be lumped into the global category "popular music," as if the entire age group shared a music monoculture. When adults have asked adolescents to sketch their music circles, they have often been amazed at the degree to which adolescents can detect subtle nuances among substyles within popular music.

After adolescence, music preferences may begin to broaden with age and experience. When Julie, a music teacher in her 30s, compared her music circles with those of her students, she became more aware of how her preferences had changed over time: "As I get older, my musical interests and tastes move farther from Pop and Rock, and closer to music from other cultures as well as folk music. As a music teacher, your role is to provide musical experiences for your students that lay a good foundation for their 'tapestry of experience.'"

In this chapter, you have been encouraged to examine your music background, preferences, and formative experiences. The insights you gain from this exercise may reveal (a) what you consider to be "good" music, (b) the pool of musics from which you may be inclined to draw examples for the classroom, and (c) the modes in which you feel comfortable interacting with music. When you compared the music circles of students with your own, did you find more intersections or contrasts? The intersections among your sets of circles can point to comfort zones from which you can launch into explorations of less familiar music. At first, the contrasts between your sets of circles may appear too great to find that comfortable common ground. The contrasts, however, may provide an opportunity to explore the diversity of music knowledge and skills that are present in any classroom. They can point to student expertise and interests on which you can build to enrich the learning environment.

In Chapter 2, our attention turns from music in our personal lives to music in the curriculum. We address how music is an essential component of school experience and discuss the roles of classroom teachers and music specialists in providing meaningful and imaginative musical experiences for students.

REFERENCES

Crafts, S. D., Cavicchi, D., & Keil, C. (1993). *My music*. Hanover, N.H.: Wesleyan University Press.

LeBlanc, A., Sims, W. L., Siivola, C., & Obert, M. (1996). Music style preferences of different age listeners. *Journal of Research in Music Education* 44:49–59.

May, W. V. (1985). Musical style preferences and aural discrimination of primary grade school children. *Journal of Research in Music Education* 33:7–22.

chapter 2

MUSIC AND THE
INTERDISCIPLINARY CURRICULUM

Visualize a scene set in the days of the Roman Empire, conjuring up individuals standing in small horse-drawn, two-wheeled carts, poised for the race of their lives. Just before the race begins, a stirring fanfare is heard, which signals the horses and riders to run toward the distant horizon with determination and courage. Each driver directs the horses and guides the cart through the smoothest parts of the terrain, leaving impressions of the chariot's wheels in the ground to mark the path of the journey. The word for the vehicle you are imagining is *curricle,* and the course on which the chariot runs is called the *curriculum* (*Compact Edition of the Oxford English Dictionary,* 1971, p. 1271). Curriculum, the word we use so frequently in education to describe the scope and sequence of study, is quite literally a path or course of action.

For purposes of illustration, we could suppose that the terrain represents the totality of human experience and the chariots represent various forms of that experience: social, political, scientific/technological, economic, cultural, and aesthetic. Or, to parallel the way those forms are addressed as school subjects and disciplines, we could imagine the chariots as music, art, dance, literature, theater, history, science, mathematics, language, physical education, or geography. Since we're already taking liberties with this scene, let's turn our attention to the drivers. The charioteers in these vehicles feel a strong obligation to find the most direct and expeditious routes to follow. They have traveled this way before, so they are well acquainted with the terrain. Sometimes chariots travel alongside one another in parallel motion; at other times, the paths intersect.

Transform the imagery in this visualization to set the stage for what is to come. Suspend the breakneck pace of the drivers and watch them pull back on the reins. Change the tempo and character of your imagined scene from a competitive race to a more relaxed and observant journey. At this calmer pace, the drivers begin to notice interesting features of the terrain that were previously blurred and vague. In time, the drivers start to entertain notions of traveling toward different inviting vistas, even though the paths are less well traveled and are in need of clearing. At a rest stop, after a welcomed stretch of the legs and some water for the horses, several drivers discuss the possibilities of alternate paths and agree to embark together on an exploration toward new destinations.

The curriculum is both the terrain and the journey combined, or, in educational terms, a blend of content (knowledge and understanding) and process (teaching and learning). Further, the curriculum takes on meaning because it is designed for and takes place in particular settings (the school context and community). Teachers, charged with the responsibility to make informed decisions about content and process, articulate goals and chart courses of action in the form of educational experiences. The path of the curriculum is not a straight-and-narrow race toward the horizon, however. A curricular course of action may be adjusted and redesigned as teachers encourage and accommodate student interests. Particular features of the educational setting—schedules, resources, policies—also influence the curriculum by offering both opportunities and constraints for action. Of particular interest to this chapter are the points at which teachers decide to set out in new and interesting directions, especially when they consider how music and other subject areas can be brought together in meaningful ways.

In this chapter, we address central questions and issues related to curriculum work of teachers and the role of music in interdisciplinary study. These central questions include:

~ What is curriculum work and what views of knowledge are expressed in teachers' curricular beliefs and practices?

~ What is meant by a disciplinary or interdisciplinary focus toward the curriculum?

~ Why should music be considered an integral part of the general curriculum?

~ Why should disciplines in addition to music be featured as integral components of the music curriculum?

~ How do current curricular practices reflect various orientations toward music in the curriculum?

~ What are the characteristics of teachers' work when they create exemplary interdisciplinary curricula?

The Questions of Curriculum

The term *curriculum* is used in many ways and contexts by participants in the educational process. Although the chariot metaphor begins to address the defining question "What is curriculum?" we might also productively ask "Where is the curriculum?" or "Where does the curriculum reside?" From the following list of possible locations, which description most closely matches your typical or customary view of the curriculum?

~ The goals and standards written and endorsed by professional associations, teams of teachers, or policy-making agencies such as state departments of instruction or accrediting bodies

~ The manuals, outlines, handbooks, teacher editions, student textbooks, and curriculum guides that organize the scope (what is to be included) and sequence (the progression or order) of crucial ideas, concepts, and topics

~ The lesson plans (written and enacted) that teachers design as they prepare and direct educational experiences

~ The experiences of students in classrooms as they come into contact with activities, materials, ideas, influential adults, and peers in order to acquire skills and understanding

~ The expectations for learning held by parents, administrators, and members of the school community

~ The tangible forms of evidence that point to the strengths of a school program, such as the accomplishments and performance of graduates, test scores, and public recognition for the work of students and teachers

~ The overall plan of studies including all of the courses, course content, activities, and events that mark a student's progression from elementary to middle to high school, often followed by college and university programs

~ The lasting, long-term effects and enduring impressions of school experience—what we take with us long after the immediate course, class, or lesson ends

The curriculum can be represented in many forms—through actions in classrooms, documents, articulated beliefs, intentions, and memories. Many voices enter into the conversation about curriculum as they discuss what schools should teach and what students should know and be able to do in order to grow and thrive as individuals and as members of a larger community. You may have noticed that hardly a day passes without some public debate in newspaper reports, journal articles, features, and interviews in broadcast media over the nature and purposes of the curriculum. The study of curriculum—its principles, content, processes, products, values, goals, participants, and dilemmas—captivates the attention of critics of the educational process as well as teachers, administrators, and parents (who often function as critics, too). Critics point out the beliefs and assumptions that many of us have begun to take for granted by calling them into question. If we take the criticism seriously, we wrestle with the questions, brush the dust from our assumptions, and engage in curriculum inquiry.

At the heart of these representations, conversations, and debates is an elegant and simple idea: The curriculum becomes real through the work teachers and students do in pursuit of understanding, defined by Gardner and Boix-Mansilla as "the capacity to use current knowledge, concepts, and skills to illuminate new problems or unanticipated issues" (Gardner & Boix-Mansilla, 1994, p. 200). Teachers have primary stewardship over the nature and character of this work; their intellectual and personal energies are directed toward the creation and sustenance of vibrant and compelling environments for learning. Curriculum documents and standards developed by others are useful as general outlines or descriptions of possible choices, helping to shape our broad conceptions and purposes with greater clarity. But teachers—aware of their own interests, needs, and talents and of how these attributes complement the interests, needs, and talents of students—create plans for learning to suit the particular characteristics of school communities. Sizer (1985) compares curriculum making to the work of an artisan: "The construction of the subject matter of any curriculum is a task of cabinet making, not of prefab carpentry. The pieces *have* to fit the conditions peculiar to each school. Master plans for cities, states, and the nation that standardize instruction are certain to be inefficient: no one set of procedures can serve most students well" (p. 115).

Teachers design, invent, implement, assess, and critique the curriculum in never-ending cycles of action and reflection. To do so, they must operate from their own conceptions of what curriculum work entails and what the curriculum is. An individual teacher's view of the curriculum is contextually bound and dependent upon that person's values, past experiences, and theories of "how the world works." This explains why you might hear such diverse and almost contradictory views of curriculum when talking with teachers. Epistemology, a branch of philosophy concerned with the nature, forms, and limitations of human knowledge, addresses general metaphors and systems of thought. For example, contrast a view of knowledge as fixed and static (what we know about a subject has already been discovered and sequentially arranged; the primary task of the learner is to acquire that clearly defined structure of knowledge) with a view of knowledge as dynamic and fluid (what we know about a subject is constantly being defined, expanded, and redefined; learners have to make sense of this rich but ill-defined universe of knowledge from their own perspectives). In the first view, the learner's mind is a container to be filled with information; in the second, the learner actively builds a system of new understanding using available information. These views influence the way we think about knowledge in art forms and the way we design educational experience with artworks[1] (Parsons & Blocker, 1993).

Kliebard (1989) reminds us that for the products and processes of curriculum planning and evaluation to be valid, we must critically examine our assumptions and beliefs about the nature of educational experience. This will help us to clarify our personal theories of knowledge and to acknowledge the way those theories are revealed in daily classroom practice. Curriculum inquiry challenges us to make informed choices about goals for our classrooms while exercising our critical and creative powers. The time we spend asking questions about the purposes of a new curricular initiative may be more important to the final outcomes than the nuts-and-bolts tasks of writing objectives, lesson plans, and long-range sequences. Kliebard identifies four primary areas for curriculum inquiry: "why certain things should be taught, who should get what knowledge, what rules should govern teaching school subjects, and how the components of the curriculum should be interrelated." He continues: "Curriculum development requires sophistication, judgment, and intelligence and only secondarily technical skill" (p. 5).

The components of the curriculum and their relationships are addressed in the next section of this chapter. But first, let's take a tour of a typical school setting to see what a classroom can tell us about the curriculum.

Take a Tour . . .

It can be difficult to find an elementary or middle school that is empty by 5:00 or 5:30 because many teachers prepare for the next day's activities after the school buses depart and committee meetings end. But let's assume that we can find a school where we are free to take an uninterrupted stroll through classrooms and wander through the colorful spaces.

In a cheerful, well-organized fifth-grade classroom, we start with the ubiquitous schedule written on a white marker board, the more contemporary counterpart of the classic chalkboard. Here, the entire day is partitioned into smaller chunks of time. Although the schedule is not the same every day, we find we have stumbled upon a day of the week when some subjects, the "specials," are grouped together to allow classroom teachers a block of joint planning time with other teachers in their grade-level teams.

Opening	8:15–8:30
Reading	8:30–9:45
Recess	9:45–10:00
Math	10:00–11:15
Circle	11:15–11:30
Lunch	11:30–12:00
Recess	12:00–12:15
Specials:	
Music	12:15–12:45
P.E.	12:45–1:15
Art	1:15–2:15
Library	2:15–2:45
Journals	2:45–3:00

We know this particular schedule doesn't reflect the entire program because we find folders in student cubicles marked "Science," "Social Studies," and "Health" along with the subjects listed for this particular day. Letters neatly stacked beside the cubicles are ready to send home to parents, with checklists of school subjects to discuss with the teacher at the upcoming parent-teacher conferences.

The music room is down the hall and easy to spot from the telltale staff-and-treble-clef banner across the door. Since no one is around, you succumb to temptation, pick up a pair of mallets, and improvise on the xylophone for a minute. The music teacher's weekly schedule is posted near the desk at the back of the room, with the names of 9 or 10 teachers per day written in the grid to correspond to the parade of 30-minute classes. This afternoon's schedule looked like this: 5C—Hutton; 5B—Stein; 3A—Naughton; 3B—Ehly; 4D—Clark; Kindergarten—Kolarik. Under a border of composers' portraits, you notice samples of listening maps created by students of different grade levels and photographs from the last all-school program. Rows and rows of smiling singers show full or partial sets of front teeth.

Finally, you peek into the teachers' workroom/lounge where notices of upcoming in-service sessions and workshops are posted above the photocopier to catch the attention of teachers: "Connecting the Curriculum through Whole Language," "Assessing the Integrated Curriculum," and "Arts across the Curriculum."

Disciplinary and Interdisciplinary Curricula

Can you recall an instance from your own school experience when several ideas that seemed unrelated suddenly fell into place, forming a larger pattern that you had never considered before? Do you remember how it felt to make such a satisfying connection? Do you recall what circumstances led up to the new understanding? This natural sense-making tendency to connect, relate, associate, and join features of experience is a hallmark of a capable learner. The cultivation of this sense-making tendency is one of the primary occupations of teachers. In the broadest sense, such connections constitute the fundamental rationale for interdisciplinary study in schools.

Few would argue against such connections. Teachers celebrate and fondly recall moments when the "lightbulb goes on." But how does the way a school is organized or the way the curriculum is structured make these connections more or less likely? In the scenario above, the school's organization seems to partition school subjects by time of day or week, location within the building, and teacher. It would be easy to assume that these partitions make it difficult for students to form powerful connections that cross disciplinary boundaries. But that assumption does not necessarily hold true if teachers keep these questions in mind as they design educational programs: How can schools emphasize meaningful relationships among forms of knowledge? How can students be encouraged to see the big picture and address interdependent, complex problems? Perkins (1992) suggests that if these connections are not explicitly addressed by the curriculum, teachers should not assume that they will spontaneously occur in the thinking of students. "Knowledge," he cautions, "does not pop up reliably" (p. 49).

"The intellectual world is full of disciplines, subdisciplines, and disciplinary combinations simply because there are so many ways to look at things," Hope reminds us (1994, p. 39). In elementary and middle schools, disciplines often come packaged in the form of school subjects. (Some of these subjects, like the "social studies," are already labeled in an interdisciplinary fashion.) Each discipline or school subject has its own central concepts, vocabulary, treasured examples, key figures, traditions, problems, and forms of experience. These conventional categories are useful to help us impose order on the world and on the school day, as well. But these disciplines and categories of knowledge can also cloud our perceptions by separating what could be related.

Most elementary and some middle-school teachers identify strongly with their chosen affiliation as curriculum generalists (the "classroom teacher" whose professional preparation features a broad range of subjects) or as curriculum specialists (such as music, art, dance, physical education, or theater teachers whose teacher education program looks quite different from that of the generalists). In this book, we argue that students' educational experiences are strengthened when both generalists and specialists attend to the potential of disciplines within the curriculum to connect and cohere. For interdisciplinary understanding to flourish, teachers must share a collective responsibility for and commitment to integrated forms of study.

Creative curriculum design requires effort, creativity, insight, and desire. The rewards must be worth the hefty personal and professional demands of time and energy for teachers. In the next two sections, we will argue for the benefits of such work from the perspective of both classroom teachers and music specialists.

Examining Musical Connections in Educational Practice

As the day's schedule on the marker board in "Take a Tour" suggests, it is quite common for school subjects to be taught separately in their allotted blocks of time. We know from our own school experience, though, that this compartmentalized schedule doesn't prevent savvy teachers from bringing school subjects together in creative and informative ways.

Think about your own educational history to identify examples when musical subjects have been addressed in other classes or when music classes have been enriched by attention to other subjects. You may also be able to cite examples from your own teaching or the classroom practice of teachers you have observed. One teacher, for example, recalled how his high school English literature teacher had played musical examples from the Elizabethan period that could have been incidental music for Shakespeare's plays. Another teacher described how the study of the music of Spain had enriched her foreign language classes by emphasizing cultural traditions. In a choir setting, an expert on Old English literature and language was invited to the rehearsal to explain and authenticate the pronunciation of a choral text. Another director sent students to the library to find interpretations of Dylan Thomas's poem, "Do Not Go Gentle into That Good Night," a text they were preparing to perform.

In what ways has interdisciplinary study been a part of your school experience? What was the impact of this study on your interests and understanding? What examples of meaningful connections have you noticed in your classroom observations and conversations with other teachers?

Music in the General Classroom

Music is just too powerful to be confined to a certain space in the school, block of time in the day, or particular teacher alone. Classroom teachers who weave music throughout the school day open opportunities for students to make connections to many forms of experience. The fundamental rationale for broadening the scope of topics and activities to include music is this: *A comprehensive general curriculum is incomplete without music, because music is central to personal and shared experience.*

In the first chapter of this book, we encouraged you to investigate the role of music in students' lives by asking students to complete the circles exercise. Their responses testify to the ubiquitous presence of music in students' surroundings and the ways personal identity and experience are marked, deepened, and remembered through music. Students use music as a frame of reference to organize their personal histories. As teachers

Figure 2.1
A Class of Second Graders Playing the Singing Game Charlie over the Ocean. Photo by Sandra Norstrom.

seek ways to honor diverse backgrounds and to acknowledge individual differences, they may ask students to describe their musical interests and activities. This act moves conversation from the general to the specific, and from the impersonal to the personal. When we reveal our favorite performers, songs, or compositions or tell stories about past musical involvement, we discover new avenues for discussion and exploration. Insight into students' musical lives is not limited to verbal responses alone, however. Young children often become engrossed in classroom activities and may spontaneously break out in song or rhythmic chants that are natural and charming extensions of their interest and enthusiasm. Through these personal expressions, teachers and students may find a common ground for interpersonal understanding.

Traditions, rituals, ceremonies, celebrations, and customs are part of communal experience, which is enriched by the inclusion of music. Noteworthy events and achievements are set apart with fanfares; losses or tragedies are commemorated with appropriate tributes. When a community of teachers and learners makes music together, social bonds and affiliations are strengthened. Performing in groups is especially satisfying because individual efforts contribute to the success of the whole ensemble. Teachers have observed the power of music making to knit a collection of individuals into a close community.

Another compelling reason for including music in classrooms relates to its potential for cultivating perception. In our daily lives, music is everywhere and readily accessible, but random environmental exposure is insufficient to educate students in the richness and depth of musical experience. Because schools are committed to educate the mind, body, eye, hand, ear, and feeling, teachers seek to develop students' abilities to perceive and discriminate keenly among forms of experience. In a world bombarded with sound, students must learn to listen with focused attention and intelligence. The sheer quantity and variety of images and sensations in modern life make it imperative for teachers to help students make sense of the jumble and learn to sort and sift among the choices. When classroom teachers use musical examples alongside narrative accounts, folktales, poetry, paintings, sculpture, videotapes, films, and CD-ROM programs, they provide multiple paths of introduction to important ideas and valuable opportunities to exercise perceptual skills.

The arts in general have long been heralded as a domain where creativity flourishes and personal interpretation is respected (as in the popular exhortation "there's no one right answer"). When assignments or projects are open-ended, such as ones that encourage students to write songs or to choose representative musical works to perform or describe, creative expression and interpretation flourish. Musical understanding, however, requires a balance of both creative and critical thought. Students learn important lessons of evaluation and aesthetic criticism as they analyze and reflect upon their creative output. A fuzzy attitude toward musical products ("anything goes") upsets this balance by downplaying possibilities for improvement. Whenever musical activities are incorporated in the curriculum, therefore, teachers must account for the ways students form standards of judgment and develop foundations of competence with the materials and tools of the discipline.

Interdisciplinary study demands attention to the quality of the relationships among the areas we seek to connect, a matter of integrity we will address in subsequent chapters. Teachers often raise valid concerns about the purposes of interdisciplinary experiences; cautionary voices help us refine our beliefs and clarify practices. Many educators are justly concerned when it appears that a discipline is corrupted or trivialized as an attachment or window dressing to other areas of study. Schwab (1978) speaks of a "perversion… [which consists of] degrading subject matter to the role of servant" (p. 377). A related criticism, reminiscent of this chapter's opening description of the curricle, is launched by May (1993): "Typically, one subject and its concomitant activities turn out to be nothing more than a recreational vehicle (RV) for the other, to make the other a palatable or interesting excursion for students." She warns, "Serious distortions and misconceptions can occur" (p. 185). Arts educators are particularly sensitive to these distortions because the full range of extrinsic and intrinsic rewards of engagement in the arts seems stereotyped and diminished if the arts are included solely for their entertainment or utilitarian value. These cautions and concerns reinforce the need for interdisciplinary projects informed by the knowledge, wisdom, and professional expertise brought to the curriculum by both generalists and specialists.

The Interdisciplinarity of Music Education

Out of necessity and passion, music educators are very protective of one of their most precious resource, instructional time in the curriculum. Leonhard (1991) conducted a national survey of arts education in American public schools and found that school schedules devote only one hour per week on average to music instruction at the elementary level. By the end of the first full week of school, the classroom teacher may have nearly as much contact with a student than the music teacher will have over the course of a typical 32-week year. At the middle school level, only 28.6 percent of small middle schools (fewer than 500 students) and 30.8 percent of large middle schools (more than 500 students) require music classes, although many schools offer band, orchestra, or chorus as electives. It is not hard to see why the wise use of instructional time is of great urgency and importance to music teachers. For that reason alone, many music educators are understandably cautious about interdisciplinary plans, weighing their justification carefully in light of the ambitious goals and scope of the music curriculum.

How likely is it, then, for the music specialist to incorporate the study of other disciplines into the music curriculum? We believe it is very likely, if practice is based on this premise: *A truly comprehensive music program is already interdisciplinary in nature because musical understanding draws upon many forms of knowing and understanding.* Strong programs in music education draw from varied sources of insight and information to enhance the musical understanding of students. When this enrichment brings about breadth and depth in the performance, analysis, and creation of music, while at the same time illuminating the social, historical, and aesthetic dimensions of music making, the music program justifiably earns the label **comprehensive.** Hope (1994) argues that this comprehensive nature is true of study in all of the arts, suggesting that "the intellectual functions of art, science, history, and philosophy [come] together with the knowledge, skills, subject matters, and purposes of dance, music, theatre, and the visual arts" (p. 40). In the following paragraphs, we describe these interdisciplinary dimensions of music education.

When students perform, create, and respond to music, understanding is enhanced through attention to style. Teachers can emphasize the origins and genesis of a work, the conditions of its creation, and how those characteristic features of time and place influence the performance of the work. A technically accurate realization of pitches and rhythms can fail to move us if these crucial stylistic elements are ignored. Through authentic and stylistically accurate performances of music, students are led to wonder about the individuals or groups who expressed ideas in sound. This natural curiosity establishes a purpose for finding out more about the people behind the music, and lures us to "travel" to other settings, periods, and regions.

Often when teachers and students find out more about the origins of a work, they attend to those impulses that moved composers and musicians to create in the first place. The impetus for creation might reside in an intriguing text, a tempting commission, a technological advance in sound production, the virtuosic abilities of particular performers, the desire to commemorate an event, the challenge to portray a story, or the urge to represent a feeling or idea. Each story of creation becomes an opportunity to delve into other disciplines and forms of human experience. Discoveries about the birth and pedigree of a musical work fold back into our music making and strengthen it.

Just as music reflects the social world, it is also firmly situated in the physical world. Musicians develop skills and techniques that rely on the recognition, control, and manipulation of sound. Music educators teach students how to differentiate among sounds with perception and refinement, how to produce them with accuracy and precision, how to organize, balance, and blend sounds in satisfying arrangements. The roots of this sensitivity to sound are fascinating, indeed. From infancy, children learn to recognize the distinctive qualities of timbre in their parents' voices. Soon, children gleefully discover the satisfaction of making varied sounds, which adults hear in their early vocalizations and baby babble. Learning to control the production of that sound is a prerequisite to tuneful singing in later years. Children also respond to intriguing sounds in their environment and learn the joys of making sounds themselves by banging on pot lids, dropping car keys, and playing with other delightfully noisy objects. Later, students learn to discriminate among and label hundreds of timbres produced by instruments and voices and develop finely tuned abilities to recognize certain performers or instruments by their distinctive sound qualities. The science of sound, *acoustics,* and the expressive creation and organization of sound, *music,* are closely related.

Figure 2.2
Third Graders Playing a Singing Game. Photo by Sandra Norstrom.

Music is also physical as it relates to the body, to movement and kinesthetic feeling. From the early Greeks onward, music frequently has been
touted as a means to enhanced physical well-being through control of the
breath, muscles, skeletal system, tongue, and larynx. The underlying beat
in a musical composition parallels the rhythmic regularity of the heart-
beat and respiration. As children grow, they become more coordinated,
develop fine motor skills, and increase their breath capacity. Through
expressive movement to music, singing, and playing, students use their
bodies to learn about music, internalize rhythm, and relate sound and
gesture. Even musical activities we usually think of as developing "naturally," like singing, are complex, coordinated systems of aural perception,
physical production of sound, and cognitive engagement.

Music is a form of cognition, involving processes of thinking *in* sound
and *with* sound. Composition, improvisation, performance, analysis, representation, reflection—all of these musical activities depend upon mental skills and strategies that are particular to the discipline. When students
are engaged in music making, they perceive patterns and structures in the
music, compare new sounds with previously heard melodies, rhythms,
and harmonies, and respond with new creations, interpretations, and real-
izations. Amazingly, this system of complex mental activity works so fluidly and dynamically that we see, on the outside, what appears to be
effortless performance. Because of the complexity and immediacy of
musical thought, cognitive psychologists have turned to music as a fascinating subject for study and examination. Music educators especially welcomed the inclusion of musical intelligence in the list of multiple intelligences described by Howard Gardner in his now-famous book, *Frames of
Mind* (1985). As new findings in cognitive science enlarge our understanding of the way the mind works, we may eventually form a clearer
picture of the role music plays in cognitive development.

Finally, music is an expressive art, with repertoires of works, conventions, traditions, and common practices as well as groundbreaking developments, revolutions, and innovations. We examine the purposes and
processes of artistic creation through our study of musicians and their
works. We also study the expressive kinship of music to other art forms.
Ballet, musical theater, films, and opera are inherently interdisciplinary as
they draw upon sound, images, text, gesture, and narrative in original and
provocative combinations. The intersections and interactions of art forms
are fertile ground for curriculum inquiry and development.

Even though these interdisciplinary aspects of music suggest multiple
associations with other subjects, not all music educators are quick to
adopt this emphasis in their teaching. Some caution that overenthusiasm
for the interdisciplinary nature and benefits of music, when coupled with

Figure 2.3
A Second Grader Performing "Ode to Joy" Using Graphic Representation. Photo by Sandra Norstrom.

the limitations of resources and shifting school policies toward the arts, could weaken the position of music in the schools. These cautionary voices are worth heeding.

One argument contends that the arts are a special province of understanding with forms of representation, perceptual skills, abilities to produce works, and evaluative capacities that take years to develop. Within the limitations of time and resources, proponents of this position argue, teachers would be wiser to concentrate on building their own competence and the competence of students in a primary art form. As programs or curricula broaden from this specialized base of experience, the fear of superficiality sets in. What if programs are so general and intermittent that students develop only a cursory acquaintance with art forms? What if students' misconceptions about the arts are strengthened rather than corrected? Smith (1995) warns that "when the arts are channeled into the mainstream and made part and parcel of everything, arts education becomes dangerously diffused" (p. 24). As the arts successfully permeate the entire curriculum, arts educators begin to worry that integrated programs may be seen as a replacement or substitute for comprehensive arts curricula. To counter these fears of superficiality, diffusion, and replacement, we believe that arts specialists should have primary responsibility for developing regular and sequential programs of instruction. This is not to suggest that the arts are the exclusive province of specialists, though. General classroom teachers and arts specialists can collaborate on projects that complement both the arts programs and other areas of the curriculum, strengthening the overall educational experience for students. A broad focus on "arts *across* the curriculum," however, must not compromise the depth of "arts *within* the curriculum."

Figure 2.4
A Music Teacher and an Art Teacher Engaged in Collaborative Planning. Photo by Sandra Norstrom.

Multiple Perspectives on Music in the Curriculum

In the following section, we are introduced to four different teams of teachers who are engaged in curriculum planning around a conference table in the media center of their schools, listening in on their conversations just at a point when the question of the use of music comes up in the discussion. Some of these teachers are classroom teachers; others are music specialists. Their particular roles and identities are not as important, however, as what the conversations are meant to illustrate: the various ways music is incorporated into the educational program. See if you can identify the perspectives of the teachers in each team after you read each scenario.

Team A

"It just seems that after I finish planning for science, math, social studies, language arts, health, and everything else, that I've used up all of the day," Ann moaned. "So, to incorporate music somewhere, I have started to collect recordings of songs that have something to do with the topics and themes of other lessons. Every now and then, I use one of the songs I've found in my collection of cassettes and CDs to introduce the theme of the day, for example. I know we don't sing as often as we could, but I notice that each time we do, my third graders seem to perk up. It really doesn't take all that much time, but at least there is some music in the day."

"I know what you mean," said Alicia. "I do the same thing. I've found that certain children in my class who may be having difficulties in other subjects, like math or reading, join in with confidence whenever we sing together. I think they feel better about themselves when they feel like part of the group, and singing is such a good group activity. Some of the songs even help them remember facts about math, science, or social studies, too."

Team B

"Do your kindergarten students seem really frazzled by the end of the day since we switched to this new all-day, everyday kindergarten plan?" Bridget asked Ben. "My class hasn't settled into a productive schedule yet." "Absolutely," he replied. "Sometimes they get so wound up by the middle of the afternoon, it's hard to get anything accomplished. But I've finally hit on an idea that seems to be working. It seemed to me that my class needed an outlet for their energy and creativity, so I've incorporated 'Expression Time' every day around 1:30 or so. The children find places at the tables or on the floor with big sheets of newsprint and crayons or markers, and I play soothing, classical music in the background. The kids spend about 15 minutes drawing to show how the music makes them feel. As I watch them, I can just see them settle down. And you should see some of their colorful drawings! We hang them up all over the room." "What happens next?" asked Bridget. "Do you talk about the drawings or the music?" "We could, but I don't want the children to think there is only one right way to show their ideas," replied Ben. "Each drawing is so special and unique that I'm just pleased the children have an outlet for their creativity. Since the class always seems so much more focused and ready to concentrate after Expression Time, I usually take the opportunity to introduce a new math or social studies lesson while their minds are still fresh."

Team C

After some pleasant chitchat, Chris called the small group of teachers to order. "We really outdid ourselves last fall at Parents' Night, didn't we? I had so many comments from parents who enjoyed watching their children perform. By the way, I still have the parrot in my room and I'd be glad to donate him to another classroom for a while."

"Sorry, two gerbils and a hamster are enough for me," Carla said. "I agree about the program, though. I've even had parents mention our Rainforest Review when they brought their children to school this September. I think they will be expecting another grand gala this year. And I think I've hit upon just the right angle," she said with a twinkle.

"I was thinking about the opening of the new Community Senior Center, and I came up with the idea, 'Generations of Entertainment,'" Carla continued. "What if we sang songs of different decades, worked on a big time line of events during those decades, found costumes to wear for different songs, and invited grandparents and guests from the senior center as well as the parents to see the children perform?"

Charles interjected, "You know, we could even ask for some audience participation in the songs or dances of various periods. Wouldn't it be terrific to have the whole school singing at the same time with the audience?"

"I think an intergenerational program would feel like a wonderful celebration and a way to bring the whole community together," said Chris. "And besides, I can't think of any way that this theme would involve classroom pets. Let's get started."

Team D

"Japan. Hmmmm . . . Japan." Darlene, David, and Diane fell silent. "Let's think carefully about this," Darlene said, reviewing the main points of the conversation. "This invitation from the educational director of the Art Center for the sixth graders to participate in the Museum Outreach Program is intriguing. The theme of the exhibit, 'Water, Air, Fire, Earth,' certainly has lots of potential, and the fact that it coincides with a performance of the Kodo drum ensemble at the Civic Center is almost too good to be true. But I don't want to agree to participate unless we can really figure out a way to weave our middle school goals for social studies, literature, art, and music with these special events in a meaningful way. Remember how we felt about the African mask exhibit? It was wonderful, but it didn't seem to align with our curriculum in the way we had hoped it might. How will this approach lead students to a deeper understanding of Japanese culture and tradition?"

"I think we need to start by asking some essential questions," offered Diane. "For instance, I would want students to answer the question 'How do Japanese people express ideas about nature through poetry, art, and music?' and also 'What are cultural traditions and characteristics of Japan?'"

David said, "I think we should pull out our original goals for the year and see how this project works with what we've already planned. In my case, I'll be ready by that time to focus on tone color by teaching a unit on orchestral instruments. But I have some recordings of koto and shakuhachi music, so I might open it up to include instruments of the world. We can extend what students know about sound production in orchestral instruments to our study of Japanese instruments. Perhaps I could tie into the elemental theme by showing how the instruments are made from natural materials. If I can find recordings of the drumming ensemble, we can prepare for the Civic Center performance. I wonder if the drumming has a particular significance within the culture? I think I have some background reading and listening to do!"

"I'll do a library search of artworks and literature to see what I find," said Diane. "I remember seeing a terrific video series in the library catalog when I was browsing through it last week. The first connection that pops out at me is something to do with representations of nature, but I have to get deeper than that. What makes a Japanese wood print so particularly Japanese? I especially need to think about the direct ways students will be involved in studying representative works and also in creating their own. Let's take a few days to gather resources before we come together for our next planning session."

For interdisciplinary curriculum work to be meaningful, teachers must address questions of purpose, balance, and relationship among disciplinary areas. There is no question that all of the teachers in these scenes included music in the design of classroom experiences, but they used music to different degrees, for different reasons, and, most likely, to varying ends. Certainly, music can be used as an effective strategy for memorizing facts, an especially pleasurable form of group activity, an outlet for creative ideas, or a focal point for community gatherings. These useful functions, as admirable or desirable as they may be, are inadequate to serve as primary reasons for the inclusion of music in the curriculum. In the absence of a stronger rationale, teachers could be led to a false sense of accomplishment, assuming that music is being *taught* or *learned* when it might be more accurate to say that music is being *used*. What is the distinction? A comprehensive program attends to the quality of students' experiences with music by addressing the ways students learn to perform, describe, and create music; the use of carefully chosen musical examples to study; the development of perception; and the cultivation of expressive responses to music.

From 1987 to 1990, the National Endowment for the Arts and the U.S. Department of Education sponsored an ethnographic study of the way the arts are taught in elementary schools (Stake, Bresler, & Mabry, 1991). The study described how art, music, dance, and theater are addressed in the schools by classroom teachers, arts specialists, and artist-in-residence programs. From this investigation of regular, ongoing practice, Bresler (1995) identified four styles of arts integration in the elementary curriculum: (a) subservient; (b) affective; (c) social; and (d) coequal, cognitive. As you read the description of each style, you may want to refer to the conversations from the teams of teachers as described above, which were written to illustrate these views and perspectives.

In the **subservient style,** the arts are used primarily *in the service of* other subjects to enliven lessons and to aid memory, but are not necessarily taught as subjects in and of themselves. In other words, activities in the arts, such as singing songs with topical lyrics, or coloring, cutting, and pasting pictures related to chosen themes, are seen as sufficient ways to address teaching music or art. The arts are used to "spice" other subjects (Bresler, 1995, p. 33), or, to use Wanda May's analogy, they act as "recreational vehicles." The primary reasons cited for including musical activities in this style were to save time by superimposing musical activities on top of other subjects of study and to improve students' self-esteem by allowing for other forms of classroom experience besides words and numbers. Ann and Alicia, the teachers in Team A, deserve commendation for incorporating recordings and songs in the flow of the day, but from this limited excerpt of conversation, we might wonder what musical understandings are being addressed or cultivated.

Teachers who exemplify the **affective style** see music as a way to change the overall mood or tone of the classroom, using musical activities as a change of pace or break in the day. Music may be played as a background to other activities, such as working on math problems or completing seat-work assignments. Another attribute of this style involves the use of music to invite creative, individual response. This practice provides blocks of time or opportunities for students to respond to recorded music by drawing pictures, engaging in movement, or describing how the music makes them feel. Open-ended responses by the children provide outlets for individual ideas and reactions. Bresler suggests that teachers who incorporate musical activities in this way do so to *complement* the structured and highly organized "regular" curriculum by including opportunities for students to respond in a free, unstructured manner. However, they stop short of asking the kinds of questions or of drawing attention to detail that would lead to the development of artistic perception and technique. In the example of Team B, then, Ben might enrich "Expression Time" by directing attention to particular features of the music and asking children to describe how their drawings reflect those features.

The **social integration style** emphasizes the role of music in the social fabric of schooling. Music is seen as an integral way to build community among students, teachers, administrators, parents, and community members. Chris, Carla, and Charles exemplify this style as they describe the goal of the intergenerational program as a vehicle for bringing the children and the community together. School ceremonies, rituals, and traditions reflect the beliefs and values of school communities and also shape cultural expectations and norms (Barresi & Albrecht, 1988). Again, music is viewed as complementary to the overall curriculum as a means to entertain and to build cohesion. These social functions of music are very important but cannot stand alone as a foundation for musical learning.

Figure 2.5
A Third Grader Spinning a Dreidel While Classmates Dance the Hora. Photo by Sandra Norstrom.

The **coequal, cognitive integration style** emphasizes "active perception and critical reflection on the technical and formal qualities" of music (Bresler, 1995, p. 34). In this approach, teachers draw students' attention to the aesthetic content of works, leading them to identify characteristic features of the music and refining the quality of perception. This style was least commonly found among the teachers in Bresler's study; those teachers who exhibited these practices either had extensive backgrounds in the arts or worked in close consultation with other teachers to provide a complementary range of skills, interests, and abilities. In the scenario, Darlene, David, and Diane consider the overarching goals of their programs, the selection of representative, engaging works, the degree to which disciplines and works are related, and the kinds of experiences and involvement that will lead students to deeper understanding of Japanese culture. In planning, they inventory their own knowledge and engage in additional study and research. Time, effort, professional judgment, and collaboration are key ingredients to the success of such ambitious and worthy initiatives.

Teachers and Exemplary Interdisciplinary Curricula

Bresler's study of practice shows the range of meaning possible in the phrase "integrating the arts into the curriculum." By describing the four styles as they are found in schools, she portrays a range of beliefs and gradations of depth in school programs that profess to teach music. We can form opinions about the quality of these programs by identifying the function that music serves in each classroom setting. We can also see how the process of clarifying educational purposes is crucial to the design of an interdisciplinary curriculum.

Insight for curriculum work also comes from identifying characteristic patterns in the most inclusive, rigorous, inventive, and strong programs. From observation of such programs and reflection on the qualities of the teachers who design them, we have generated a list of characteristics of teachers who create exemplary interdisciplinary curricula. As you read the following characteristics, turn your thinking from the current status of schools, *what is,* to the possibilities and potential for growth and change, *what could be.*

~ **Curiosity and an intellectual disposition to seek connections.**
   Teachers who are prone to look for, listen for, and think about relationships, patterns, influences, and coherent meaning act as models of intellectual curiosity for students.

~ **Attention to reciprocal and complementary relationships between and among disciplines.**

Insights from related disciplines—social studies, art, dance, or literature, for example—strengthen understanding in music. In turn, teachers carefully consider how experiences in music enhance or strengthen understanding in the related disciplines. This synergistic affinity dissolves confining borders between subject areas and opens up fresh possibilities for investigation and experience.

~ **Sensitivity to a balance of time and emphasis.**

Factors of quantity and quality of time are crucial. Teachers note the frequency and duration of student engagement in a discipline and the portion of the day or week devoted to such work. They also address the degree to which students attend to significant works, processes, and products in the complementary disciplines. Music is not used as window dressing for social studies, for example, or vice versa. Because representing the essential nature of disciplinary knowledge is a weighty responsibility for those whose primary training has been in another area, teachers often turn to quality resources or seek collaborative input.

~ **Depth of understanding.**

Interdisciplinary experiences go beyond shallow exposure to deeper forms of understanding, which includes knowing in more than one way. In particular, teachers design educative experiences that allow students to study a work, theme, topic, or problem from many perspectives. In the arts, these perspectives may be addressed by studying a work's structure and content, origin and context of creation, and capacity for expressive meaning.

In Chapter 3, we will turn our attention to matters of quality when designing curriculum around music and other subjects. For educationally sound programs, teachers must consider the essential elements of musical experience, the strength of connections between and among disciplines, and broad goals and aims for the curriculum. As teachers imagine and evaluate, create and critique curriculum, they must test the soundness and validity of educational ideas and initiatives.

References

Barresi, A., and Albrecht, G. (1988). School culture. In G. Olson (ed.), *Looking in on music teaching: The context book.* New York: McGraw-Hill.

Bresler, L. (1995). The subservient, co-equal, affective, and social integration styles and their implications for the arts. *Arts Education Policy Review* 96 (5): 31–37.

Compact edition of the Oxford English dictionary. (1971). Oxford: Clarendon.

Elliott, D. J. (1995). *Music matters: A new philosophy of music education.* New York: Oxford University Press.

Gardner, H. (1985). *Frames of mind: The theory of multiple intelligences.* New York: Basic Books.

Gardner, H., & Boix-Mansilla, V. (1994). Teaching for understanding in the disciplines—and beyond. *Teachers College Record* 96 (2): 198–218.

Hope, S. (1994). Making disciplinary connections. In B. O. Boston (ed.), *Perspectives on implementation: Arts education standards for America's students* (pp. 38–46). Reston, Va.: Music Educators National Conference.

Kliebard, H. M. (1989). Problems of definition in curriculum. *Journal of Curriculum and Supervision* 5 (1): 1–5.

Leonhard, C. (1991). *The status of arts education in American public schools.* Urbana, Ill.: Council for Research in Music Education.

May, W. T. (1993). Why teachers cannot respond to Leonhard's proposal. *Bulletin of the Council for Research in Music Education* 117: 167–191.

Parsons, M. J., & Blocker, H. G. (1993). *Aesthetics and education.* Urbana: University of Illinois Press.

Perkins, D. N. (1992). *Smart schools: From training memories to educating minds.* New York: Free Press.

Schwab, J. J. (1978). *Science, curriculum, and liberal education: Selected essays.* Chicago: University of Chicago Press.

Sizer, T. R. (1985). *Horace's compromise: The dilemma of the American high school.* Boston: Houghton Mifflin.

Smith, R. A. (1995). The limits and costs of integration in arts education. *Arts Education Policy Review* 96 (5): 21–25.

Stake, R., Bresler, L., & Mabry, L. (1991). *Custom and cherishing: The arts in elementary schools.* Urbana, Ill.: Council for Research in Music Education.

chapter 3

INTEGRITY IN THE
INTERDISCIPLINARY CURRICULUM

At the end of the first day of the August teacher in-service meetings at Four Winds School, Nina Farraj, a music specialist, felt frustrated. During the day, her principal had shown a series of videotapes on interdisciplinary teaching and how it had been implemented in a variety of schools. In the videotaped programs, music was mentioned only superficially or was poorly portrayed. The featured musical examples consisted mostly of nursery songs to which new words had been added, and music teachers were never shown as members of curriculum planning teams. The cumulative effect of these examples seemed to short-change the role of music across the curriculum.

Driving home, Nina mulled over the concept of interdisciplinary teaching. "I can see how there would be some real advantages to that approach," she thought, "but I must convince my colleagues that music can be incorporated in a meaningful way that doesn't compromise music itself."

How do teachers integrate the curriculum well? Ackerman (1989) recommends that teachers consider validity within a discipline, validity for the disciplines, and validity beyond the disciplines when evaluating the intellectual and practical sense of interdisciplinary curricular programs. To judge a program as valid suggests that it is sound or well reasoned. This soundness is crucial to disciplinary and interdisciplinary curriculum planning. We have chosen, however, to cast Ackerman's basic notion of validity in a slightly different way, by referring instead to the **integrity** of curriculum. Integrity connotes sound and valid ideas as well, but also suggests the "state of being whole, entire, undiminished" (Flexner, 1987, p. 990). Curriculum plans, then, whether involving just one discipline or more than one, must be evaluated as full and coherent wholes. **Integrity within the discipline** occurs when teachers plan and conduct instruction in a manner that upholds standards of quality in a particular field of study. Curriculum work in two or more content areas makes sense when teachers attend to natural and organic connections to preserve **integrity between or among disciplines. Integrity beyond the**

disciplines is addressed when teachers consider the broad goals and purposes of schooling and the way the attainment of these goals contributes to the students' general development and quality of life.

Integrity within the Discipline of Music

One of the most important roles of the teacher is to identify what is essential in understanding any topic, subject area, or discipline. To return to the metaphor of curriculum as a path discussed in Chapter 2, we might ask what assumptions or principles guide teachers as they navigate through the territory of all that is possible to explore, ultimately selecting the most important routes for exploration. If educational experiences in a discipline are to have integrity and meaning for students, we must always be asking the essential question, What are the fundamental components and forms of experience in the discipline?

Although it sounds redundant, teaching or learning music is dependent upon engagement *in music*. This means that active music making is the highest priority for both teachers and students, as opposed to learning about music through other, less immediate means such as reading about it in books, playing computer games with musical symbols, or listening to someone else discuss how they make music. Insight can be gained from these secondary sources, certainly, but *to know music is to do music*. This mission of working in, around, and within real music encompasses three intertwining branches of content: (a) musical examples or music literature, (b) the elements and structure of music, and (c) the processes of music making.

Examples/Literature as the Content of Music. Music is a body of works, although the number of works and range of styles are ever expanding. These works may be centuries old or the immediate product of a class improvisation. They may be easily recognized by many people (the "warhorses" of the literature) or may be known to a relative few. They may be organized in familiar and predictable ways or may challenge our perceptions and expectations. They may remain in our memory for decades or may dissipate the second the last pitch is sounded. Whatever their staying power or influence, musical examples are not just vehicles through which teachers teach about music; they are music.

Bamberger (1991) reflects on the all-too-common dinner party conversation when individuals claim that they "don't know anything at all about music" even when they can recall a substantial number of tunes, hum or whistle parts of them, and possess a rather extensive collection of musical recordings. This paradox may reflect people's beliefs about musical knowledge and the common assumption that only certain kinds of knowledge "count" toward musicality (being able to sing or play fluently, for example). An individual's personal repertoire is one valid form of musical knowledge.

What body of works will we choose for the classroom? Criteria for the choice of musical examples often include the appropriateness of the example for the students; the inclusion of a wide menu of types, genres, and styles of music; and the quality of the musical example itself.

Appropriateness for the students includes a judgment of the example's possible appeal. In the teacher's professional opinion, will this music engage the interest of students? The answer to this question often depends upon particular classroom settings and the knowledge the teacher has of the students' preferences and past reactions to musical works. If the work is a song, the text must be considered. Is the subject matter of the text appropriate and interesting for students? School policies and community expectations should also be considered when choosing literature, as teachers strive to exercise cultural sensitivity in the selection of works to study and perform. The length of the musical example is often a prime factor, as teachers select shorter or longer pieces based on their knowledge of the students' attention, endurance, and skill. The complexity of the musical example is also important. If students will be asked to perform the work, teachers analyze how the technical and expressive demands of the piece provide a challenge suited to the skills and capabilities of the student. This can vary, though, with the type of interactions children have with the music. Students may listen to a recording of a work, for example, that is beyond their performing abilities but not beyond their skills of comprehension and response.

The realm of possible musical works spans the globe and extends through centuries of human experience. Access to this musical panorama is expanding as technology makes the preservation and transmission of works commonplace. To be knowledgeable about music, students need to be familiar with a wide variety of musical styles and genres, such as representative works from various historical eras and diverse cultural traditions.

Teachers make informed judgments about the quality of the music they select for the curriculum. Within the plethora of possibilities and the limited constraints of time, there are works that deserve our attention and works that are too trivial, objectionable, or mundane to consider. A framework for judging the quality of artwork, including music, is provided by Reimer (1991): (a) craftsmanship, the "expertness by which the materials of art are molded into expressiveness"; (b) sensitivity, "the depth and quantity of feeling captured in the dynamic form of the work"; (c) imagination, which refers to the "vividness of an art object and its performance"; and (d) authenticity, the "genuineness of the artist's interaction with his materials in which the control by the artist includes a giving way to the demands of the material" (pp. 332–336). Although in later chapters we will refer to authenticity in terms of the cultural origins and contexts of a work, Reimer's use of the term suggests the presence of the artist's ideas within the work as echoes of the artist's distinctive personal signature within a medium. Teachers continually define and redefine personal and professional standards of quality as they note the lasting appeal and endurance of works, student engagement and interest, and richness of content that invites new interpretation.

Elements and Structure as the Content of Music. Music is organized sound. When we perform, create, or listen to music, we notice patterns and regularities in the sound—aural (heard) features that make the music comprehensible and meaningful to us. Music interests us because these patterns can be heard and felt on many different levels, in many schemes of organization, and in infinite combinations. Sometimes the patterns are so characteristic that we can identify a particular composer's style, or the work's affiliation with a particular region or group of musicians. The way a performer or composer works with these structures of sound by emphasizing, minimizing, repeating, changing, or highlighting nuances within the patterns is a reflection of the musician's craft or fluency.

We refer to these patterns and structures as the **elements** of music, and we label them by categories of rhythm, melody, harmony, form, tone color, and texture (see Table 6.3 for a useful review of these elements). We use these categories to draw attention to particular features of a musical example. After encountering many examples of these elements as they are embodied in varied types of works, we form **concepts** of music. These mental structures allow us to make sense of new works because we have built a good general sense or concept of how melodies go, how beats might be grouped into meters, how harmonies pull the music toward or away from important tonal centers, or any other relationships of sound. Verbal labels and terms for these features expedite our conversations about music with other individuals.

The teaching of music has integrity when teachers give attention to these elements so students can form music concepts. Instruction often focuses on musical examples that highlight these elements, which helps students acquire a vocabulary of representative patterns and structures, along with labels for identification. For example, teachers might begin by presenting a song in ABA form, with very distinct differences in the B section to set it apart from the A section. Later, students might attend to the phrases within a section, labeling smaller groupings of musical ideas as same or different. Or, more subtle differences in a phrase might lead to a categorization scheme of same, similar, or different, with a corresponding set of labels, a, a', or b. Perceptions become more acute as we learn to attend to simultaneous layers of musical events while, at the same time, we notice additional musical details and nuances.

Fluency with these elemental building blocks includes our ability to recognize and label what we hear, but also extends to what we can do with music as we work within the grammar or syntax of a musical style. How does rhythm work when we improvise in a blues style or play a Sousa march? How does rhythm work when singing a spiritual, or a work song, or other songs in an oral tradition? How does rhythm work when we play an accompaniment to an African story song or tap repeated patterns on a drum for a Renaissance dance? These elements of rhythm, melody, harmony, form, and so on are universal in that they can be found in many styles of music, but they are at the same time particular when they are used in the "language" or syntax of a musical style.

Figure 3.1
Fifth Graders Performing with their Teacher in an Ensemble. Photo by Sandra Norstrom.

Processes as the Content of Music. Musicians demonstrate an incredible range of musical actions and activities. To encourage such fluency in the music classroom, teachers provide many options for music making and offer a diversified approach to musical development. Students gain competence and skill in performing by learning to sing or play. Students also create new musical ideas through improvisation, composition, and interpreting and arranging the compositions of others. Producing sound is central to musicianship. Teachers strive to develop students' sensitivity to the relationships, qualities, and subtleties in sound. As students notice how a work is organized, how characteristic elements can be heard in the music, and how these elements are used expressively, they show how acutely they perceive sound. New works are learned and created as students observe and imitate the music making of others, using the ear, hand, and voice to learn "by ear." To develop music literacy, students learn how to represent sound in various forms, which includes reading and writing using both graphic and conventional symbols for music. Finally, learners think about their musical experiences as they direct their efforts, monitor what they have learned and what yet needs to be mastered, evaluate music and their performances of it, and consider how the works they perform, create, analyze, or represent fit within the stylistic contexts they seek to understand. This realm of activity encourages deliberate reflection upon sound. Comprehensive music programs give students experiences with all of these processes. Students who learn to produce, perceive, represent, and reflect upon sound become well rounded and accomplished musicians.

Production, perception, representation, and reflection broadly encompass the fundamental processes of music. Consider how these four broad processes are incorporated into the nine content standards for music in the 1994 National Standards for Arts Education (Table 3.1) (Consortium of National Arts Education Associations, 1994).

Table 3.1 *Content Standards in Music*	1. Singing, alone and with others, a varied repertoire of music 2. Performing on instruments, alone and with others, a varied repertoire of music 3. Improvising melodies, variations, and accompaniments 4. Composing and arranging music within specified guidelines 5. Reading and notating music 6. Listening to, analyzing, and describing music 7. Evaluating music and music performances 8. Understanding relationships between music, the other arts, and disciplines outside the arts 9. Understanding music in relation to history and culture

Students engage in these forms of musical activity to acquire skill, develop technique, heighten perceptual abilities, make novel contributions, evaluate progress toward goals, and most importantly, begin to define their competence and identity as musical individuals. Through thoughtfully selected and arranged experiences in the classroom, students acquire the skills and dispositions to move toward independent musicianship. The satisfaction that comes from mastering new challenges encourages students to take on new musical ventures. Note that standards 8 and 9 also refer to the music's relationship with other disciplines, as necessary understanding for informed musicianship.

In summary, educational experiences in music have integrity when students and teachers are engaged in processes of producing, perceiving, representing, and reflecting on sound, while attending to the elements of sound that make musical works expressive and give them significance in our lives. Whether the classroom is inhabited by five-year-olds or college students, the impact of the experience will depend upon the choices teachers make from the infinite varieties of musical works, elements, and forms of musical engagement.

Figure 3.2
A Third Grader Locates Ghana on the World Map Before the Class Sings a Song from Ghana. Photo by Sandra Norstrom.

Later in the year, Nina Farraj found herself sitting beside her colleagues in the front of the room during parent-teacher night. Her principal had organized this meeting so the teachers could describe some of the innovative and collaborative projects they had designed. As Nina listened to her colleagues, she was pleased to hear them describe how they had incorporated music in thoughtful, expressive ways into their study of literature, dance, art, and social studies. Nina's zeal in communicating the essential components of instruction in music had paid off, but in turn, she had also learned more about the essence of teaching other subjects in the curriculum. The teachers at Four Winds had spent many hours of planning and preparation to coordinate their efforts, and as a result, their ideas were inventive, lively, and powerful.

When it was Nina's turn to talk about the changes in the music program brought about by the interdisciplinary initiative, she began by describing how this year had been full of new discoveries as she consulted historical and cultural sources to enhance her understanding of the origins of musical works. She told the parents how the students had suggested placing a time line around the perimeter of the music room as a record of the different works they had studied. She also displayed the large world map that helped the children locate the musical traditions of other cultures. Nina also described how she had learned much from her colleagues in art and literature as they found meaningful connections among works of art and explored those connections with students.

Integrity between and among Disciplines

In the previous chapter, we stated that teachers must address issues of purpose, balance, and relationship when designing interdisciplinary curricula. Whether a teacher is planning innovative lessons individually or working collaboratively within a team, great new ideas are accompanied by a flurry of important questions: Why are we doing this? What is the significance of these ideas? What forms of experience and classroom activities are most useful in gaining new understanding? Why put these particular ideas or works together? Are we giving equal time and emphasis to each area we've incorporated into the curriculum? For each new plan or idea we add to the curriculum, what will be replaced or eliminated? Do we have the resources and materials we need? How will we really know what the students learn through their participation in these lessons? What do we know about this topic already? What do the students know? Will they be interested in these ideas and find them useful? These questions are important to the issue of integrity between and among disciplines.

An English logician named John Venn used interlocking, overlapping circles to represent the degree of relationship between and among sets of objects or ideas. We can borrow this graphic organizer from mathematics to test the validity of ideas between and among disciplines. Representing the relationship between ideas with circles is nothing new in interdisciplinary work; in fact, various diagrams, webs, and graphics are used in different models of curriculum planning (Fogarty, 1991; Jacobs, 1989; Kovalik, 1992). Venn diagrams are a simple yet powerful tool to test the strength of connections and related ideas.

To begin, consider that music can be taught as a discrete subject, apart from other areas of the curriculum. If students happen to make a connection between music and another area, it comes as a result of their own process of discovery rather than any intentional act on the part of the teacher or school to stress the relationship.

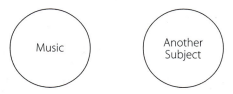

Figure 3.3
Music and Another Subject

One very common framework for interdisciplinary work uses a topical theme as the integrative area (oceans, transportation, animals, the circus, etc.):

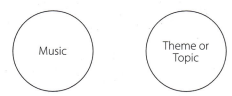

Figure 3.4
Music and Theme or Topic

In many of the topical units that we have examined, it appears that music is related to the general model only through the texts of songs chosen to relate to the theme. If you can "animate" the two circles above, move them together and overlap them only slightly to show the degree of their true relationship. In this instance, we might imagine the two circles with a very small shared area because only the words of the song relate to the topical theme:

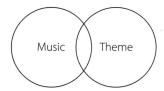

Figure 3.5
Music and Theme with Minimal Overlap

To move beyond this rather superficial "words about X" context, choose two subject areas with a truly complementary overlap of content, such as music and social studies. When students are learning about the lives of people in the Civil War era, music may be used as a means to show the depth of feeling and intensity of emotion. Here, the two areas are drawn together with almost a magnetic pull, since studying the music of the Civil War illuminates that time in history, and understanding the circumstances of the Civil War helps us to understand and perform the music of that time with greater sensitivity.

Figure 3.6
Music of the Civil War and History of the Civil War

Finally, it is certainly possible to design interdisciplinary curriculum units in which more than two subject areas are related in reciprocal, complementary fashion. Art forms that are intrinsically multidisciplinary, such as ballet, are prime candidates for three- or four-ring Venn diagrams. To understand a ballet, students might study the music, the choreography, and the visual elements of costume and set design. Each area is integral to the holistic form, so the circles move together and overlap in close proximity.

Figure 3.7
Music, Dance, and Visual Elements

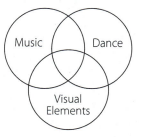

Venn diagrams can be useful tools to evaluate the intersections of content found in single lessons, entire units, or year-long curricular programs. We have found this strategy helpful in the early exploratory phases of idea generation, as well as later stages of review and evaluation. As teachers reflect on curriculum projects to evaluate why they worked so well or what should be modified in the future, the strength of content relationships is assessed. In collaborative efforts, this exercise encourages teachers to forge a consensus about the purposes of the plan. Sketching out these circles and thinking about the ways they overlap clarifies the nature and extent of mutually complementary relationships between and among disciplines.

After several years of teaching at Four Winds School, Nina decided to return to school in the summers to complete a graduate degree in music education. She found the whirlwind of classes, readings, and papers to be stimulating and worthwhile. Her interdisciplinary experiences had prepared her well to think about the Big Picture of education. Nina felt a sense of satisfaction as she reflected on the ways that her classroom practices, her strong beliefs about the power of music, and important educational theories aligned.

In courses on the foundations of education and curriculum development, Nina thought about the relationship of her carefully designed music program to the interdisciplinary focus of her school. She confirmed her belief that music allows children to acquire knowledge and skills in ways that match their learning characteristics and personal styles. She thought ahead to her students' years in middle school, high school, and college, and hoped that they would continue to show enthusiasm for learning music and seek out new experiences in the future, whatever their professional goals might be.

Integrity beyond the Disciplines

The philosopher John Dewey conceived of education as growth, a process of "continual reorganizing, reconstructing, and transforming" (1944, p. 50). He called upon educators to examine the needs and capacities of students in order to plan curriculae that are "flexible enough to permit free play for individuality of experience and yet firm enough to give direction towards continuous development of power" (Dewey, 1938, p. 58). For students to realize their intellectual and personal power fully through educative experience, teachers must contemplate the overarching purposes of education and the curricular decisions and actions that lead to the attainment of those purposes. We might ask: How does an interdisciplinary emphasis in curriculum move students closer to the realization of their potential as individuals? How might the cultivation of this potential eventually lead to important advances in knowledge and the amelioration of social problems? How does a teacher ever really know the long-lasting effects and ultimate outcomes of classroom experience?

Earlier in the chapter, we suggested that integrity beyond the disciplines involves consideration of the broad goals and purposes of schooling, as well as the way the attainment of these goals contributes to the students' general development and quality of life. Educational thought and discourse revolve around complicated issues and essential questions embedded in these two interrelated areas. Many educational theorists have contemplated these aims of education, publishing arguments and frameworks against which teachers can assess beliefs and practices. This relationship of theory and practice is mutual, however, because educational theories often arise from practice in the first place. These important ideas and questions can stimulate lively conversations about the curriculum. Goodlad (1984) grouped the purposes of schooling into four categories: (a) academic goals; (b) vocational goals; (c) social, civic, and cultural goals; and (d) personal goals (see Table 3.2).

Table 3.2
The Purposes
of Schooling
(Goodlad)
	A. Academic Goals
	    Mastery of basic skills and fundamental processes
	    Intellectual development
	B. Vocational Goals
	    Career education
	C. Social, Civic, and Cultural Goals
	    Interpersonal understandings
	    Citizenship participation
	    Enculturation
	    Moral and ethical character
	D. Personal Goals
	    Emotional and physical well-being
	    Creativity and aesthetic expression
	    Self-realization

How do these worthy goals, which we often view as the culmination of experience from kindergarten through college, play out in the everyday reality of lessons and classes? Interdisciplinary study may be crucial to the attainment of these large purposes by dissolving boundaries between subjects and allowing teachers and students to work together on large, complex problems and issues.

Another view of the mission of schooling especially relates to the arts in the overall experience of schools. Eisner (1991) proposes six aims of schooling that hold profound implications for school life and interdisciplinary curriculum development. He suggests that these ideas are the most valid and worthwhile lessons we could teach, including (a) the idea that "the exploration of ideas is sometimes difficult, often exciting, and occasionally fun," (b) learning "how to formulate [our] own problems and how to design the tactics and strategies to solve them," (c) encouraging the "development in the young of multiple forms of literacy," (d) "teaching the young the importance of wonder," (e) "helping children realize that they are part of a caring community," and (f) "teaching children that they have a unique and important personal signature" (pp. 13–16).

Eisner's aims inspire us to provide students with imaginative and expressive experiences in music, art, theater, dance, and literature. To design these experiences with creativity and insight, teachers need to consider how they come to know new works fully and comprehensively, which is the subject of Chapter 4. Personal insights may lead to pedagogical insight in preparing to teach those works to students.

REFERENCES

Ackerman, D. B. (1989). Intellectual and practical criteria for successful curriculum integration. In H. H. Jacobs (ed.), *Interdisciplinary curriculum: Design and implementation* (pp. 25–37). Alexandria, Va.: Association for Supervision and Curriculum Development.

Bamberger, J. (1991). *The mind behind the musical ear: How children develop musical intelligence.* Cambridge: Harvard University Press.

Consortium of National Arts Education Associations. (1994). *National standards for arts education: What every young American should know and be able to do in the arts.* Reston, Va.: Music Educators National Conference.

Dewey, J. (1938). *Experience and education.* New York: Collier.

Dewey, J. (1944). *Democracy and education: An introduction to the philosophy of education.* New York: Free Press. (Originally published 1916.)

Eisner, E. W. (1991). What really counts in schools. *Educational Leadership* (February): 10–17.

Flexner, S. B. (ed.). (1987). *The Random House dictionary of the English language* (2nd ed.). New York: Random House.

Fogarty, R. (1991). *The mindful school: How to integrate the curricula.* Palatine, Ill.: Skylight.

Goodlad, J. I. (1984). *A place called school.* New York: McGraw-Hill.

Jacobs, H. H. (ed.). (1989). *Interdisciplinary curriculum: Design and implementation.* Alexandria, Va.: Association for Supervision and Curriculum Development.

Kovalik, S. J. (1992). *Integrated thematic instruction.* Village of Oak Creek, Ariz.: Books for Educators.

Reimer, B. (1991). Criteria for quality in music. In R. A. Smith & A. Simpson (eds.), *Aesthetics and arts education.* Urbana: University of Illinois Press.

⊰ chapter 4 ⊱

GETTING TO KNOW A WORK OF ART

Sometimes Running

Sometimes running
to yes nothing and
too fast to look
where and at what
I stand and there
are trees sunning
themselves long a
brook going and
jays and jewelry
in all leafages
because I pause

John Ciardi

In his poem, "Sometimes Running," John Ciardi (1962) reminds us that if we don't take time to examine the world *around us* and the world *within us,* we will miss the opportunities for awe and wonder that life can offer. The arts—music, painting, sculpture, poetry, dance, and theater— can be powerful antidotes to our stress-filled, fast-paced, quick-fix, sound-byte culture. Thomas Moore, in his book *Care of the Soul* (1992), asserts that "we'll feel empty if everything we do slides past without sticking." The arts are important because they arrest attention and "invite . . . us into contemplation—a rare commodity in modern life. In that moment of contemplation art intensifies the presence of the world" (p. 286). When we are participating in the arts as creator, performer, or perceiver, we are able "to see more in our experience, to *hear* more on normally unheard frequencies, to *become conscious* of what daily routines, habits and conventions have obscured" (Greene, 1995, p. 379). To achieve this heightened awareness, one must make a commitment of time and effort. Georgia O'Keeffe, who painted spectacular canvas-filling flowers, said, "Still—in a way—

nobody sees a flower—really—it is so small—we haven't time—and to see takes time, like to have a friend takes time" (cited in Hecht, 1995, p. 4). Just as O'Keeffe took the time to observe every minute detail of the flowers she painted, we viewers must take the time to "see" what she presents to us. So while the arts can serve as a catalyst for contemplation, they cannot automatically offer their full benefits if they are encountered only casually. To derive full value from the arts, we must be willing to become actively engaged with them over time.

Art, as a refinement and intensification of our human experience (Dewey, 1934), is a magnifying glass for the soul. A magnifying glass can be used to bring cloudy images into focus. It can also be used to focus sunlight with enough intensity that it can burn a hole in paper. The artist, through visual images, melodies, physical gestures, or poetic language, not only helps us clarify our thoughts about life experiences, but also helps us distill and intensify the feelings of joy, sorrow, wonder, or amusement we associate with those experiences. Consider, for example, some ways music serves to add meaning to an experience or to intensify its emotional impact. We sing "Happy Birthday" to make a birthday celebration even more festive. Quiet, reflective music adds solemnity to a funeral. Film soundtracks pique our anticipation, raise our anxiety level, or allow us to relax in a flood of relief as the violins soar, assuring us of a happy ending.

Our intense responses to the arts often provoke a desire to convey our newly discovered insights to others. Our verbal attempts to do so, however, lack the forms of representation in sound, space, and time that are the qualitative dimensions of artistic experience. Words seem like straitjackets when compared with the fluid, lively, and simultaneous elements of a folk dance, jazz quartet, opera chorus, or grand finale in the musical theater.

Still, we are compelled to attempt to represent our experience in words, as much to ourselves as to others. For ourselves, we seek to articulate our understanding and to observe our processes of engagement in the hope that future encounters with artworks will be as intense, enjoyable, and profound. In our roles as teachers, friends, or family members, we describe our most vibrant responses so that others might seek similar opportunities for artistic experience. Leonard Bernstein (1959), as gifted as anyone in pointing the way to musical experience through words, resigned himself to "joining the long line of well-meaning but generally doomed folk who have tried to explain the unique phenomenon of human reaction to organized sound" (p. 11). He summarized the necessity and inevitability of the challenge:

> Ultimately one must simply accept the loving fact that people enjoy listening to organized sound (*certain* organized sounds,

anyway); that this enjoyment can take the form of all kinds of responses from animal excitement to spiritual exaltation; and that people who can organize sounds so as to evoke the most exalted responses are commonly called geniuses. These axioms can neither be denied nor explained. But, in the great tradition of man burrowing through the darkness with his mind, hitting his head on cave walls, and sometimes perceiving a pinpoint of light, we can at least try to explain; in fact, there's no stopping us. (p. 11)

Attending a concert, dance, or play is an opportunity to observe our own process of engagement with works of art. In the next scenario, compare this description of engagement with arts performances you have attended.

Several months ago, you purchased tickets for a performance of Shakespeare's Twelfth Night *by an acclaimed acting company. You have anticipated this performance for weeks (whenever you've had a tiny crevice of time to think about your cultural agenda in the midst of your hectic schedule). Now, on the evening of performance, your frustration mounts as unsolicited phone calls cause a chain reaction of delays, compounded by heavy traffic and packed parking ramps. As the usher escorts you to your seat and hands you the playbill, you consider speed-reading the synopsis, just so you'll be better prepared to understand the roster of players and enjoy this comedy. "Perhaps I should have checked out a copy of the play from the library," you think with a twinge of regret, just as the hall lights dim.*

"If music be the food of love, play on." The opening line only serves to remind you that you didn't have time for dinner after work. For the first 10 minutes, you struggle to calibrate your ear to the rhythms and vocabulary of this rich linguistic feast. "Maybe I'm just too frazzled for Shakespeare tonight," you think with resignation, still working diligently to catch the flow of the story and the relationships of the characters. "I'll go along for the ride, but they'll have to lug me along with them." Then, the miraculous happens as the preoccupations of the day fade and you find yourself caught up in Shakespeare's web of words. In the crazy mix-up of identities, you want to call out to warn Olivia that her beloved is not Cesario, but Viola in disguise. You sense that it is inevitable that Malvolio will fall right into the trap of vanity set for him by Sir Toby Belch and his drunken cohorts. You listen with rapt attention as Feste, the jester, addresses the central flaws and features of the human condition. By the end of the play, you feel uplifted, transformed, and thankful that even though your life is complicated and fast moving, the problems you need to solve are far less messy than the tangled webs of deceit and dirty tricks portrayed in this comic tale.

The Individual and the Artwork

The preceding scenario depicts the power of artwork to *engage* and *move* an individual, not just in the sense of deep emotional response, but also in the sense of the individual's relationship to the work of art. To discuss this relationship, the metaphor of location, in which distance or position signifies engagement and understanding, will be used. At the beginning of the play, this person was fully "outside" the play, caught up in the vicissitudes of modern life that contributed to the sense of distance from deep comprehension of meaning or personal response to the work. If you can imagine yourself as the playgoer in this scenario, we might say at the outset that you are as **removed** as possible from *Twelfth Night*.

Figure 4.1

"Removed" from the Work

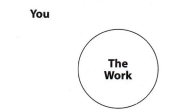

This distance brings detachment and objectification. You look on the work as an important cultural artifact to be preserved or studied, but this preservation or study exists apart from your rich, subjective inner life. You may examine the work, but you aren't led to examine yourself in the process. Or, it is certainly possible, when you are in the "removed" state, that you have little interest in the work at all, viewing it as an extraneous frill or idle amusement.

In contrast, search your personal experience to recreate the sense of being fully **within** a work—engaged in comprehension, personal response, or dialogue with the work or the impulses of its creator. Recall a time when your senses were heightened and your perceptions were clear while performing, listening to, creating, evaluating, viewing, or examining a song, play, poem, sculpture, dance, or other work. The distracting barriers that held you at arm's distance were removed, and the dimensions of the experience were expanded. For a time, you were transported to the center of the artistic experience. When the encounter with the work ended, you may have felt a sense of returning to the world of reality. Although we may not be able to articulate how we arrived at this "place," we remember the vitality, the sense of personalization, heightened awareness, and enhanced meaning.

Figure 4.2
"Within" the Work

The business of philosophy, psychology, sociology, and the hybrid discipline of education in the arts is to describe both the "removed" position and the location of "within" and also to address *how an individual moves from one to the other.* Since location is our current metaphor, we are going to call this notion the idea of **transport.**

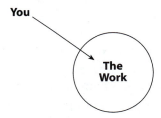

Figure 4.3
Transport from "Removed" to "Within" the Work

Transport is concerned with an individual's progression from detachment to engagement, from superficial acquaintance to deep comprehension, from transitory encounter to long-lasting ownership. When students encounter the arts in classroom settings, teachers have opportunities to observe and reflect upon the degrees of engagement, comprehension, and ownership among students. We sense occasions when students are removed, confused, or disaffected; we also feel the exhilaration of connectedness.

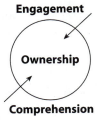

Figure 4.4
Engagement with and Comprehension of the Work

As we orchestrate educational experiences for the classroom, we can direct our reflective effort to pay attention to the forces or conditions that allow or even propel movement from "without" to "within." In turn, our insights may strengthen the quality of students' encounters with music, theater, art, dance, and literature.

Examining Personal Experience

The Transport Exercise

One way to gain insight into teaching and learning is to attend with care and deliberation to the quality of your own personal experience. Through this examination of your thoughts and responses, you may find parallels to important puzzles of curriculum design and instructional strategy. Play with the notion of transport by choosing a musical work that you don't know well but have been attracted to in passing. (You could either choose a recording to study or a musical example to perform.) Set a limited period of time—a weekend, perhaps—to chart your own progress from "removed" to "within." Use your strategic thinking and available resources to move yourself from superficial acquaintance with the work to fuller, deeper understanding. Make note of your path and the moves you make toward understanding in an attempt to monitor your own responses to the process. When you think you've arrived in the center of understanding the work (as centered as possible in this short window of time), summarize what you learn about the means of transport you used to get "within." If an illustration conveys the best sense of the journey, draw a map of your process. Engage in this experiment before you read the remainder of this chapter. You may find the following questions helpful in thinking about the task:

~ How do you define "within" and "without" in your own terms?

~ How do you know when you reach a point where you are able to think and feel "within" the music?

~ Can you fall out of that center place? Does the depth of experience endure or fade? Why?

~ What about the rate of transport? Sometimes we "get it" immediately. Sometimes works grow on us. Does it make any difference whether you get "within" at a snail-like 35 miles per hour or a speedy 65?

~ What helps you to understand the music? What blocks transport? How do you eliminate distractions along the way?

Stages of a Relationship with a Musical Work

There are, no doubt, as many paths from "without" to "within" as there are combinations of individuals and musical works. Teachers probably cannot predict or prescribe how quickly students will be ready to perform or understand a work, or when they will come to "own" it. Generalizations about the process of getting to know a work are tricky because each individual relates the new work to the pool of works already known (what cognitive psychologists called schematic knowledge). The depth and width of this known pool vary among individuals, of course. Personal histories act as lenses, filters, or mirrors for new experience.

For the purpose of illustration, however, entertain the possibility that any individual may go through various stages of a relationship with a work[1] (see Table 4.1), just as friendship or courtship may go through a progression from initial introductions to deep intimacy. Although the idea of stages implies that everyone passes through each stage in the same sequence, an itinerary that is certainly too rigid and linear for describing artistic experience or personal relationships, a general map of the changes in the quality of experience might illuminate varying levels of engagement with a work. For this description of a deepening relationship, assume that the individual first hears a recording or live performance of a musical composition.

Stage	Description of Stage
0	**No relationship.** You have no contact with nor interest in the work. You have never heard it, or you have heard it and do not care to hear it again.
1	**Personal, incidental relationship.** In public or private settings, you have heard the work and recognize it, either by sound, title, or association. You recognize the work whenever you encounter it in your everyday experience.
2	**Personal, intentional relationship.** In private settings, you seek out the work so that you can hear it more often. You listen *for* it on the radio, or perhaps you make note of the title so you can purchase a recording of it. You find yourself humming the melody, singing some of the words, or tapping the rhythm as you bond with the work. The important element of personal choice is exercised at this level; *you* take the initiative to select this work over others.
3	**Public relationship.** You commit to a public declaration of your enjoyment of or interest in the work by telling your friends, colleagues, or students about it. Perhaps you endorse a particular recording or play the work for them to see how they respond. You make your preferences public.
4a	**Performing relationship.** You expend the effort to learn the work so that you can play it or sing it without the recording or score—that is, you memorize it. You also bring your own interpretive ideas to the performance.

Table 4.1

Stages of Interaction with a Musical Work

continues

Stage	Description of Stage
	Table 4.1 *Stages of Interaction with a Musical Work (continued)*
4b	**Pedagogical relationship.** You know the work so well you decide to teach it to others so they will be able to listen to it with understanding or be able to perform it. You determine how you will teach it and how you will enhance the students' learning by providing information about the sociocultural context of the work. You engage in research about the work to understand it origins and structure.
5	**Long-lasting personal and professional relationship.** You come back to the work time and time again for further levels of understanding and enjoyment. The work takes its place in your personal repertoire of known works. Students, friends, or colleagues may associate this work with you—"This is Michael's favorite song" or "I performed this work with Ms. Howard in high school."

Certain themes that run through this progression suggest principles to consider when constructing curriculum in music: repetition, choice, identity, context, elements/structure, performance, critique/evaluation, creative response, and resources. A common theme is **repetition,** the opportunity to become familiar with a work by hearing it many times. Multiple encounters are often necessary, for just as the creator of a work may persevere at the task of bringing a work of art to fruition, perceivers may need patience and time to cultivate a relationship with a work. Some individuals experience sudden, immediate, and profound insights on a first hearing of a composition; for others, meaning is revealed in layers as the listener comes back to the work again and again. The speed of revelation may depend on features of the work as well as the perceptual skills and prior knowledge of the listener. Through repeated encounters, we incorporate the images, sounds, and patterns from the work into our "interior" until we sense that we know the work. Like the nearly obsessive process of playing a new recording over and over, we know we are "within" the music when we hear the sound of the next selection in the silences between tracks of the compact disc.

Choice implies a level of personal commitment. When we seek out a particular work and select it over other possible works, we have already made tentative connections with the work. Attraction and interest, piqued by the title, composer, or familiarity with similar works, lead us to take the initiative to hear the work again and again. In classrooms, it is typical practice for teachers to select the musical material to study or perform, so this desire for another encounter with the piece must be kindled by some other means (planning the introduction of the piece to pique students' curiosity, for example). If listening stations are available, students can make their own decision to hear works again and again, or to select something new. **Identity** is another theme. We respond to the work as a listener, performer, or composer, or as a teacher imagining how our students would respond. We can direct our attention toward the work in different ways depending upon the personal or professional hat we are wearing at the time. The **context** of a work is important in situating the example in a time or place and in addressing its power in the lives of individuals and groups.

Through heightened perception of **elements,** we notice how the work is constructed, or focus on the constituent parts that make up the whole. We may approach the work from various perspectives of personal experience, or stances of **performer, critic,** or **creator. Resources** are also important. We can turn to liner notes, commentaries, analyses, scores, other recordings, other musicians and teachers, or biographies to assist our interpretation or process of understanding.

Studying our responses to and engagement with a work may be a necessary prerequisite to teaching that work. If we notice how we become enamored or intrigued with a work to the point where we decide to bring it into the classroom, we may be able to communicate the intensity of our relationship with it as we introduce it to students.

A Teacher's Path from "Outside" to "Inside" in Preparation for Curriculum Development

As teachers, we have observed classroom experiences that struck us as particularly innovative and engaging, bearing the imprint of a creative, thoughtful teacher. We have also read impressive, carefully designed, and thoroughly researched lesson plans, which have inspired us to explore new ideas in our classrooms. It is not as common, however, to be able to eavesdrop on the birth of the ideas that lead to these experiences and plans. How are little sparks of ideas fanned by teachers into the vivid realities of classroom practice? What goes on behind the scenes in the mind of a teacher who is casting about for ideas in preparation for classroom experiences?

In the following excerpt from the journal of an experienced teacher, Joanna describes her process for understanding a work of interest, the *Concerto Grosso 1985* by Ellen Taaffe Zwilich. Joanna's entries describe her encounters with Zwilich's work as a series of phases. As we read, we notice how she remains open to the possibilities for imaginative curriculum design that stem from her own curiosity and engagement as a learner.

Joanna's Journal

Phase one: I listen to the music a couple of times while reading the sparse notes with the recording. I know I do this to get the big picture without trying to understand any components. I notice a few things. I can hear the Handel influence. I think Zwilich's music sounds like a scribble.

Phase two: Another day. I have some more information now from the notes. First, I read that Zwilich was commissioned by the Washington Handel Society for a piece commemorating Handel's 300th birthday. I found out that Zwilich played the violin and loved the sonata she quotes in the music. Armed with a little more information, I listen again, but still am not ready to follow the score. I want to see if my ears can hear the juxtaposition of old and new in the music. They can—very easily. I now have the hook to hang my teaching hat on. I'll have the students listen for and compare the old and the new. I like how Zwilich's music flows into Handel's and back again.

Phase three: I listen three times with the score in front of me to see if I can come up with a plan of the piece. It's pretty simple and one that fifth graders can discover. After an introduction of long tones, the Zwilich sound takes off. Soon a violin breaks in with Handel's theme, taking us back 300 years. The late-twentieth-century sounds return. The two eras flow back and forth—yes, the kids will really be able to hear this, and it sounds neat. I know that what I'm doing here is putting on my "kid ears," which is when I try to hear the piece as my students would, figuring out what catches my attention first.

Phase four: After letting the piece jell in my brain, I listen once just to enjoy it. This is the place where I know I am inside the music because my brain is full of the fun it will be to introduce this music to the kids. Then I start to sketch out my curriculum. My own path from "outside" the work to "within" looks like this:

Figure 4.5

Joanna's Path from Outside to Within

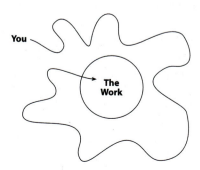

We can identify Joanna's process of bonding with the work through repetition, her pedagogical stance as she considers how the students will respond and "get it," and her intentional use of resources to expand her knowledge of the composer's creative intent. She finds the process of preparation and discovery to be enjoyable, and hopes students will experience the same pleasure in learning as they form a new relationship with Zwilich's composition.

In the lesson plan below, students are encouraged to describe their process of coming to know a new work. As they reveal their ideas, teachers can look for signs of transport from outside to inside.

Lesson Plan
Honoring the Past through Quotation

Rationale Musical style arises from using complex blends of sound in characteristic ways. Style involves relationships in sound, sometimes obvious, sometimes subtle, that lead us to recognize the influence of a particular time, place, composer, or related group of musicians. We recognize and categorize styles by perceiving the musical vocabularies and grammars of the composers and performers who make music in that "language." Style is perhaps one of the most difficult concepts to describe verbally, although it is often far easier to sense when we encounter a distinctive style in sound. Juxtaposing two different styles of music is an especially useful strategy to help students hear stylistic differences. In this lesson, students are asked to identify style in the form of quoted musical material from the Baroque period found embedded in a twentieth-century work by Ellen Taaffe Zwilich.

Suggested Grade Level Fifth through Eighth

Objectives Students will

- ~ identify contrasts in Baroque and twentieth-century style through listening.
- ~ discuss ways in which quotations can pay tribute to voices from the past.
- ~ show the stylistic changes in the Zwilich *Concerto Grosso 1985* through movement.
- ~ create a musical map to show the contrasting ideas in a concerto grosso.
- ~ compose a musical "conversation" with another student in class.
- ~ reflect on the process of becoming acquainted with a new musical work.

Materials
~ A sample of quotations students are likely to recognize

~ Recordings: Zwilich, E. T. (1989), *Concerto Grosso 1985,* conducted by Zubin Mehta with the New York Philharmonic, on *Ellen Taaffe Zwilich* [CD], New York: New World Records; Handel, G. F. (1994), Sonata in D major, HWV371, Op. 1, No. 3, performed by R. Terakado, C. Rousset, H. Suzuki, and K. Uemura, on *Sonatas for violin and basso continuo* [CD], Japan: Denon

~ Paper for student responses, two file cards per student, large sheets of paper and markers for musical maps, streamers

~ Classroom instruments or instruments the students bring to class for the composition exercise

Introducing the lesson

1) Begin by reading a sample of familiar quotations that students are likely to recognize. Encourage students to identify the person quoted, if possible. (Suggestions include the "I Have a Dream" speech of Martin Luther King Jr., John F. Kennedy's inaugural speech "Ask not what your country can do for you," and any recognizable phrases from individuals in your school community.) Note how quotation marks set apart the quoted material. Draw attention to "quotes within the quote." (King used phrases from the Declaration of Independence; Kennedy's speech was said to be based on John Greenleaf Whittier's funeral oration.) *Why do people quote other people's words?* (Because the person quoted has said profound and inspiring things or has said them in elegant ways; perhaps the people quoting might wish to pay tribute to the life of the person quoted or to show they are familiar with important ideas, etc.)

Developing the lesson

2) *Composers can quote musical ideas, too. In the composition we are about to hear, the composer, Ellen Taaffe Zwilich, has woven her own ideas with the musical ideas of another composer. Listen the first time to familiarize yourself with the entire piece.* Play the entire first movement, "Maestoso," of Zwilich's *Concerto Grosso 1985,* which lasts for 2 minutes, 41 seconds. Ask students to write a short sentence describing their responses to the piece on the first hearing.

3) Ask students to decorate one file card with the label "new" and another with "old." *As we listen a second time, see if you can recognize when Zwilich is composing in the twentieth-century, "new" style, and when she is quoting the ideas of another composer. Hold up your cards to show what your hear during the piece.* Play the entire movement. *Jot down what you heard this time that was different from your first hearing. Just as quotation marks set up an expectation for the reader that someone else's ideas are being cited, before the violins*

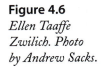

Figure 4.6
Ellen Taaffe Zwilich. Photo by Andrew Sacks.

COURTESY OF ANDREW SACKS AND THE NEW YORK TIMES.

play the quoted theme, another instrument plays a musical quotation mark in this composition. What is it? (Answer: The harpsichord arpeggio before the first occurrence of the Handel theme.)

4) *When we don't have differences in words to help us figure out who is speaking, how do we recognize a musical quote? In this case, Zwilich, a contemporary composer using contemporary musical ideas, is quoting from George Frideric Handel, a composer from the Baroque period 300 years ago. Zwilich even borrows the title* Concerto Grosso, *which describes a Baroque form built on the idea of contrast—a small group of instruments pitted against the large group* (the Latin word *concertare* means "to contend with" or "to fight"). *She shows that her composition includes a new "voice," too, by adding* 1985 *to the title. Why might Zwilich chose to quote Handel?* (The liner notes from the Zwilich recording calls this composition "a friendly handshake across the centuries" [Rich, 1989].) Establish the context for the composition by reading this note from the score of the *Concerto Grosso 1985* (Preston, 1985):

> In 1984 the Washington Friends of Handel commissioned New York composer Ellen Taaffe Zwilich to write a work in commemoration of the three-hundredth anniversary of Handel's birth. Ms. Zwilich almost immediately thought to base her own

work on that composer's D-major Violin Sonata. "I performed the work many years ago," she said. "And I especially love the opening theme of the first movement—the striking head motive and the beauty of the generative tension between the theme and the elegant bass line." The resulting composition, she says, is a "twentieth-century response to the spirit of George Frideric Handel. My concerto is both inspired by Handel's sonata, and, I hope, imbued with his spirit." (Zwilich, cited in Preston, 1985, p. 4)

5) *As we listen to this piece for the third time, does this knowledge about Zwilich's ideas change what you hear? Write down what happens as you listen, now that you know some of the reasons Zwilich quotes Handel.*

6) Divide the students into two groups, distributing different-colored streamers to each group. Realize the "Maestoso" through movement by asking one group to move fluidly during the Handelian passages and another group to show the angular "chase" of Zwilich's ideas.

Example 4.1
Zwilich's Theme from Concerto Grosso 1985 *by Ellen Taaffe Zwilich. Copyright © 1985 by Mobart Music.*

Example 4.2
Zwilich's Quote from the First Movement of the Sonata in D Major for Violin by Handel. Copyright © 1985 by Mobart Music.

7) Invite students to create a map of this dialogue between two musical styles by choosing one color of marker for Zwilich's themes and another for Handel quotes. *As we listen again, draw as much detail as you can to show what you hear.* (If students are new to mapping, you may direct them to think about the upward and downward contours, distance between sounds or intervals, or musical thoughts or phrases.) Students may need several hearings before their maps are finished. (You may wish to play the recording once for the students to draw the Zwilich, then again to add the Handel.) *On another time through, label the instruments you hear or add any phrases to your map that might help another listener to follow your diagram. Exchange your map with another student and see if you can follow the other's work.*

Figure 4.7
Sample No. 1:
Musical Map of
Concerto
Grosso 1985

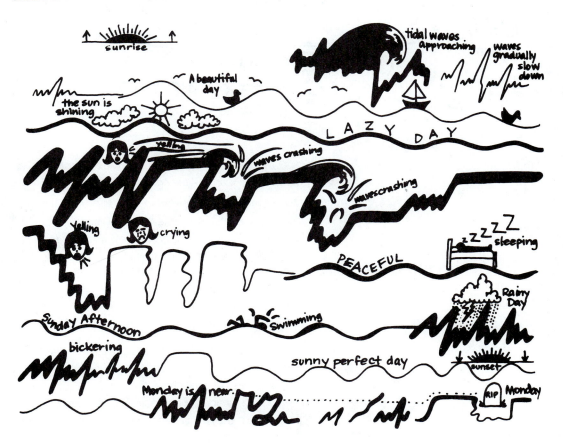

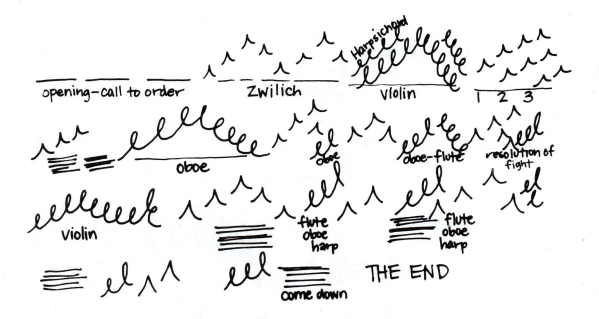

Figure 4.8
Sample No. 2:
Musical Map of
Concerto
Grosso 1985

How does this process of mapping help you to focus on the contrasting styles?
Do they look as different as they sound? Write again.

8) At the premiere performance of *Concerto Grosso 1985,* the original Handel
sonata (HWV371, Op. 1, No. 3, first movement) was played before the
Zwilich. *Let's listen to the two pieces in that order to see how the order of per-*
formance influences our ability to hear the quotes in the Zwilich. How does this
strengthen the contrast between the Baroque style of Handel and the twenti-
eth-century voice of Zwilich? How does Zwilich keep the composition "togeth-
er," even with the quoted material? Write or discuss.

Closing
the lesson

9) Invite each student to compose a short piece using available classroom
instruments, instruments students bring to class, or voices, in a way that
will show their own musical ideas or style characteristics. (This activity may
be extended over several class periods.) Then pair students and ask them
to blend their compositions so they make a new, longer one with recognizable shifts between one person's style and the other person's style.
Perform these musical conversations. Can other class members tell when
the identity of the composer changes? As a variation, students could also
compose a short piece to alternate with quotes from some known musical work. *Whose musical ideas will you honor in this manner?*

Assessment

~ Can students identify contrasts in style by showing where the quotations occur in the first few hearings of the piece?

~ Do the students move expressively to reflect changes in style, articulation, dynamics, and contour?

~ Collect the musical maps and study them to determine how students are able to represent multiple aspects of the composition, for example, melodic contour and interval, timbre, and phrases.

~ How articulately do students describe differences in perception when they hear the original Handel before the Zwilich?

~ Do students reveal characteristic compositional personalities in their musical conversations?

~ What do students conclude about the process of becoming acquainted with a new work, especially one in the twentieth-century style?

Extending the lesson

~ Find other examples of the old juxtaposed with the new. Can you find other instances of paying tribute through quotation in music, art, poetry, dance, and theater? How do changes in the creator's use of the medium "move" the reader, listener, or viewer across decades or centuries?

~ Read more about Zwilich's processes of composition, as described in "Conversations with American Composers: Ellen Taaffe Zwilich" (Grimes, 1986).

~ Identify other musical compositions that are based on quoted material, such as Copland, *Lincoln Portrait* ("Camptown Races"); Ives, Second Symphony and *Fourth of July*; and Schuman, *New England Triptych* ("Chester").

~ On other occasions, listen to the entire Zwilich work, which consists of five movements in arch form (the first movement and the last are paired, the second and fourth are paired, the third is the center of the arch). Listen to a concerto grosso by Handel after listening to Zwilich's *Concerto Grosso 1985*.

STRATEGIES

Guiding Listening

Music listening experiences in the classroom are most successful when the music is engaging and the listener's attention is directed in some way to the important features of the music. Here are some tips for planning listening experiences:

~ Keep listening experiences brief. Outside of the classroom, students tend to listen to popular songs that rarely exceed three minutes in length. In a sense, their attention spans have been trained to that length of time. While it is a goal to increase students' capacity for extended listening, it is wise to start with brief compositions or musically meaningful excerpts from longer works.

~ Provide opportunities for repeated listening. Music exists in time: We hear it, then it's gone. Because we can't create a "freeze-frame" of music, we need to hear it more than once to be able peel away the layers of complexity. Generally, the more we listen to a complex piece of music, the more we grow to like it. Make friends with the music; listen to it several times.

~ If a composition is based on a song, sing the song before listening to the composition.

~ The only thing that students should listen to while the music is playing is the *music*. Avoid talking about the music while it is being played. Written or pictorial guides allow the students' listening to be guided without creating an overload of aural information.

~ Use listening guides or activities to point out the important features of a composition. Printed listening guides allow the students to follow the descriptions as they listen. Listening activities may be designed so that students have to make decisions about what they are hearing in the music. Remember that musical events can go by very quickly, so when designing activities that include opportunities to respond, limit the number of responses students have to make.

~ If students have been asked to answer questions about what they have heard, provide an opportunity for them to listen again to compare their answers with your answers. Marking papers for the correct answer will have no learning value if the students do not have an opportunity to associate the proper responses and labels with the sounds they hear.

References

Bernstein, L. (1959). *The joy of music.* New York: Simon & Schuster.

Ciardi, J. (1962). *In fact.* New Brunswick, N.J.: Rutgers University Press.

Dewey, J. (1934). *Art as experience.* New York: G. P. Putnam's Sons.

Elliott, D. J. (1995). *Music matters. A new philosophy of music education.* New York: Oxford University Press.

Greene, M. (1995). Art and imagination: Reclaiming the sense of possibility. *Phi Delta Kappan* 76 (5): 378–382.

Grimes, E. (1986). Conversations with American composers: Ellen Taaffe Zwilich. *Music Educators Journal* 72 (6): 61–65.

Hall, G. E., Loucks, S. F., Rutherford, W. L., & Newlove, B. W. (1975). Levels of use of the innovation: A framework for analyzing innovation adoption. *Journal of Teacher Education* 26 (1): 52–56.

Handel, G. F. (1994). Sonata in D major, HWV371, Op. 1, No. 3, performed by R. Terakado, C. Rousset, H. Suzuki, and K. Uemura. On *Sonatas for violin and basso continuo* [CD]. Japan: Denon.

Hecht, A. (1995). *On the laws of poetic art.* Princeton: Princeton University Press.

Moore, T. (1992). *Care of the soul.* New York: HarperCollins.

Preston, K. K. (1985). *Notes for* Concerto Grosso 1985 (Ellen Taaffe Zwilich). Hillsdale, N.Y.: Mobart Music.

Rich, A. (1989). Liner notes for Mehta, Zubin (conductor) & New York Philharmonic, Concerto Grosso 1985. On *Ellen Taaffe Zwilich* [CD]. New York: New World Records.

Zwilich, E. T. (1989). Concerto Grosso 1985. Conducted by Zubin Mehta and the New York Philharmonic. On *Ellen Taaffe Zwilich* [CD]. New York: New World Records.

{ chapter 5 }

EXPLORING RELATIONSHIPS
AMONG THE ARTS

The various manifestations of the arts, among them music, painting, literature, sculpture, dance, and theater, reside in the world of expression. They allow us to express in a powerful, concentrated way the ideas, emotions, and events about which we humans care most deeply. Musicians, painters, poets, sculptors, dancers, and playwrights have celebrated, interpreted, and preserved the great historic and mythic events and personas of human civilization. They have addressed the profound human themes of love, worship, relationships with nature, conflict, and death. Whether we are experiencing someone else's artistic expression or creating our own, the arts help us explore the connection between our outer and inner lives.

In this chapter and the next, we will be examining commonalities and differences between and among the arts. We, the authors of this book, are music educators, so our discussions of other art forms will often be cast in relationship to music. Visual artists, poets, dancers, or playwrights would probably bring different perspectives and emphases to the topics we will address. You, the reader, may have in-depth experience with one or more of these art forms. As you encounter the ideas presented in this chapter, think about examples from the art forms with which you are most familiar that you could add as illustrations of the ideas.

There are many examples of how people working within one art form have been profoundly influenced by other art forms. Sometimes the influence is revealed by the metaphors they use to describe their own art. Sharon Olds's description of poetry as "singing the language without melody" (Gross, May 19, 1995/June 29, 1988) is one such example. Wassily Kandinsky used music as a metaphor for his painting: "Color is the keyboard, the eyes are the harmonies, the soul is the piano with many strings. The artist is the hand that plays, touching one key or another, to cause vibrations in the soul" (cited in Cole, 1993, p. 53).

Sometimes specific works inspire new creations in other art forms. Modest Mussorgsky composed *Pictures at an Exhibition* after seeing an exhibition of paintings and sketches by his friend, Victor Hartmann. William Carlos Williams's poem "The Dance" was inspired by Brueghel's painting *The Kermess*.

Collaborative projects such as ballets, films, and musicals integrate the work of writers, choreographers, composers, and designers. Consider the collective artistic energy in the Ballet Russe's production of *Pulcinella* with music written by Igor Stravinsky and production design by Picasso; the combined efforts of composer Aaron Copland and dancer/choreographer Martha Graham that resulted in *Appalachian Spring;* and the collaboration between Wynton Marsalis and choreographer Garth Fagan in the contemporary ballet *Griot New York.* The music of John Williams has played an integral role in films directed by Steven Spielberg such as *Close Encounters of the Third Kind, Schindler's List,* and *Raiders of the Lost Ark.* The realm of musical theater abounds in collaborative teams of composers and lyricists such as Richard Rodgers and Oscar Hammerstein, George and Ira Gershwin, and Leonard Bernstein and Stephen Sondheim.

Making connections between and among the arts can be exciting and revelatory; it seems like a very natural thing to do in the classroom. Each student in a class, because of differences in previous experiences, individual proclivities and interests, or school instruction, has an individual profile of familiarity, understanding, and comfort with various art forms. Relating two or more art forms provides students the opportunity to learn by analogy and metaphor—to learn something new by relating it to something they already know. Access to quality experiences with the arts strengthens students' capacity to see or hear beyond the surface so that they may deepen their understanding of the arts and how they work.[1]

The teacher who wishes to design curriculum to lead students on their own paths of discovery must understand what kinds of classroom connections between and among the arts promote understanding and insight and what kinds of connections are shallow and misleading. An important first step is to become aware of the ways art forms are distinct as well as similar. In this chapter we will explore those areas of similarity and difference and propose a model to assist teachers in discovering meaningful intersections between and among the arts.

Josh wrinkled his nose and forehead in concentration. With great intensity, he studied a painting of a woman in a brightly colored robe sleeping on desert sand with a lion, a jug, and a lute-like instrument nearby. He was trying to see what that painting had in common with the lively music pouring from the CD player. Finally, he raised his hand and shared his conclusion: "The paint-

THE MUSEUM OF MODERN ART, NEW YORK. GIFT OF MRS. SIMON GUGGENHEIM. PHOTOGRAPH COPYRIGHT © 1977 THE MUSEUM OF MODERN ART, NEW YORK.

Figure 5.1
Henri Rousseau.
The Sleeping
Gypsy. *1897.*
Oil on canvas,
51" x 6'7" (129.5
cm x 200.7 cm).

ing has an instrument in it, and you have to have instruments to play music."
Josh's teacher looked crestfallen. She was disappointed because her students just
didn't seem to make the expected connection that both the painting and the
music had something to do with night.

The intention of Josh's teacher was to design a learning experience
leading toward one of the music achievement standards from the
National Standards for Arts Education: "Compare in two or more arts how
the characteristic materials of each art (that is, sound in music, visual
stimuli in visual arts, movement in dance, human interrelationships in
theater) can be used to transform similar events, scenes, emotions, or
ideas into works of art" (Consortium of National Arts Education
Associations, 1994, p. 45). She had chosen Henri Rousseau's *The
Sleeping Gypsy* and *Eine Kleine Nachtmusik* (A Little Night Music) by
Mozart as examples from two different art forms that relate to the theme
of "night." Unfortunately, she did not consider that these two works,
while related by title, are not closely related in mood, style, or structure.
Rousseau's painting evokes hushed tension, while Mozart's lively music
is more suggestive of celebration. Because *Eine Kleine Nachtmusik* and
The Sleeping Gypsy have little in common beyond the nominal theme of
night, it is understandable that Josh could not easily draw meaningful
parallels between them.

How Do the Arts Differ?

Perhaps before we look for commonalities among the arts, we would do well to explore how the arts differ. One basic difference among the arts is how the dimensions of time and space come into play. In Table 5.1, physical dimensions of time and space are listed in the column on the left. For each of the art forms listed in the top row, consider which physical dimensions are integral to the experience of the art form, then mark the appropriate cells in the chart to indicate the relationship. You may also find it useful to imagine yourself as the viewer, listener, performer, creator, or critic to examine your ideas from different perspectives. The first cell, time and music, has already been marked for you. After you have completed this exercise, compare your responses with others. You may find that the exercise leads to clearer understanding but also, perhaps, to additional questions as you consider certain types of works that seem to be special cases.

Table 5.1

Physical Properties of the Arts

	Music	Poetry	Dance	Painting	Sculpture
Exists in time	√				
Exists in two-dimensional space					
Exists in three-dimensional space					

What did you discover as you completed this exercise? Here are some ideas that have emerged when others have thought about these properties.

Music and dance are temporal experiences: They have a beginning, a continuation, and an ending. In live performances, they are here and gone. One can study a music score or dance notation, but the experience will not be the same as the performance. Kinetic sculpture (sculpture that moves) is much like music and dance in that it unfolds and changes over time. Although painting and nonkinetic sculpture do not change perceptibly over time, the element of time is involved as the viewer scans different portions of a canvas or examines a sculpture from all sides.

Poetry, in its spoken form, exists in time; in its written form, it exists in two-dimensional space. There are some aspects of poetry that must be heard or imagined in the "mind's ear" to be appreciated, such as the rhythm and the sounds of words; some aspects of poetry must be seen to be appreciated, such as visual rhyme and the placement of the lines on the page.

Most painting can be characterized as existing in two-dimensional space, but this characterization is not without exception: Heavily textured paintings take on a third dimension, as layers of paint add depth. Three-dimensionality, however, is most usually associated with sculpture and dance. Because of this characteristic, sculpture and dance are best experienced firsthand; photographs and videos do not allow us to have the experience of three-dimensional space necessary to understand these art forms fully.

Each mode of artistic expression involves the senses in a slightly different way. Sight is employed in the perception of painting, sculpture, and dance, and in the reading of poetry. We hear music and poetry, and sometimes we hear the rhythms of the body in dance. Even some sculptures are meant to be heard. The tactile sense is important in appreciating sculpture and weaving; even when we cannot actually touch the works, we can imagine how they would feel.[2] The kinesthetic "sense," that is, the vital experience of rhythmic movement in one's own body, comes into play when a dancer dances, a musician plays, a painter paints, an actor acts, or a sculptor sculpts. Their movements, and the results of their movements, may also evoke a sympathetic kinesthetic response from the viewer. This is the phenomenon James Laughlin describes in this line from his poem "Martha Graham": "music moves moving from her into us" (Laughlin, 1988, p. 17). Visual art can arouse a similar response: "The body of the viewer reproduces the tensions of swinging and rising and bending so that he himself matches internally the actions he sees being performed outside" (Arnheim, 1989, p. 26). The rhythms of poetry can also evoke a kinesthetic response from the listener or reader.

Because art forms differ in their physical properties and the way they engage the senses, each art form provides its own unique lens on experience. Each also has its own limitations on what it can "say" to us. As an illustration, consider three works on the subject of swans: *The Ugly Duckling* by Hans Christian Anderson; a painting of a swan; and a composition for cello and harp, "The Swan," from *Carnival of the Animals* by Camille Saint-Saëns. What aspects of "swanness" can be expressed by each? If we had never seen a swan before, Anderson's descriptions would allow us to piece together in our imaginations our own idea of what a swan looks like and how it moves. In a painting, we can observe a swan's appearance and its environment. The painter, by choice of color and line can also communicate something of a swan's peaceful grace as it swims in a lake. As we listen to the composition by Saint-Saëns, we cannot learn anything about what a swan looks like, but its graceful, flowing movement is suggested by the cello's gently undulating melody. If we listen carefully to the harp accompaniment, we can hear patterns of cascading tones that might suggest shimmering water.

Common Terms but Different Phenomena

When the arts are described, identical words are sometimes used to characterize very different phenomena. This practice may trick us into making invalid conclusions about commonalities among the arts unless we take into account the different characteristics of the media (Thomas, 1991). **Rhythm** is a term that is used in characterizing music, poetry, dance, painting, and sculpture. In music and poetry, rhythm is an aural phenomenon that exists in time; in painting and sculpture it is a visual phenomenon that exists in space. In dance, rhythm can be perceived visually and, sometimes, aurally. **Color** is another example of a word that refers to different phenomena. In painting, color refers to pigment or hue. In music, however, the term *color* can be used in reference to the characteristic sound of instruments or perhaps the harmonic characteristics of certain chords or intervals. So while it may appear at first glance that terms such as *rhythm* and *color* may point to meaningful relationships between and among the arts, in reality, they may not. Other terms that pose similar problems are listed in Table 5.2.

Table 5.2

Common Terms/Different Phenomena

	Music	Poetry	Dance	Visual Art
Rhythm	patterns produced by groupings of tones of varying duration and stress	sense of movement created by patterns of strong and weak elements in the flow of sound and silence in speech	organization of movement patterns in time	regular occurrence of similar visual elements
Texture	pattern of sound created by melodic lines, a succession of chords, or a combination thereof	the elements of poetry such as imagery, rhythm, meter, alliteration, etc., that cannot be paraphrased		visual or tactile surface characteristics

(continues)

Table 5.2 *(continued)*

	Music	Poetry	Dance	Visual Art
Line	rhythmic succession of tones; the contour of a vocal or instrumental part and its horizontal motion	a unit in the rhythmic structure of poetry that is formed by the grouping together of a number of the smallest units of the rhythm (syllables, stress groups, metrical feet)	movement that connects two points to take the body through space; the shape of a dancer's body	outline or contour; the defining border between areas
Gesture	movement of a musical line that suggests a physical action		movement of the body or parts of the body for communication of qualities, ideas, or emotions	the artist's brush strokes or other marks on the work that might provide insight into the artist's way of working
Color	(tone color) characteristic sound of instruments or voices	figures of speech; vividness or variety of emotional effects of language	qualities, mood, or emotion evoked by movement	hue or pigment
Consonance	combination of musical tones felt as satisfying and restful	repetition of similar or identical consonants or words whose main vowels differ		
Composition	the act of creating music; the work thus created		the organization of movements into a form or structure with a sense of wholeness	the organization of visual components to form a unified whole
Movement	a division of an extended composition such as a symphony, sonata, or concerto; the forward motion of music through time	rhythmic flow of words	interactions of energy and space through the medium of the body	representation of motion

Before we begin a discussion of how to integrate the arts most fruitfully, one additional caution should be raised. Music, like each of the other arts, is a unique discipline that must be taught through a rigorous, structured curriculum to be grasped fully. Like each of the other art forms, it has its own materials, processes, and structure. Learning to use sound, paint, words, clay, gestures, and movement in expressive, artistic ways are very different ventures. So while interdisciplinary instruction can be tremendously valuable, it must be based on strong sequential programs of instruction in the individual art forms.

Making Connections

How can we as educators go about exploring connections among the arts and then use that knowledge to provide meaningful experiences for our students? Generalizing across art forms is complex and difficult because the arts press out against boundaries, which results in frequent exceptions to any generality. Then we risk misunderstanding rather than enlightenment. What is a thoughtful teacher to do? David Best (1995) contends,

> Cooperative, interdisciplinary ventures can be highly successful. But their educational value *always* depends upon the *particular* possibilities of greater understanding implicit in *particular* cases. That is, it depends upon the enrichment of understanding for students that is inherent in *particular cases,* where working together from different disciplines offers really fruitful, imaginative educational enlightenment. (p. 88)

If greater understanding comes from the study of particular cases, then a full exploration of the many dimensions of a painting, a piece of music, a poem, or other artistic expression is an important place to start in any interarts curriculum planning.

Sometimes, thinking in terms of models kindles our imaginations and provides structure for our explorations. One day, we, the authors of this book, were idly playing with some plastic geometric toys while brainstorming. One of those toys, a polyhedron, inspired the concept of **facets** as a model for developing a fuller understanding of a work and for pointing to possible intersections among the arts.

The Facets Model for Exploring Connections

Consider the sparkling diamond, ruby, and emerald: These gems are cut with many facets so that when the light enters the top facets of the stone, the other facets reflect it back to the eye. This reflection causes the sparkle that we value so highly in gems. The value we assign to these precious stones is evident in the way we use them as tokens of love and affection, and in their price.

The arts, too, are gems with many facets. Their facets provide manifold ways for us to peer into works of art so that understanding can be reflected back to us. Indeed, the multifaceted nature of art forms is what makes our experience of them so rich—it is what makes them "sparkle" for us. It is from an exploration of these facets that revelations about relationships between or among the arts may emerge. Some of the facets of any particular artistic expression can be revealed by answering these questions:

~ Who created it?
~ When and where was it created?
~ Why and for whom was it created?
~ What does it sound or look like?
~ What kind of structure or form does it have?
~ What is its subject?
~ What is being expressed?
~ What techniques did its creator use to help us understand what is being expressed?

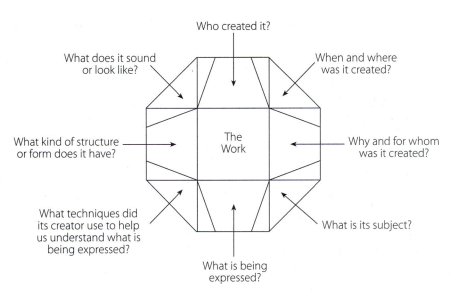

Figure 5.2
Facets of an Artistic Work

Let's apply the facets model to a well-known composition, "Variations on Simple Gifts" from *Appalachian Spring* by Aaron Copland. Imagine three people—a music teacher, a fourth-grade classroom teacher, and a composer—sitting around a table. The music teacher has featured "Variations" in past lessons. The classroom teacher has heard the composition before but was not particularly familiar with it. The composer has studied the composition in great depth and has performed it many times as a bass player in an orchestra. Together they listen to a recording of the music, watch a film of the ballet, read the liner notes to the recording, and generate a list of ideas in response to the questions posed in the facets model. Here is their list:

~ It was written for a ballet choreographed and danced by Martha Graham.

~ The story of the ballet concerns preparations for a pioneer wedding.

~ It was written by Copland, who wanted to write music that was uniquely American.

~ It was completed and first performed in 1944.

~ It is based on the Shaker tune "Simple Gifts."

~ It is in major mode and duple meter.

~ The texture is primarily linear and contrapuntal.

~ The music is in the form of theme and variations.

~ It begins simply then gets more active and complex, like a sunrise before an active day.

~ The accompaniment to the tune in the opening section features the interval of a fifth, which evokes associations with country fiddling.

~ The pauses in the music are relaxing.

~ Watching the ballet distracts my attention from listening.

~ Watching the ballet enhances my listening.

~ The tune is used in a television commercial to sell cars.

Upon examination of this list, the various facets identified for "Variations" fall into three interdependent categories: (a) facets that relate to the properties of the work itself, (b) facets that relate to the context in which the work was created, and (c) facets that relate to an individual's experience of the work. From these facets emerge new insights about how "Variations on Simple Gifts" from *Appalachian Spring* might serve as a springboard for interarts explorations.[3] Here are some ideas:

~ The piece is in the form of theme and variations. How is the theme and variations technique used in other art forms?

~ Copland wrote the music in collaboration with Martha Graham. How does composing music for movement influence a composer's choices?

~ Does the choice of the tune "Simple Gifts" have any symbolic meaning when considered in light of the story of the ballet? What symbols of the pioneer myth can be found in the choreography and stage set of the ballet?

Applying the Facets Model to Music

Now use the facets model yourself. Choose a piece of music, perhaps the same piece you explored in the "transport" exercise in Chapter 4, and see how many of the questions posed in the facets model you can answer. Some of the questions will require you to consult reference materials such as the liner notes of recordings, music textbooks, biographies, music dictionaries, and encyclopedias. Other questions can be answered only as a result of careful listening and reflection on your part. Does investigating the questions posed by the facets model help you understand the piece more fully? Do facets of the piece suggest links and intersections with other art forms, either with particular works or through general concepts?

Exploring the Intersection of Facets

As we have seen in the discussion of "Variations on Simple Gifts" from *Appalachian Spring,* the facets model can be very helpful in exploring the multiple dimensions inherent in any work of art. It can also be helpful in pointing toward potential relationships between and among the arts. These relationships can occur on several planes. Singing a song about rain and then reading a poem about rain demonstrates a simple intersection of facets on the topical plane. When you compare the balanced, symmetrical form of the architecture of the Cathedral at Reims or the U.S. Capitol with the ABA form of a Mozart minuet, you are exploring intersections of facets on the structural plane. Additional planes of intersection may be the context of history (such as studying the political messages conveyed by paintings of the American Revolution or by various versions of "Yankee Doodle") or culture (such as studying the relationship between the geography of Andean countries and the kinds of instruments and weavings made there).

Discovering relationships, even when they appear to be confined to only one plane of intersection, can open possibilities for expanding knowledge and understanding. Even more exciting and rich possibilities present themselves when we look for additional planes of intersection beyond those that are most obvious at first glance.

As an illustration, consider the poem "I Am Growing a Glorious Garden" by Jack Prelutsky (1990, pp. 12–13).

I Am Growing a Glorious Garden

I am growing a glorious garden,
resplendent with trumpets and flutes,
I am pruning euphonium bushes
I am watering piccolo shoots,
my tubas and tambourines flourish,
surrounded by saxophone reeds,
I am planting trombones and pianos
and sowing sweet sousaphone seeds.

I have cymbals galore in my garden,
staid oboes in orderly rows,
there are flowering fifes and violas
in the glade where the glockenspiel grows,
there are gongs and guitars in abundance,
there are violins high on the vine,
and an arbor of harps by the bower
where the cellos and clarinets twine.

My bassoons are beginning to blossom,
as my zithers and mandolins bloom,
my castanets happily chatter,
my kettledrums merrily boom,
the banjos that branch by the bugles
play counterpoint with a kazoo,
come visit my glorious garden
and hear it play music for you.

Jack Prelutsky

It is obvious that one of the facets of this poem is its topic of musical instruments. Is the author really planting instruments in his garden? Of course not: The instruments in the garden are metaphorical. Why is this metaphor so pleasing? One reason is that music and flowers are both prized for their life-enhancing qualities. They both are often present at important life events such as graduations, courtships, weddings, funerals, and civic occasions. Why is this metaphor so amusing? Although we know no one would really plant instruments in a garden, the power of the author's imagination and description allows us to envision the improbable garden of "staid oboes in orderly rows" and bassoons "beginning to blossom."

This connection between gardens and instruments can be explored further. Often gardeners artfully "orchestrate" their flower beds to create a harmonious mix of colors, shapes, and sizes of flowers. They choose flowers not only for their individual beauty but also for the way they coordinate with other flowers in the garden. Each variety of flower has its own particular presence and power: Some flowers, like hollyhocks, are particularly striking so that only a few are needed in a garden, whereas other flowers, such as tulips, create a better effect when planted in abundance. This process of planning a garden is similar to the process a composer undertakes in orchestrating a composition. In a symphony orchestra, the strings are often the predominant "color," while the wind and percussion instruments provide striking aural contrasts. Although a single trumpet can be heard over many string instruments, a single violin would get lost if many trumpets were playing. Just as red roses, orchids, and chrysanthemums can each convey a different message from the sender to the receiver, so can the composer convey particular moods or messages to the listener through careful orchestration. Certain instruments may conjure up specific images, such as the horn with its hunting and pastoral associations. If a composer wants to create an exotic atmosphere, the melody might be given to the oboe instead of the flute.

When trying to find just the right word for a poem, the poet considers not only what the word means, how many syllables it has, and its potential for rhyme, but also other aspects of its sound. In "I Am Growing a Glorious Garden," Prelutsky takes great care in selecting words for how they sound, using the poetic devices of **assonance** (the repetition of vowels sounds with varying consonant sounds) and **alliteration** (two or more words begin with the same sound). Assonance is featured in the lines "an arbor of harps by the bower" and "there are violins high on the vine." Alliteration is found in the lines "My bassoons are beginning to blossom" and "sowing sweet sousaphone seeds." The way a poet chooses particular words for their sound qualities is similar to the way a composer chooses particular instruments for their **timbre,** or tone color.

There is yet another important facet of "I Am Growing a Glorious Garden" that intersects with music. That facet has to do with how the poem itself is constructed. The first line of the poem has an accent scheme of x x x́ x x x́ x x x́ x, which is analogous to musical meter in three, with two unaccented beats preceding the accented beat. The meter and the rhyme scheme are part of the architecture of the poem; they help provide the structure that holds the poem together.

Figure 5.3

Facets of "I Am Growing a Glorious Garden"

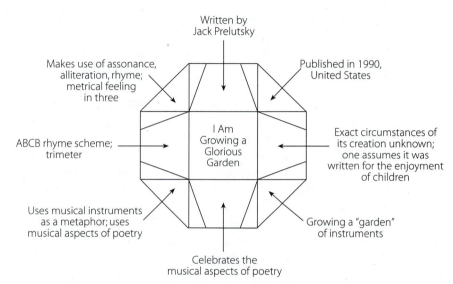

Written by Jack Prelutsky

Published in 1990, United States

Makes use of assonance, alliteration, rhyme; metrical feeling in three

ABCB rhyme scheme; trimeter

I Am Growing a Glorious Garden

Exact circumstances of its creation unknown; one assumes it was written for the enjoyment of children

Uses musical instruments as a metaphor; uses musical aspects of poetry

Growing a "garden" of instruments

Celebrates the musical aspects of poetry

So, as we can see in this example, by digging beneath the surface of what at first seemed a single facet of intersection between "I Am Growing a Glorious Garden" and music—that is, the subject of musical instruments—we can discover even richer and more satisfying relationships. The more planes of intersection shared by two art works, the more power each has to illuminate the other. In Chapter 6 we will explore in greater depth those facets that relate to the qualities inherent in a work itself, and in Chapter 7 we will show how explorations of those facets can lead to lessons that help children discover relationships among the arts.

REFERENCES

Arnheim, R. (1989). *Thoughts on art education.* Los Angeles: Getty Center for Education in the Arts.

Best, D. (1995). The dangers of generic arts: Philosophical confusions and political expediency. *Journal of Aesthetic Education* 29 (2): 79–91.

Cole, A. (1993). *Color.* New York: Dorling Kindersley.

Consortium of National Arts Education Associations. (1994). *National standards for arts education: What every young American should know and be able to do in the arts.* Reston, Va.: Music Educators National Conference.

Gross, T. (May 19, 1995). Radio interview with Sharon Olds. *Fresh Air.* Philadelphia: WHYY. (Originally aired June 29, 1988.)

Haack, P. A. (1970). A study involving the visual arts in the development of musical concepts. *Journal of Research in Music Education* 32: 195–204.

Laughlin, J. (1988). Martha Graham. In L. Morrison (ed.), *Rhythm road.* New York: Lothrop, Lee & Shepard.

Prelutsky, J. (1990). *Something big has been here.* New York: Greenwillow.

Thomas, T. (1991). Interart analogy: Practice and theory in comparing the arts. *Journal of Aesthetic Education* 25 (2): 17–36.

⁂{ chapter 6 }⁂

PERCEPTIONS, PATTERNS, AND PROCESSES

Celia McCarthy attended an unusual concert at Big Rapids High School at the invitation of her former student, Jason. First a string quartet played a fugue while four other students danced the interplay of the instrumental lines as the fugue subject passed from instrument to instrument. Then a trumpet player performed a composition in the form of a theme and variations while a collage she had constructed to demonstrate theme and variations was displayed. At the end of the concert, Jason read a poem he had written about the high school football team's learning ballet. He explained that the scenario in his poem was inspired by the humorous nature of his double bass solo, which he then performed.

By watching and listening to the ways the students demonstrated aspects of their understanding of the music in conjunction with other modes of artistic expression, Celia found that her own experience of the music was heightened. She was fascinated by the discovery of the many ways the arts parallel each other. "Music, poetry, and art already play an important role in my classroom," she mused. "How could I design experiences that would help my students understand how the arts relate to each other?"

In Chapter 5, the facets model was proposed as a way to examine a work in depth and to explore productive intersections between it and other works or forms of art. The facets model encourages us to look at works of art (music, dance, visual art, literary arts, and theater) from different points of view and to consider the aesthetic qualities inherent in the works, the context of their creation, and our reactions to them (see Figure 6.1).

In this chapter, we will discuss in greater depth those facets that relate to the aesthetic qualities inherent in the work itself. These facets are represented by the following questions:

- ~ What is its subject?
- ~ What is being expressed?

Figure 6.1

Facets of Artistic Expression with Emphasis on Structural and Expressive Facets

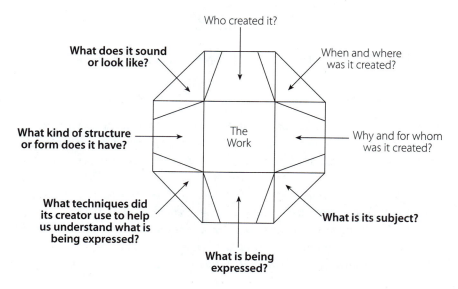

~ What does it sound or look like?

~ What kind of structure or form does it have?

~ What techniques did its creator use to help us understand what is being expressed?

The answers to these questions can be a starting place for discovering analogous relationships between and among the arts and identifying ways that the various art forms share artistic principles or processes.

Applying the Facets Model to Other Art Forms

In Chapter 5, you were encouraged to apply the facets model to a musical example of your choice. Prelutsky's poem "I Am Growing a Glorious Garden" showed how the facets model could be applied to poetry as well. In this chapter, the concepts and terms used to refer to analogous relationships in the arts will have more meaning and clarity if you also select and examine a work from another art form, such as a painting, sculpture, play, or dance, for possible comparisons with music. Surround yourself with interesting examples to consider, and compare your perceptions of artistic elements with others, when possible.

What Is the Subject and What Is Being Expressed?

For some artworks, the answer to the question *What is the subject?* may seem readily apparent. When we see a rose portrayed in a painting or listen to a poem or song about a rose, we will answer the question by say-ing, "The subject is a rose." Artistic representations, however, are not slavish copies of an actual rose or simply exact descriptions of a rose. "Artistic representations give us insights that actual things do not. They have an 'aboutness,' which of course actual things do not . . ." (Parsons & Blocker, 1993, p. 84). When we consider this "aboutness," a new level of thinking about the subject may reveal itself. As we begin to look deeper, beyond what on the surface may present itself as the subject, we may find alternative subjects as possibilities. "Paintings are not about concrete objects so much as about what can be thought or felt and must be apprehended inwardly. They express aspects of experience, states of mind, meanings, emotions; subjective things. . . . Often, we call them feelings; often, ideas or points of view" (Parsons, 1987, p. 70).

What is the subject of music that doesn't have any lyrics? Sometimes a subject is implied through the use of a "program," that is, a title or description that accompanies the work. Music of this type is therefore referred to as **program music.** When one listens to the first movement of Vivaldi's concerto for three violins, *Spring,* one may hear suggestions of twittering birds, flowing streams, and thunderstorms. Someone listening to the music without knowledge of its title, however, might not interpret the music in the same way at all. The title predisposes us to hear the extramusical associations in the music. A similar phenomenon exists in ballet. With prior knowledge of the story of *Swan Lake,* the actions and interactions of the dancers will be seen to tell a story, but without that knowledge, and without clues provided by costumes and sets, the subject of the ballet may be less apparent.

Sometimes the subject of an art work is more abstract: The elements of the art form and their manipulation become the subject. The subject of a symphony by Mozart, for example, is the elements of melody, rhythm, and harmony and their development within a particular form. Music of this type is referred to as **absolute music.** Some examples of program music and absolute music are listed in Table 6.1. Notice that the titles of the program music examples suggest a scene or story whereas the titles of the absolute music examples refer to the musical form or genre.

Program Music	Absolute Music
Vivaldi, *The Four Seasons*	Bach, Prelude and Fugue in D Minor
Beethoven, *Pastoral Symphony*	Mozart, Symphony No. 41 in C
Debussy, *La Mer* [The Sea]	Brahms, Quintet for Clarinet and Strings
Mussorgsky, *Night on Bald Mountain*	Stravinsky, Octet
Saint-Saëns, *Carnival of the Animals*	Zwilich, *Concerto Grosso 1985*

Table 6.1

Examples of Program and Absolute Music

Analogs to absolute music are found in all of the other art forms as well. The subject matter of a dance can be "pure" movement unrelated to a story or theme. The subject for a sculpture can be the relationships of texture, line, form, and space rather than a recognizable object. There are even some analogous examples in poetry, such as poems by Gertrude Stein in which the sounds of words, rather than their meanings, are of primary interest.

What Does the Work Sound or Look Like?

In Chapter 4 we discussed the process of moving from "without" to "within" a work. Part of this process includes developing a deeper personal understanding of the work, then finding ways to share that understanding with others. This involves learning to see what there is to see and hear what there is to hear, and learning how to verbalize those perceptions. Each art form has a specialized vocabulary that helps us communicate about that art form. There is a mutual relationship between our ability to use this vocabulary with care and precision and our abilities to perceive with greater clarity and depth.

Imagine you are looking at a painting and are being asked to describe what you see. You probably would respond first with a description of the painting's subject. With further prompting, you might comment on the colors that are used or the types of lines or shapes that are prominent in the painting. You might also begin to notice how the different components of the painting are grouped. Continued examination would yield new discoveries that were not apparent in the initial viewing and description. The same is true in all of the arts. The outlines in Table 6.2 suggest some of the basic elements that can be perceived in music, dance, visual art, and poetry. The elements in the dance list were derived from the chart of skills and concepts for dance formulated by Adshead, Briginshaw, Hodgens, and Huxley (1982); the elements for visual arts were derived from a similar chart formulated by Ralph A. Smith (1989).

Let's look at the elements of music in greater detail. As you examine Table 6.3, see if you call to mind music that illustrates the characteristics of the elements that are described. Could you provide similar elaborations on the elements of dance, poetry, and visual art listed in Table 6.2? If you need more information to be able to do that, the resource list at the end of this chapter will point you toward books that will help you and your students become more familiar with how artists, dancers, choreographers, and poets use these elements in their work.

Music

melody	rhythm
contour	beat
interval	tempo
register	meter
range	duration—melodic rhythm
melodic sequence	accent
articulation	tone color
staccato/legato	vocal tone colors
attack/sustain/decay	instrumental tone colors
dynamics	harmony
static dynamic levels	chords
changing dynamic levels	tonality

Poetry

sounds of the words	rhythm
rhyme	accents
alliteration	meter
assonance	line length
consonance	
onomatopoeia	figures of speech
	simile
	metaphor

Dance

movement	dancers
spatial elements	numbers and gender
shape	role—lead, subsidiary
size	
pattern/line	visual setting
direction	set
location in performance space	light
dynamic elements	costumes and props
tension/force	
speed/tempo	aural elements
duration	sounds
rhythm	spoken word
clusters of movements	music

Table 6.2

Elements of Music, Poetry, Dance, and Visual Art

continues

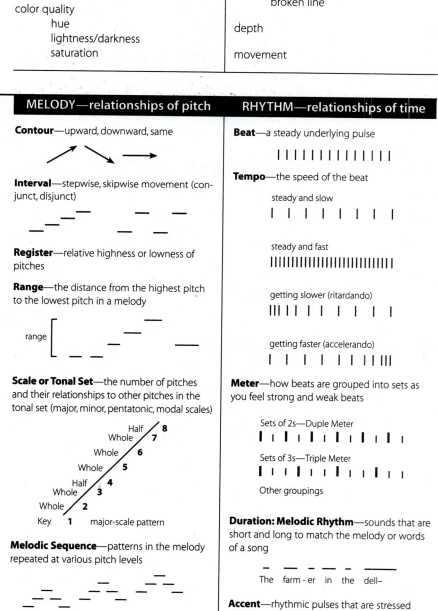

Table 6.2

Elements of Music, Poetry, Dance, and Visual Art, continued

Visual Art	
shape	complexes (clusters of elements)

size	line
	    line area
	    boundary line
	    broken line

position	

color quality
    hue
    lightness/darkness
    saturation
	depth
	
	movement

Table 6.3

A Listener's Compendium of Musical Elements

MELODY—relationships of pitch	RHYTHM—relationships of time
Contour—upward, downward, same	**Beat**—a steady underlying pulse
Interval—stepwise, skipwise movement (conjunct, disjunct)	**Tempo**—the speed of the beat steady and slow steady and fast getting slower (ritardando) getting faster (accelerando)
Register—relative highness or lowness of pitches	
Range—the distance from the highest pitch to the lowest pitch in a melody	**Meter**—how beats are grouped into sets as you feel strong and weak beats Sets of 2s—Duple Meter Sets of 3s—Triple Meter Other groupings
Scale or Tonal Set—the number of pitches and their relationships to other pitches in the tonal set (major, minor, pentatonic, modal scales) Half / 8 Whole / 7 Whole / 6 Whole / 5 Half / 4 Whole / 3 Whole / 2 Key 1 major-scale pattern	**Duration: Melodic Rhythm**—sounds that are short and long to match the melody or words of a song The farm-er in the dell–
Melodic Sequence—patterns in the melody repeated at various pitch levels	**Accent**—rhythmic pulses that are stressed

TONE COLOR— the quality of sounds	HARMONY—"vertical" pitches

Vocal Timbres
solo or ensemble
classifications:
    soprano, alto, tenor, bass
 	
Instrumental Timbres
by specific instruments (flute, guitar, piano, trumpet, violin, snare drum)
 	
by families of the orchestra (string, woodwind, brass, percussion)
 	
by Sachs–von Hornbostel system:
    aerophones: vibrating column of air
    chordophones: vibrating stretched strings
    membranophones: stretched membranes
    idiophones: unstretched vibrating substances
    electrophones: electronically generated sounds
	Chords
	(major, minor, diminished, augmented)
	harmonic progressions
	harmonic rhythm
	
	"Key" Feeling—Tonality
	feeling of a key or tonal center (tonal)
	
	no feeling of key (atonal)
	
	shifting key feelings (modulation)

DYNAMICS—volume or intensity	ARTICULATION
Dynamic Levels—*pp* (very soft); *p* (soft); *mp* (medium soft); *mf* (medium loud); *f* (loud); *ff* (very loud) **Changing Dynamic Levels**—*crescendo* (gradually getting louder); *decrescendo* (gradually getting softer) 	**Legato**—smoothly connected path from one pitch to the next **Staccato**—pitches detached from each other **Attack/Sustain/Decay**

As you examined the elements of the various art forms, you may have noticed that some terminology in the music section of Table 6.2 appeared again in the poetry, visual art, and dance sections. Shared terminology in the arts is quite common. Sometimes the use of the same terms points to similar phenomena across the arts, but as was demonstrated in Chapter 5, the terms can sometimes represent very different phenomena.

Even though differences in media make it impossible to draw direct parallels across art forms, many elements can be understood by way of interarts analogies. The properties related to the broad category of

rhythm are a logical starting place. Most music, dances, and poems have a sense of steady pulse that serves as the reference point for all other aspects of rhythm. Some of those pulses are stressed or accented more than others. When we discover a pattern of stressed and unstressed beats, we become aware of **meter.** A couple dancing a waltz performs a regular repeating pattern of three steps. The beats of the music to which they dance (also called a waltz) are grouped in threes. In a waltz, or any other piece of music in triple meter, a stronger beat is followed by two weaker beats. We may perceive the first beat as being stronger because it is louder than the other beats, because it is higher or lower than the other beats (the oom-pah-pah bass of a waltz, for example), and/or because the harmony changes. Poetry, too, has meter. In poetry, metrical "feet" are organized around accented syllables. Poetry's equivalent of the waltz is dactylic meter: x́ x x. Poems written in dactylic meter often evoke a physical response of swinging or swaying. It was no accident that Robert Louis Stevenson chose that meter for his poem "The Swing": "Hów would you líke to go úp in a swíng?"

    Tempo is the term used to indicate the speed of the beat in music and the speed of movement in dance. In music, the tempo for performance may be indicated by a metronome marking showing the number of beats that are to be performed in a minute (mm = 120), or it may be indicated more generally by words (often in Italian) that designate a range of tempos from slow *(adagio)* to very fast *(presto)*. Poems, like music and dance, also have a range of tempos. These tempos, however, are implied, rather than specified. Speak these excerpts of poetry aloud:

> Clickety-clack / Wheels on the track, /
> This is the way / They begin the attack[1]

> Slowly the tide creeps up the sand /
> Slowly the shadows cross the land[2]

Did you read the second excerpt more slowly than you read the first? Seeing the word "slowly" probably influenced your choice of tempo. Now try this experiment: Read the first excerpt slowly and the second excerpt quickly. What happens? Does your tongue become impossibly tangled when reading the second excerpt? The poet used a combination of vowel and consonant sounds that must be spoken slowly to be enunciated. Thus, through his use of phonetic sounds, he established a tempo that enhances the literal meaning of the words.

    When we speak the excerpts from "Song of the Train" and "Slowly," the ways we use our mouth, tongue, and teeth to articulate are very different. In "Song of the Train," the articulators create consonant sounds of *c, k,* and *t.*

These sounds have a crisp, explosive, detached quality. In "Slowly," more liquid sounds are created by the *s, sh, l, n,* and *w* consonants. These differences in word articulation are analogous to the **articulation** of tones in music that may be characterized as **staccato** and **legato.**

Let's explore further the musician's and the poet's use of the sensuous quality of sound. The musician selects instrumental or vocal **tone colors** to convey a particular mood or feeling. The poet, too, is concerned with the quality of sound and uses devices that emphasize the interest and meaning inherent in the sounds of words. These devices include **rhyme** (words with final syllables that have the same or similar vowel and consonant sounds), **alliteration** (repeated initial consonant sounds), **assonance** (repeated vowel sounds), **consonance** (repetition of similar or identical consonants or words whose main vowels differ), and **onomatopoeia** (word sounds that are similar to the actual sounds they represent). Can you find examples of each of these four devices in the lines from "Song of the Train"? Here are some instances you may have identified: (a) rhyme (cl*ack,* tr*ack,* att*ack*), (b) alliteration (*cl*ickety-*cl*ack), (c) assonance (cl*i*ckety, th*i*s, beg*i*n), and (d) onomatopoeia (clickety-clack). These devices, along with meter, suggest the sound and movement of the train. If you wanted to imitate the percussive articulation of the words of this poem in music, what kinds of instruments would you use? How would those instruments be played? Percussion instruments would be an obvious choice. A violin would also be a possibility if it were played with the wood instead of the hair of the bow *(col legno)* or if it were plucked with the fingers *(pizzicato).* Now contrast how the violin might play to imitate the words of "Slowly." The player would slowly draw the hairs of the bow across the strings to play smooth, legato phrases.

In music, dance, and visual art we speak of shape and direction in lines. Making a connection between lines in music and lines in painting and sculpture is tempting, but also fraught with difficulties. Musicians may refer to a "rising" melodic line or a bass voice that sinks down for a "low" pitch. The spatial connotations of these words are simply a convention, though. Pitches that are "high" differ from "low" pitches in that they have more sound cycles per second. It would be more true to their physical properties to say that "higher" pitches have a greater frequency of cycles per second. But even the terminology that is used to refer to the acoustic properties of tones makes reference to "high" and "low" frequencies. So, it appears that even when speaking in acoustical terms we cannot escape the reference to high and low.

Musicians and music educators regularly draw on the association of pitch level with high and low. Imagine watching the great operatic tenor Luciano Pavarotti ending an aria on a high note. What would he be doing with his arms? He would probably raise them as he ends the aria with a flourish. Now imagine that his aria ends on a low note. Where would his arms be? We would probably find it incongruous if he raised them. Sometimes composers use pitch direction to create the effect of "tone painting." In the Christmas carol "Joy to the World," for example, Handel symbolizes the descent of Jesus to earth by beginning the song with a descending scale. The musical line would be represented in notation by eight notes descending from a high position on the staff to a low one. That graphic representation of high to low might be echoed physically by a teacher coaching a group of singers who traces the descending melodic line with her hand to remind them of the melodic contour of the phrase.

What Kind of Structure or Form Does the Work Have?

A fragment of melody may be beautiful, a gesture graceful, or a metaphor evocative, but these bits of raw material do not become art until they are manipulated and combined with other bits in a meaningful way to create a coherent, expressive whole. In music, the concepts that are related to how musical elements are combined to create the coherent, expressive whole of a composition are **texture** and **form.** (See Table 6.4)

Texture in music is manifested in the way that musical lines are performed either alone or in simultaneous combination with other musical lines. The terms that are commonly used to describe the basic musical textures are **monophony, homophony,** and **polyphony.** When a single singer or a group of singers performs the melody of "Row, Row, Row Your Boat," for example, a monophonic texture is created. If a pianist were to accompany the singing of the melody with chords, that texture would be described as homophonic. If one singer began singing "The Farmer in the Dell" while another sang "Row, Row, Row Your Boat," the result would be a polyphonic texture. If one singer began singing "Row, Row, Row Your Boat," then another began the same song four beats later, a special variety of polyphonic texture, known as a **round,** results. If the pianist were to add chordal accompaniment to the performance of the round, a hybrid of polyphonic and homophonic texture, or **mixed texture,** would be created.

In composing "Farandole" from *L'Arlésienne Suite No. 2,* Georges Bizet made use of all of these types of textures. Listen to the "Farandole" while following the descriptions in the listening chart in Table 6.5. You will notice that Bizet saved the most complex texture for the climax of the composition.

Analogs to polyphony in music can be found in dance and poetry. The relationship of two or more dancers through time can reflect the relationship of polyphonic musical lines; music and dance share the same

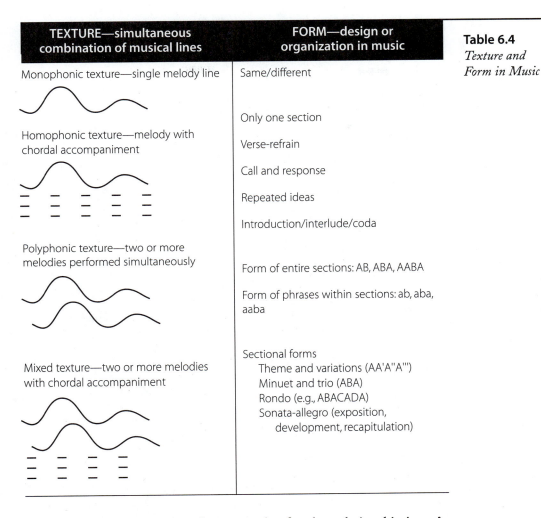

TEXTURE—simultaneous combination of musical lines	FORM—design or organization in music
Monophonic texture—single melody line	Same/different
Homophonic texture—melody with chordal accompaniment	Only one section
	Verse-refrain
	Call and response
	Repeated ideas
	Introduction/interlude/coda
Polyphonic texture—two or more melodies performed simultaneously	Form of entire sections: AB, ABA, AABA
	Form of phrases within sections: ab, aba, aaba

Mixed texture—two or more melodies with chordal accompaniment	Sectional forms
	    Theme and variations (AA'A''A''')
	    Minuet and trio (ABA)
	    Rondo (e.g., ABACADA)
	    Sonata-allegro (exposition,
	        development, recapitulation)

Table 6.4
Texture and Form in Music

labels for these relationships. One example of such a relationship is **osti-nato,** where an individual or a group performs a repeating pattern in movement or sound that underlies the ongoing movements or sounds of the other performers. Another is **canon,** in which everyone performs the same movements or melody, but each performer or group of performers begins at a different time. The characteristic of simultaneity that is the essence of polyphony is rare in poetry, but it can be found. If, for example, a poet wants you to consider two different points of view simultaneously, those points of view might be expressed in two parallel poems placed side by side. Paul Fleischman (1988, 1989) has written two books of poems for two voices, some of which are nearly canonic. One such poem is "Whirligig Beetles," which is the focus of a lesson plan presented in Chapter 7.

		Farandole from *L'Arlésienne* Georges Bizet (1838–1875)		
Table 6.5 *Listening Chart* *for Texture in* *Music*[3]	1 :00 Theme A; minor mode Homophonic texture	4 1.28 Theme A; minor mode Monophonic texture
	2 :17 Theme A; minor mode Polyphonic texture; canon	5 1:38 Theme B; transformed to minor mode
		6 1:44 Theme A; minor mode Begins in monphonic texture, becomes homophonic
		7 1:54 Theme B; minor mode
	3 :34 Theme B; major mode Homophonic texture	8 2:16 Theme A in major mode and Theme B in major mode com- bined with harmony Mixed texture
		9 2:46 Coda

One of the overarching principles in artistic form is the interplay between similarity and difference. Artists walk a tightrope between similarity and difference to achieve cohesiveness and maintain interest in their work. The process of variation is one way artists negotiate that tightrope. In the process of variation, similarity and difference exist simultaneously as some elements of a theme or idea remain constant while other elements undergo change. A dancer, for example, can perform a basic series of movements—a theme, if you will. That movement theme can be varied by making it larger, smaller, higher, lower, stronger, weaker. It can be inverted (high becomes low, forward becomes backward) or performed in retrograde (reverse order). Parts of the movement series can be subtly changed or ornamented. Through all of the variations, however, the relationship to the original theme should be discernible.

Artists also employ the principle of variation in their work. Sometimes a series of variations on an object or abstract pattern is presented within the context of a single work. Sometimes variations are achieved through a series of works in which the presentation of a single subject is varied across works. Study the photographs of the series of bronze reliefs, *Back I, Back II, Back III, Back IV* by Henri Matisse (Figure 6.2). What is the theme of these reliefs? How is that theme varied? You'll notice that the theme, a woman's back, becomes increasingly abstract.

COURTESY OF HIRSHHORN MUSEUM AND SCULPTURE GARDEN, SMITHSONIAN INSTITUTION, GIFT OF JOSEPH H. HIRSHHORN, 1966. PHOTOGRAPH BY LEE STALSWORTH.

Figure 6.2
Henri Matisse.
Back I, Back II,
Back III, Back IV.
ca. 1959–1960.
Bronze relief.

In music, composers achieve variation by ornamenting a melody; presenting it in a different mode; inverting it; changing its tempo, rhythm, and meter; setting it in different textures; and using alternate harmonizations. The more familiar the listener is with the original theme, the greater the possibility for delight in tracking the ways the composer manipulates the theme. Many of the compositions listed in Table 6.6 use familiar songs as the basis for variation, which makes them especially appropriate for initial experiences with theme and variations.

Table 6.6

Music in the Form of Theme and Variations Suitable for Young Listeners

Composer	Composition
Wolfgang Amadeus Mozart	Variations on "Ah, vous dirai-je, Maman" (same tune as "Twinkle, Twinkle, Little Star")
Aaron Copland	Variations on "Simple Gifts" from *Appalachian Spring**
Charles Ives	*Variations on America*
Morton Gould	*American Salute**
Benjamin Britten	*Young Person's Guide to the Orchestra*

* A lesson plan that features Copland's *Variations on "Simple Gifts"* is included in Chapter 7; a lesson plan that features *American Salute* can be found in Chapter 10.

Like theme and variation, the compositional device of **motive** consists of a core idea that undergoes successive transformation. A line or shape, gesture, or brief musical idea can constitute a motive that is repeated and developed to create larger structures. In Seurat's *Sunday Afternoon on the Island of La Grande Jatte,* for example, the arc is used as a motive throughout the painting. We see the arc repeated in the shape of umbrellas, dogs' tails, women's bustles, a monkey's arched back, the crook of a cane, hats and heads, sails, and a bit of a cloud. In music, undoubtedly the most famous use of motive is the initial four notes of Beethoven's Symphony No. 5 in C minor. The melodic shape and rhythm pattern of those four notes provided Beethoven with enough raw musical material to sustain an entire movement. The motive is presented in various guises: at higher and lower pitch levels, inverted, augmented (twice as slow), with altered pitches, and with pitches added or subtracted.

Another way that similarity and difference come into play in artistic form is in the repetition of ideas and the juxtaposition of those ideas with contrasting ideas. **Repetition** and **contrast** can occur on both small-scale or large-scale levels. In poetry, for example, repetition and contrast occur on a small scale when final vowel and consonant sounds are repeated to create rhymes. Those rhymes are contrasted with other lines of the poem to create rhyme schemes that contribute to the larger architecture of the poem.

Repetition and contrast contribute to the sense of balance in a work of art. That balance may be achieved through the equilibrium of exact or similar elements in **symmetry,** or through the use of unequal parts or elements in **asymmetry.** The most common type of symmetrical balance is characterized by ABA form whereby identical or similar parts frame a contrasting part. In music, the sections may consist of only a few phrases or many phrases that combine to create a larger section.

Let's examine how the elements of repetition and contrast, form, and balance operate in the simple song "Twinkle, Twinkle, Little Star." The lyrics of the song follow an *aabbaa* rhyme scheme (see Table 6.7)

a	Twinkle, twinkle, little star,	**Table 6.7**
a	How I wonder what you are.	*Rhyme Scheme of*
b	Up above the world so high,	*"Twinkle, Twinkle,*
b	Like a diamond in the sky.	*Little Star"*
a	Twinkle, twinkle, little star,	
a	How I wonder what you are.	

The last two lines of the lyrics are a literal repetition of the first two lines. This is also true of the phrase structure of the song; therefore, the song's musical form would be labeled ABA (see Example 6.1).

Example 6.1

Phrase Structure of "Twinkle, Twinkle, Little Star"

If we examine the song's structure on a smaller scale, we notice a different scheme of repetition and contrast (see Example 6.2). In the first phrase of the song, the two subphrases are contrasting (a and b), but in the second phrase, the subphrases are identical (c and c). The return of the first full phrase provides a sense of symmetry and completion to the song. We also can find interplay between repetition and contrast in the rhythm and melody of the song. Within each subphrase we see the same rhythm pattern of short and long sounds (six eighth notes and a quarter note). The repetition of the rhythm pattern throughout the entire song provides unity while the contrasting melodic phrases provide variety. The subtle balance between repetition and contrast at both the smaller and larger scales in "Twinkle, Twinkle, Little Star" is one of the reasons that this simple song is regarded as a classic.

Example 6.2
Subphrase Structure of "Twinkle, Twinkle, Little Star"

Because of its temporal nature, music makes more use of repetition than do the visual and literary arts. We can go back and reread a line of poetry or scan a painting again to reinforce our understanding and memory of it. But the sounds of music vibrate in the air, then dissipate. In live performances we can't call them back to listen to them again. That is why composers rely on repetition to familiarize us with the main musical ideas. The next time you are listening to popular music on the radio, try this experiment. When you hear a new song, listen for how many times the refrain of a song is repeated. By the end of the song, can you sing the refrain along with the recording? The refrain you are singing is often referred to as the "hook." By repeating the hook many times throughout the song, the composer "hooks" you into familiarity with the song, thus promoting quicker understanding, and, it is hoped, enjoyment of the song.

What Techniques Did the Creator Use to Help Us Understand What Is Being Expressed?

Every day we express our feelings and emotions by uttering sounds and words, adopting particular postures and facial expressions and using gestures. Sounds, words, postures, gestures, and facial expressions are also raw materials for artistic expression. What differentiates the way those expressive elements are used in daily life from the way they are used in the arts? One difference is that the artist has an aesthetic intention: He or she is deliberately setting about to make art. In the process of making art, the artist's privately held ideas, emotions, and feelings become public expressions created within the constraints of a particular form or medium, such as a song, sonnet, watercolor, or ballet. Another difference is that artists use or create rules to provide structure for their expression. Only within the context of these aesthetic rules does expression become art. John Ciardi, discussing the discipline necessary to create art, said, "Communication of feeling is a skill—a way of doing. It involves pain; it involves difficulty. Robert Frost spoke of 'the pleasure of taking pains.' That is the aesthetic joy" (Ciardi, 1989, p. 13).

An artist starts with an idea or emotion, and in the process of working it out within a particular medium, the idea or emotion becomes clarified; it takes on a form that can be better understood by the artist as well as by the viewer, reader, or listener. The work acquires its own expressive life beyond the artist's original intentions or motivations. Parsons (1987) addresses this phenomenon in the context of painting, but his ideas can be applied to the other arts as well:

> The medium itself as it appears in actual paintings determines the expressiveness, regardless of whether the artist intended precisely what it expresses. This means that the artist can express things that she was not aware of, things that have to do, for example, with her character or with that of the times. (p. 110)

If we, as viewers, readers, and listeners, wish to understand what is expressed in a work of art, we must start to pay closer attention to how artists manipulate their media. Just as the process of creation is characterized by a willingness on the part of the artist to invest hours, days, or years in molding and manipulating raw materials into an expressive work of art, we too must be willing to go beyond casual encounters with the works and invest our time and effort to understand their meaning.

One strategy devised to help learners "read" a work of art is known as **aesthetic scanning** (Dobbs, 1992). This strategy was designed by Harry S. Broudy and W. Dwaine Greer to apply to the study of visual art, but many of its components can be applied to other art forms as well. In this approach, an artwork is examined for its (a) sensory properties (e.g., lines, shapes, colors, textures), (b) formal properties (e.g., relationship of individual elements to the whole, use of theme and variation, balance), (c) technical properties (e.g., media, tools and equipment, and ways of working), and (d) expressive properties (e.g., mood language, dynamic language, and idea language). Sensory and formal properties in this model correspond to the components of the facets model discussed earlier in this chapter that are represented by the questions What does it look like? and What is its form and structure? Engaging in reflection on the technical properties of a work is equally appropriate for music as it is for art. Just as an artist selects his or her medium, masters its techniques, works within its limitations, and sometimes invents new techniques to transcend those limitations, so too do composers and performers. When someone composes music, the expressive possibilities of the medium or media—whether the voice, electronic sounds, string instruments, brass, woodwinds, or percussion—as well as the technical limitations of those media, have to be considered. The composer must understand the ranges of voices and instruments as well as the various techniques used by performers, such as bowings and articulations.

The component of aesthetic scanning that concerns expressive properties is easily applied across all forms of artistic expression. When we think about the expressive properties of a work, we often think first about the **mood** that work evokes. Beginning attempts at characterizing mood are often limited to variations on happy and sad. While it is true that many poems, paintings, musical works, and dances do express happiness or sadness, the mood palette of the arts is much more subtle and varied. Kate Hevner (1936) has compiled a set of adjectives that can be applied to the mood palette of music (see Figure 6.3). You may find this set of adjectives helpful as a starting point for refining the vocabulary you use to describe the mood or moods evoked by music.

The way an artist uses color, a composer uses tone colors, or a writer uses words with particular sound qualities contributes to the mood of their creations. The character of the **dynamic language** of the work also contributes to our perception of mood. Dynamic language refers to elements such as tension, relaxation, energy, and conflict. All works of art incorporate elements of tension and relaxation, but the balance of those elements may be skewed in such a way as to create a prevailing atmosphere of tension or relaxation. If you listen to the opening section of *Prelude to the Afternoon of a Faun* by Debussy, then listen to the "Harbingers of Spring" section of *The Rite of Spring* by Stravinsky, a distinct contrast in dynamic language will be apparent. Tempo, rhythm, accents, and harmonic tension are used in distinctly different ways to achieve the character of languid sensuality in the case of *Prelude to the Afternoon of a Faun* and brutal, primal energy in "Harbingers of Spring."

The **idea language** of a work also contributes to its potential expressiveness. Idea language includes symbols, social concepts and values, and psychological or political values. To be able to interpret the idea language of a work, we must know something about the context in which it was created. We come closer to understanding the meaning of the work when

bright
cheerful
happy
joyous
merry

agitated
dramatic
exciting
exhilarated
passionate
restless
sensational
soaring
triumphant

delicate
fanciful
graceful
humorous
light
playful
quaint
sprightly
whimsical

emphatic
exalting
majestic
martial
ponderous
robust
vigorous

calm
leisurely
lyrical
quiet
serene
soothing
tranquil

awe-inspiring
dignified
lofty
sacred
serious
sober
solemn
spiritual

dark
depressing
doleful
frustrated
gloomy
heavy
melancholy
mournful
sad
tragic

dreamy
longing
plaintive
pleading
sentimental
tender
yearning

we understand the meaning inherent in symbols or allusions used by an artist. The *1812 Overture,* for example, can be enjoyed simply for the way Tchaikovsky combines the elements of music to create stirring themes. If one is aware, however, that Tchaikovsky commemorates the defeat of Napoleon in Russia by symbolically waging a battle between the Russians and the French through the incorporation of their respective national anthems into the overture, the work will be understood in a very different way.

Figure 6.3
Hevner Adjective Circle (adapted)

Learning More about the Arts

In this chapter, we have discussed how an exploration of facets of the arts that relate to formal properties can be a starting place for discoveries about perceptions, patterns, and processes that cut across art forms. Such multifaceted examinations of the arts enhance, rather than detract from, our enjoyment of them. According to Umberto Eco (1989), "The form of the work of art gains its aesthetic validity precisely in proportion to the number of different perspectives from which it can be viewed and understood. These give it a wealth of different resonances and echoes without impairing its original essence" (p. 3).

The more you know about the various forms of art, the more readily you can see connections between and among them. To help you and your students expand your understanding of music, visual art, dance, and poetry, we provide a bibliography that includes books written for young readers as well as books written for adults. In Chapter 7 we will discuss how to plan educational experiences that will lead students to discover relationships between music and the other arts.

REFERENCES

Adshead, J., Briginshaw, V. A., Hodgens, P., & Huxley, M. R. (1982). A chart of skills and concepts for dance. *Journal of Aesthetic Education* 16 (3): 51–61.

Blishen, E. (ed.). (1984). *Oxford book of poetry for children.* New York: Peter Bedrick.

Ciardi, J. (1989). *Ciardi himself: Fifteen essays in the reading, writing, and teaching of poetry.* Fayetteville: University of Arkansas Press.

Cole, J. (Ed.). (1984). *A new treasury of children's poetry: Old favorites and new discoveries.* Garden City, N.Y.: Doubleday.

Davidson, M. C., Ferguson, N., Staton, B., & Staton, M. (1990). *Music and you.* New York: Macmillan.

Dobbs, S. M. (1992). *The DBAE Handbook: An overview of discipline-based art education.* Los Angeles: The Getty Center for Education in the Arts.

Eco, U. (1989). *The open work* (Anna Cancogni, trans.). Cambridge: Harvard University Press.

Fleischman, P. (1988). *Joyful noise: Poems for two voices.* New York: Harper & Row.

Fleischman, P. (1989). *I Am Phoenix: Poems for two voices.* New York: Harper & Row.

Hevner, K. (1936). Experimental studies of the elements of expression in music. *American Journal of Psychology* 48: 245–286.

Parsons, M. (1987). *How we understand art: A cognitive developmental account of aesthetic experience.* Cambridge: Cambridge University Press.

Parsons, M., & Blocker, H. G. (1993). *Aesthetics and education.* Urbana: University of Illinois Press.

Smith, R. A. (1989). *The sense of art: A study in aesthetic education.* New York: Routledge.

ADDITIONAL RESOURCES FOR LEARNING ABOUT THE ARTS

MUSIC

Beethoven, J., Bohn, D., Campbell, P. S., Culp, C., Davidson, J., Eisman, L., Glover, S. L., Hayes, C., Hilley, M., Hoffman, M. E., March, H., McCloud, B., Moore, M., Nadon-Gabrion, C., Palmer, M., Ravosa, C., Reilly, M. L., Schmid, W., Scott-Kassner, C., Sinor, J., Stauffer, S., & Thomas, J. (1995). *The music connection.* Morristown, N.J.: Silver Burdett Ginn.

Bond, J., Davidson, M. C., Goetze, M., Lawrence, V. P., & Snyder, S. (1995). *Share the music.* New York: Macmillan/McGraw-Hill.

Copland, A. (1988). *What to listen for in music.* New York: McGraw-Hill.

Dallin, L. (1986). *Listener's guide to musical understanding.* Dubuque, Iowa: Wm. C. Brown.

Fowler, C. (1994). *Music! Its role and importance in our lives.* New York: Glencoe.

Kernfeld, B. D. (1995). *What to listen for in jazz.* New Haven, Conn.: Yale University Press.

Spence, K. (1994). *The young people's book of music.* Brookfield, Conn.: Millbrook.

Weiss, R. (1991). *Music and expression.* Dubuque, Iowa: Wm. C. Brown.

VISUAL ART

The art of sculpture. (1993). New York: Scholastic.

Blizzard, G. S. (1990). *Come look with me: Enjoying art with children.* Charlottesville, Va.: Thomasson-Grant.

Cole, A. (1993). *Color.* New York: Dorling Kindersley.

Cumming, R. (1979). *Just look...: A book about paintings.* New York: Charles Scribner's Sons.

Davidson, R. (1993). *Take a look: An introduction to the experience of art.* New York: Viking.

Horwitz, E. L. (1976). *A child's garden of sculpture.* Washington, D.C.: Washington Books.

Isaacson, P. M. (1993). *A short walk around the pyramids & through the world of art.* New York: Knopf.

Pekarik, A. (1992). *Painting behind the scenes.* New York: Hyperion Books for Children.

Vyverberg, H. (1988). *The living tradition: Art, music, and ideas in the Western world.* San Diego: Harcourt Brace Jovanovich.

Yenawine, P. (1991a). *Colors.* New York: The Museum of Modern Art/Delacourt.

Yenawine, P. (1991b). *Lines.* New York: The Museum of Modern Art/Delacourt.

Yenawine, P. (1991c). *Shapes.* New York: The Museum of Modern Art/Delacourt.

Yenawine, P. (1995). *Key art terms for beginners.* New York: Harry N. Abrams.

DANCE

Au, S. (1988). *Ballet and modern dance.* London: Thames and Hudson.

Hayes, E. (1993). *Dance composition and production* (2nd ed.). Pennington, N.J.: Princeton Book Company.

Kerner, M. (1990). *Barefoot to Balanchine: How to watch dance.* New York: Doubleday.

Minton, S. C. (1986). *Choreography: A basic approach using improvisation.* Champaign, Ill.: Human Kinetics.

POETRY

Ciardi, J., & Williams, M. (1975). *How does a poem mean?* Boston: Houghton Mifflin.

Dacey, P., & Jauss, D. (eds.). (1986). *Strong measures: Contemporary American poetry in traditional forms.* New York: Harper & Row.

Jones, R. T. (1986). *Studying poetry: An introduction.* London: Edward Arnold.

Strauss, P. (1993). *Talking poetry: A guide for students, teachers and poets.* Cape Town, South Africa: David Philip.

{ chapter 7 }

PLANNING INTERDISCIPLINARY ARTS EXPERIENCES FOR STUDENTS

In Chapters 4, 5, and 6 we presented ideas and activities to help you deepen your understanding as you encounter particular works of music, art, poetry, or other arts. We hope that through your exploration of these works' facets, some new insights about relationships among the arts have emerged. Perhaps you are beginning to think about how the facets of a piece of music can lead you to other areas of the curriculum. Now that you have begun to make some connections, it is time to turn our attention to the question of how to design educational experiences to help students make their own connections.

In Chapter 6 we discussed facets of the arts that relate to perceptions, patterns, and processes. We did so in a way that we hope is meaningful to you, an adult reader. Because you are an adult, we have made certain assumptions related to your ability to grasp these ideas. One is that you have reached a stage of intellectual development in which you can deal with abstract concepts. Another is that, because of your own life experience, you are able to understand, relate to, and talk about a wide range of emotions. Yet another is that you have a vast storehouse of knowledge about the world including a perspective that transcends your own place in time and space. We also assume that you have had some experience with the arts as producer or performer and that you have seen and heard at least some of the works of art and music to which we have referred or are able to obtain recordings and reproductions of the works from a library or other source.

Now think about the students you are or will be teaching. Do the assumptions we hold for you also hold true for your students? If you are teaching young children, most likely not. If you are teaching students at the middle school or high school level, some of the assumptions may apply, some may not. Through careful observation of children's responses to the arts, teachers and researchers have described general characteristics of the developmental path from birth through adolescence. These generalizations help teachers tailor instructional experiences to the student, accounting for areas of cognitive, physical, emotional, social, and affective growth. Perceptive teachers will also be alert to individual variations in development, particularly as experiences in music, art, dance, or theater draw on multiple forms of understanding and skill.

Children's development in the arts is a complex issue because of the multifaceted nature of the arts themselves and because of our interactions with them. One can come to the arts as (a) a producer or performer, whereby one is "in the middle" of the work; (b) a perceiver, whereby one stands outside the work observing the components of the work and the way they interact to create meaning; or (c) a reflective inquirer, whereby one is even further removed from the work considering issues such as function or context (Wolf, 1989). Each of these artistic activities is mutually enhancing, but the relative influence and importance of each may shift as one matures.

Most of children's interactions with the arts are in the realm of production/performance and perception. Young children tend to be concerned with the aspects of art that have relevance to their own worlds and gravitate toward favorite colors, or songs, poems, or paintings about favorite things or activities (Parsons, 1987). They respond to the sensory qualities of arts experiences. Young children often react physically to the rhythmic qualities of music and poetry; children perceive differences in loud and soft and use them for expressive purposes in their own performance; they distinguish differences in tone color and begin to associate tone colors with particular instruments.

With children's increasing maturity also comes a "developmental shift from an absorption with their own individual work to an appreciation of tradition and the social aspects of their work" (Davidson & Scripp, 1989, p. 72). As children become able to consider a work of art from another's point of view, they become better able to move beyond personal preference to reflect on what a composer or artist is communicating, why a composer or artist made particular choices, and how those choices affect the expressiveness of the work. Continued instruction and maturity deepens the capacity for these reflections; this capacity continues to develop into and throughout adulthood.

Designing Interarts Experiences for Children

When designing arts experiences in the classroom, one must remember that direct experience with the arts is of utmost importance. For children to understand the arts conceptually, they must sing songs, listen to music representing a variety of styles and time periods, move—both freely and in patterned designs—view artwork in a variety of media and styles, and read and listen to vivid poetry. The teacher provides experiences that create new "worlds" for the children and enlarges their scope of experience beyond that which they encounter day to day. To create this world convincingly, it is vital that the recordings and reproductions used be of the highest quality possible.

If part of your plan includes opportunities for students to perform or create, make sure they have had the prior experiences necessary to be able to do so with skill and success. Untutored exploration of the raw materials of the arts may result in some happy and fortuitous discoveries. To sustain interest and develop skill, however, teachers need to sequence and structure the educational experience with care. How will students progress from obvious choices to artistic sophistication? How will experiences be arranged to draw on already-acquired knowledge and skill while at the same time making it possible for students to acquire new tools and enhanced understanding? How will students' reflections on the processes of performance and creation be encouraged to help them acquire the discipline and rigor necessary for excellent work?

Thoughtful, sensitive planning brings all of these factors into the foreground of a teacher's attention in the design of interarts experiences. In the next portion of this chapter, descriptions of four instructional strategies that incorporate music, children's literature, movement, and visual art will be presented. Ideas for the first strategy are provided in skeletal form. The lesson plan for the second strategy is accompanied by parallel commentary that explains the rationale behind the instructional choices made in the lesson. Fully scripted lesson plans are provided for the third and fourth strategies. These complete plans include a rationale for each lesson, objectives, assessment strategies, and ideas for extending the lesson to make additional curricular links. These plans will demonstrate applications of the facets model to planning interarts experiences.

Lesson 1
Exploring the Qualities of Sound in Poetry and Instruments

The poem "Jump or Jiggle" by Evelyn Beyer (Arbuthnot & Root, 1968) is enjoyed by young children because of its appealing subject matter, its distinct meter, and its colorful use of words. Alliteration (*worms wiggle, snakes slide*) and onomatopoeia (*horses clop, bugs jiggle*) abound in this poem. These characteristics easily lend themselves to an exploration of the musical potential inherent in the poem. The following lesson would be appropriate for students in first or second grade.

Jump or Jiggle

Frogs jump
Caterpillars hump

Worms wiggle
Bugs jiggle

Rabbits hop
Horses clop

Snakes slide
Sea gulls glide

Mice creep
Deer leap

Puppies bounce
Kittens pounce

Lions stalk—
But—
I walk!

Evelyn Beyer

---

1) Read the poem using vocal inflections that highlight the alliteration and onomatopoeia.

2) Pat hands on thighs then clap hands together to create a two-beat pattern. Perform the pattern as the poem is read so that the pat-clap pattern coincides with the metrical rhythm of the poem.

3) Experiment with ways to move that reflect the descriptions and sounds of the animals' movements.

4) Experiment with ways to play instruments to reflect the qualities, descriptions, and sounds of the animals' movements.

5) Speak a line of the poem, then play the instrument sounds for the animal described, either imitating the word rhythms or creating an appropriate rhythm to fit in the two-beat time frame.

In this lesson, the term *instruments* can be interpreted very broadly to mean any object producing a sound that can be used in a musical way. Everyday objects found around the classroom can be used as instruments. Have you ever considered a coat zipper as an instrument? How about a plastic drinking glass turned upside down and tapped on a desk? If two plastic drinking glasses are taped together with dried rice, beans, or lentils inside, you can imitate the sound of a maraca. Some types of plastic drinking glasses have ridges that can be scraped by a pencil to mimic the sound of a guiro.

In one classroom equipped with a wide assortment of traditional classroom instruments, the poem was "orchestrated" in this fashion:

Jump or Jiggle

Frogs jump	two wood blocks with different pitches
Caterpillars hump	short scrapes back and forth on a guiro
Worms wiggle	tambourine, shaken
Bugs jiggle	maracas
Rabbits hop	rhythm sticks
Horses clop	temple blocks
Snakes slide	sand blocks
Sea gulls glide	slide whistle
Mice creep	fingertips fluttering on hand drum
Deer leap	large hand drum
Puppies bounce	drum struck with a hard mallet
Kittens pounce	drum struck with a soft mallet
Lions stalk—	timpani roll
But—	foot stamps
I walk!	

Evelyn Beyer

Lesson II
Musical Improvisation and Children's Literature

Musical improvisation is also the focus of this lesson. A children's book, *The Maestro Plays* (Martin, 1994), provides the impetus for improvisation. In the book, the maestro plays loudly, slowly, swingingly, sweepingly, and so on; children will create the music they imagine the maestro is playing. A singing game, "Billy, Billy," which features movement improvisation, serves as a prelude to musical improvisation.

Example 7.1
"Billy, Billy"

Here's   the way   we Bil - ly, Bil - ly,   Bil - ly, Bil - ly, Bil - ly, Bil - ly,

Here's   the way   we Bil - ly, Bil - ly,   All   night   long! __

Verse 2:	Step back Sally, Sally, Sally Strutting down the alley, All night long!
Verse 3:	Here comes another one, Just like the other one, Here comes another one, All night long!

Formation   Players, in two lines, facing partners

Action

Verse 1:	All players "twist" with partners.
Verse 2:	Players take four steps backward. Head player improvises a movement while moving to end of opposite line.
Verse 3:	Improviser's partner imitates action while moving to end of opposite line.

The Flow of the Experience:

1) Begin with a creative movement exercise—"Billy, Billy" (in two lines with partners across from one another)

The Thinking behind the Flow:

Young children learn by doing and acting out their understanding. This movement game has structure (in verse 1 all move together) and freedom (in verses 2 and 3 partners improvise movements). Children move in response to the rhythmic character of the song.

The Flow of the Experience:	**The Thinking behind the Flow:**
2) Read *The Maestro Plays* by Bill Martin Jr. (1994). Draw attention to the illustrations.	Descriptive questions—What do you see? What do you notice? What is happening here?— build perception and verbal ability.
Transition: "But there isn't any music with the Maestro's story, so we must make our own. Can you imagine what the Maestro's music sounds like?"	This encourages students to imagine the sounds that accompany the lively text and bold illustrations.
3) Build musical vocabulary by echoing melodic and rhythmic patterns using Orff instruments set up with a limited set of pitches. Teacher plays, children echo. Use familiar labels to describe sound or ask children to describe the high/low, fast/slow, soft/loud possibilities.	Observation of a model. Children practice their skills at imitating the model using gestural, visual, and auditory cues. Labels give a name to the elements that are formed into concepts (internal mental structures).
4) Develop musical question-and-answer conversations. The teacher may play a short question phrase, which is answered, but not exactly imitated by the class. As the children catch on, encourage "paired conversations" between students.	Moving from imitation to invention. Children perceive the content of the question, and respond with a musically sensible answer.
5) Display adverbs from *The Maestro Plays* that have been printed on cards and sequenced in order of appearance. Develop a whole-class response to "proudly, loudly" and "slowly, oh——ly."	Drawing attention to adverbs and their *-ly* forms. Martin has used typical adverbs and imaginative ones, too. The *tutti* or "all together" section will help to set expectations about the length of the improvisations.
6) Invite pairs of players to select one of the adverb cards to develop into an improvisation with speech and music. Allow for time to explore, settle on ideas, and practice in pairs.	Allowing for choice helps to personalize the lesson. Pairs work cooperatively and negotiate their ideas. This is an example of musical problem solving.

The Flow of the Experience:

7) Perform the entire book. If desired, play the *tutti* sections again as an encore.

The Thinking behind the Flow:

The entire performance restores the whole of the book, now enhanced with the musical interpretation.

Objectives, Learning Activities, and Assessment

If you were to implement the preceding lessons in your classroom, what would the students be learning? How would you know if they had learned it? Although the students' and teacher's **activities** have been described, no educational **objectives** have been stated, nor have **assessment** strategies been specified.

The metaphor of a journey is helpful in thinking about the multiple dimensions of lesson planning. First of all, we need to know where we want to go. If we embark on a long journey, we break the trip up into shorter legs. Sometimes, unforeseen circumstances cause us to modify our plans. So it is with teaching. We must have a clear idea of what students should know or be able to do as a result of instruction—that is, well-articulated objectives. Long-term objectives are broken down into shorter-term objectives. A time frame for the accomplishment of those objectives is estimated, but is often modified based on students' progress.

The next question of our travel metaphor is, How are we going to get there? When traveling we have many alternatives: We may fly, drive, sail, walk, or ride a bicycle, train, or bus. We weigh the alternatives in terms of cost, efficiency, convenience, and personal preference. We use maps and guidebooks to help us make our decisions. In planning instruction we choose from among many alternatives for guiding children's interactions with the concepts or skills to be learned. These interactions may include participating in teacher-led activities; observing the teacher or another student modeling a skill, then practicing independently; solving self-selected or teacher-designed problems or puzzles in small groups; or engaging in independent research to answer questions. We choose songs, books, videos, computer programs, recordings, diagrams, and other instructional materials to help students achieve the objectives.

The final question of our travel metaphor is, How do we know when we've arrived? If we know precisely where it is we want to go, it is usually easy to ascertain if, when, and where we've arrived. Unfortunately, in our journey of learning we don't encounter large signs that read, "Welcome to New Understanding," so we have to set up our own methods for assessing our progress on the journey.

Objectives for music learning reflect the array of ways we experience and interact with music. Objectives may relate to singing, moving to music, performing on an instrument, interpreting notation, improvising and creating music, listening with understanding, making judgments about music, and understanding music's relationship to the other arts as well as its historical and cultural context. Because the purpose of teaching is to promote learning, objectives should be written in terms of what *students* should know and be able to do as a result of instruction, not what the *teacher* will do.

The method one chooses to assess student achievement should be congruent with the type of learning that is taking place. For example, if students are given guidelines for a composition task, their compositions should be assessed in terms of those guidelines. If the learning outcome states that students will synchronize body movement with the beat of the music, the teacher can assess achievement by systematically observing and noting the degree of competence of individuals' performances in a group setting. Traditional pencil-and-paper assessments can be used to assess factual knowledge; interviews and journals work well for assessing more subjective areas of learning such as aesthetic understanding. There are many excellent resources you can consult to learn about additional assessment strategies. Two such resources are *Student-Centered Classroom Assessment* by Richard J. Stiggins (1994) and *A Practical Guide to Alternative Assessment* by Herman, Aschbacher, and Winters (1992).

Now that we have completed our whirlwind tour of objectives, learning activities, and assessment, go back and read Lessons I and II again. Can you formulate learning objectives for the lessons? What strategies could you use to assess student understanding and achievement? If you would like to see models of outcomes and assessments, examine the last two lesson plans in this chapter or lesson plans presented elsewhere in this book.

Lesson III
Bach and the Beetles

Rationale   When I first read the poem "Whirligig Beetles" by Paul Fleischman (1988), I was struck by the similarities between its construction and the contrapuntal construction of a Bach invention. In these works, I found the potential for exploring principles of form shared by two different art forms. Listeners sometimes have difficulty understanding the nature of contrapuntal music because they are unused to listening to two melodic lines simultaneously. The poem serves as a vehicle for students to explore the nature of counterpoint, which they then can apply to music.

   The musical elements of counterpoint and triple meter, so prominent in "Whirligig Beetles," can also be found in Bach's Invention No. 10 in G. Similarities in the facets of these two works can be readily seen in this combined model shown in Figure 7.1.

Figure 7.1
*Facets of
"Whirligig
Beetles" and
Invention No.
10 in G*

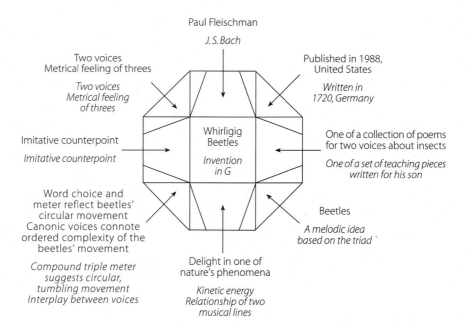

The activities in this lesson plan are designed to guide students in making discoveries for themselves about the parallels between these two works.

Grade Level   Fourth through Eighth

Objectives   Students will

- ~ identify and respond physically to the metrical feeling of three in music and poetry.
- ~ recognize the imitative contrapuntal use of voices in music and poetry.
- ~ perform a poem for two voices with expression.

Materials

- ~ "Whirligig Beetles" by Paul Fleischman (see Figure 7.2)
- ~ Recording: Bach, J. S. (1985), *Two-part inventions BWV 772a–786; three-part inventions BWV 780–810* [CD], A. Schiff, pianist, New York: London (other recordings may be substituted)
- ~ Copies for students of the first six measures of Two-Part Invention No. 10 in G by Johann Sebastian Bach (see Example 7.2)
- ~ Hand drums

COURTESY OF HARPERCOLLINS PUBLISHERS. USED BY PERMISSION.

Figure 7.2
"Whirligig Beetles"

Example 7.2
*First Six
Measures of
Two-Part
Invention
No. 10 in G*

**Introducing
the lesson**

1) Arrange four or five hand drums on the floor, heads down. Ask students to follow you with their eyes as you walk a path around and between the drums. Then ask for a student volunteer to follow you as you walk a fluid, curving path around the drums. Have another volunteer follow you as you walk a sharp, angular path around the drums. *As I read this poem, imagine in your mind's eye what kind of path the beetles in the poem might take if they were to move around the drums.* Read the third column of "Whirligig Beetles," then ask for a volunteer to demonstrate the beetles' path as you read the poem again.

**Developing
the lesson**

2) What did you hear in the poem that made you want to walk such a curving path? Students should recognize the word cues such as "swimming in circles," "turning, revolving and curving," "arcs, ovals, and loops." Some students may also identify that the rhythm of the words contributes to the feeling of circular motion. Explore this notion by having the students tap the fingertips of both hands together on the strong beat that falls on the accented syllable of the words while you read the third column of the poem. Encourage students to let their hands rebound in a circular motion after the tap, then come together again for the next beat. Ask them to lightly whisper "one, two, three" as they make their circles. *Beats grouped in threes often make us want to move in a circular motion. The waltz, for example, is a dance in three. Waltzers never dance in a straight line, but instead, spin around the dance floor. So the poet, Paul Fleischman, helps us imagine the movement of the beetles not only by using words that tell us the beetles are revolving and curving, but also by using words that help us feel the circular movement.*

3) *As you listen to this music, tap your fingertips together where you feel the beat.* Play a brief excerpt from the Bach Invention No. 10. *Did you find that your hands wanted to make a circle as they did when we tapped to "Whirligig Beetles?" Let's listen again and whisper "one, two, three" as we did before.* Play the music again. *Now, let's look at how this music is notated.* Give students copies of the excerpt from the Bach Invention No. 10. *Do you see how three eighth notes are grouped together with one beam? These were the groups of three we were counting. How many groups of three eighth notes can you find in each measure?* In every measure there are three groups of three.

4) *Let's look again at the notation. How many lines of music are there?* Two. We sometimes call these lines "voices" even though they are played on an instrument rather than sung. *Lightly connect the note heads in the top line in "dot-to-dot" fashion. The line you've drawn shows the contour, or the path of higher and lower pitches, that the music takes. Now do the same for the bottom line. Compare the contour of the top line in measures 1 and 2 with the contour of the bottom line in measures 2 and 3. What do you notice?* Students respond. *Because their contours look so similar, let's see how similar their sound is. You'll hear the top voice easily, but you'll have to listen carefully for the lower voice. How do they compare?* Play the excerpt. Students should recognize that the two voices have the same tune but at different pitch levels. *What other form of music do we know where one voice starts out singing a tune and then another starts singing the tune later? That's right—a round or a canon. Bach put these two voices together very much like a canon. Listen to the music again and see if you can hear how one voice starts an idea and the other follows along behind.*

5) *Let's go back to the "Whirligig Beetle" poem. When I read it to you before, I was only reading part of the poem. Let's look at the poem together. Can you figure out how the poem is really supposed to be read?* Students offer suggestions. *Would it help you figure out this puzzle if I told you that the author says this is a poem for two voices? Now how would you suggest we read it? What does this poem have in common with the Bach invention?*

6) Have students read one voice of the poem together slowly. *When we speak the poem slowly in unison, some of the "music" of the words gets lost. How can we make our reading more expressive?*

Closing the lesson

7) Note the places in the poem where voice 1 leads, where voice 2 leads, and where both voices are speaking together in unison. Group students as partners and let them decide who will be voice 1 and who will be voice 2. Give them time to practice speaking the poem together as written. Encourage them to capture the lighthearted fun of the poem through expressive reading. Invite students to perform their readings for each other.

Assessment

~ Do students recognize how circular movement is both denoted and connoted in "Whirligig Beetles"?

~ Do students' tapping movements show both the tempo and the character
of the Bach invention?

~ Do students recognize parallels between the construction of Bach's
Invention No. 10 and "Whirligig Beetles"?

~ When students read the poem, do the two voices show awareness of each
other by keeping the same tempo and speaking in unison when appropriate? Do they read expressively?

**Extending
the lesson**

Create a movement canon having students improvise a series of movements of
four beats' duration. To assemble the series of movements to form the canon, a
student performs his or her four-beat movement series, then everyone else imi-
tates it. The second four-beat series is demonstrated by an individual, then
learned by the class. This procedure continues until the four series are learned.
Then divide the class into two groups. The first group begins performing the
entire sequence, then, four beats later, the second group begins.

Lesson IV
"Simple Gifts" (Theme and Variations)

Rationale   By the upper elementary or middle school level, students who have participated in well-planned arts programs acquire a conceptual understanding of various elements in art and music and possess a descriptive vocabulary to represent that understanding. The purpose of the lesson is to introduce the students to the idea of variation, which they will apply in subsequent lessons by composing theme and variations and creating artworks that center around a theme. When I considered which musical composition to select as an example of that form, Aaron Copland's well-known variations on the Shaker tune "Simple Gifts" immediately came to mind. The song Copland quotes in the music for the ballet *Appalachian Spring* led to a fascinating investigation of the original tune in its distinctly American context.

Grade Level   Fifth through Eighth

Objectives   Students will

~ describe subtle differences in design in a drawing of six Shaker slat-back chairs.

~ sightread the rhythm and melody of the song "Simple Gifts."

~ listen to a recording of Shaker singing and discuss how the text of the song reflects Shaker traditions and beliefs.

~ identify the way musical elements are used in Variations on "Simple Gifts" from *Appalachian Spring* by Copland.

Materials   ~ A reproduction of the "Shakers' Slat Back Chairs, with Rockers" (Figure 7.3)

~ Student copies of "Simple Gifts" (Example 7.3)

~ Recordings: Boston Camerata, Schola Cantorum of Boston, and The Shaker Community of Sabbathday Lake (performers), (1995), *Simple gifts: Shaker chants and spirituals* [CD], Germany: Erato; and Copland, A. (1983), *Appalachian Spring* [CD], Los Angeles Philharmonic Orchestra, conducted by Leonard Bernstein, Hamburg: Polydor; or another recording of the Appalachian Spring Suite for full orchestra.[1]

~ Envelopes containing descriptions of the theme and variations on separate strips (see Table 7.3). Place the strips in the envelope in random order. You may wish to prepare the descriptions for interludes on a different color of paper to distinguish them from the theme and variations.

Figure 7.3
Shakers' Slat Back Chairs, with Rockers

The Shakers' Slat Back Chairs, with Rockers.
WORSTED LACE SEATS.
Showing a Comparison of Sizes.

No. 0	No. 1	No. 3	No. 4	No. 6	No. 7
$3.25	$3.50	$4.50	$7.00	$7.50	$8.00

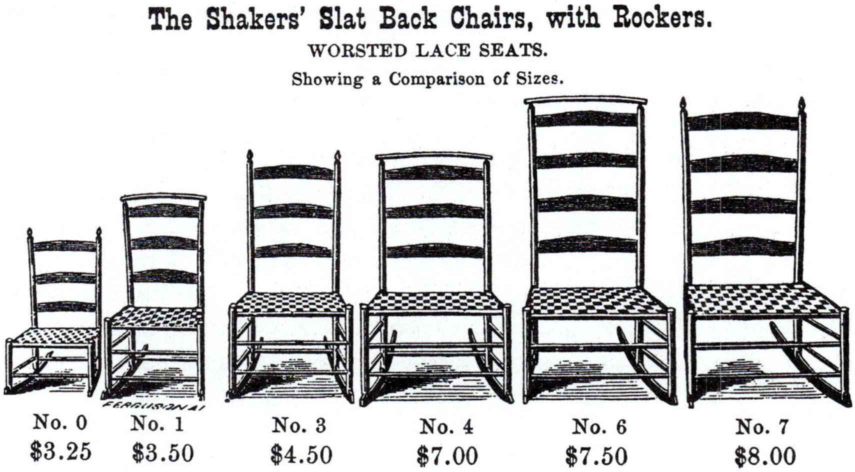

REPRINTED FROM ILLUSTRATED CATALOGUE AND PRICE LIST OF SHAKER'S CHAIRS (WASHINGTON, D.C.: SMITHSONIAN INSTITUTION PRESS), PAGE 22, BY PERMISSION OF THE PUBLISHER. COPYRIGHT © 1972.

Introducing the lesson

1) Begin by describing chairs in the classroom, drawing attention to materials, size, shape, or style. *Would you choose any of these chairs as furnishings for your room or home? What makes these chairs "school furniture"?* Display a reproduction of "The Shakers' Slat Back Chairs, with Rockers." Ask students to list all of the characteristics of these chairs (size, number of slats, finials or crossbars at the top, width of seat, height). *What do you see that remains the same from chair to chair? In what ways are they different from each other? What sort of illustration is this?* (Answer: a catalog illustration.) *When do you suppose the catalog was published?* (The prices, $3.50 to $8.00, suggest an earlier time.) *What are the practical reasons these chairs are offered in various sizes? Are they beautiful? Would you choose these as furnishings for your room or home?* Draw attention to the title of the illustration and solicit what the students know about the Shakers. Display photographs from books about the Shaker community; describe characteristic beliefs and practices.

A Brief Portrait of the Shakers

The Shakers, the common name for members of the United Society of Believers, are one of America's most notable religious and utopian communities. With beginnings in Manchester, England, in 1747, a small group of Believers arrived in the United States in 1774 under the direction of their leader, Ann Lee, referred to as "Mother Ann." Never a large group, Shaker membership peaked around the time of the Civil War at 6,000 members, with a present-day community of fewer than 10 who reside at Sabbathday Lake, Maine. The Shakers are distinguished for their tolerance, pacifism, industrious work habits, vows of chastity, devotion to community, and love of cleanliness. Because they strive for simplicity and efficiency in their work, their inventions and designs have long been prized for ingenuity, clean lines, and quiet elegance. (See "Extending the Lesson" for additional sources of information and photographs.)

Developing the lesson

2) *If Shaker buildings and furniture are prized for their simple lines and lack of ornamentation, what do you suppose Shaker songs sound like?* (Early Shaker songs, in particular, were sung in unison with no instrumental accompaniment.) *Let's look at the most widely known Shaker tune, a song called "Simple Gifts."* Read the text:

> 'Tis the gift to be simple, 'tis the gift to be free,
> 'tis the gift to come down where we ought to be;
> And when we find ourselves in the place just right,
> 'twill be in the valley of love and delight.
> When true simplicity is gain'd,
> to bow and to bend we shan't be ashamed;
> To turn, turn will be our delight
> 'Til by turning, turning we come 'round right.

What do you suppose these words mean to a member of the Shaker community? (A reminder to live in humility and harmony; "turning" refers to a turning of the spirit, as well as the characteristic dances that are part of Shaker religious services.)

Assist the students in singing the song from notation without hearing it first. *Let's start by speaking the rhythm of the song.* (Use a neutral syllable like "bah" or known rhythmic syllables; tap a steady eighth-note pulse for rhythmic continuity as the students chant.) Read the melody. Warm up the class by singing tonic patterns using numbers (1-3-5-3-1) or sol-fa syllables (do mi sol mi do). *If the first space "F" is the home tone, where does the song begin?* (On low 5 or sol.) Guide the students as they sing through the pitches at a comfortable tempo. Now put the text with the rhythm and melody. Sing again. *In what ways do the melody and rhythm match the text of this song?* (Simple rhythm patterns and simple melodic movement by steps or outlines of the tonic chord.)

3) Listen to the unison singing of men and women on the recording *Simple Gifts: Shaker Chants and Spirituals,* which features professional singers along with the remaining members of the Shaker community at Sabbathday Lake, Maine. Perform the song again, emulating the plain, strong style heard on the recording.

Example 7.3
"Simple Gifts"

'Tis the gift to be sim-ple, 'tis the gift to be free, 'tis the

gift to come down where we ought to be; And when we find our-

selves in the place just right, 'twill be in the val - ley of

love and de - light. When true sim - pli - ci - ty is gain'd, to

bow and to bend we shan't be a - shamed; To turn, turn, will

be our de - light 'Til by turn - ing, turn - ing we come 'round right.

4) *This tune captured the attention of one of our most famous American composers, Aaron Copland. He used "Simple Gifts" in the music for the ballet*
Appalachian Spring, *which was choreographed and performed by another
famous American, the dancer Martha Graham. Copland incorporated "Simple
Gifts" using a particular musical form called* theme and variations. *When we
looked at the Shaker chairs, we saw how the basic chair was varied through
repetition. After presenting the theme, the composer changes aspects of the
melody, harmony, rhythm, or other elements to create interest while still keeping the theme recognizable.*

*As we listen the first time, I'll keep track of the flow of Copland's composition by
labeling the variations or interludes between variations on the board. While
playing the recording, list the following events as they occur: Theme,
Variation 1, Variation 2, Interlude, Variation 3, Interlude, Variation 4.*

5) *What are some of the ways you would vary this "Simple Gifts" melody in a
theme and variations of your own?* Encourage students to list a number of

alterations—instruments, pitch, tempo, texture, and so on. Whenever possible, direct the class to sing a phrase or two to show how the suggested alteration would sound.

6) Distribute the "theme and variations" envelopes (see Table 7.3). *Read through the description of Copland's music on these strips.* Clarify terms such as "canon" and "augmentation" by singing or playing brief examples. *As we listen a second time, choose the strip that you think mostly closely describes what you hear in each section. To keep you on your toes, I have included a "foil" in the envelope, a description that never matches the music.* Play the recording again as needed until students seem satisfied with their answers.

LISTENING GUIDE

Table 7.3

Variations on "Simple Gifts" from Appalachian Spring

"Answer"	Description on Paper Strip
Theme	A solo *clarinet* plays the melody. *Flute, piccolo,* and *harp* punctuate. A *triangle* sounds at the start of the phrase, "When true simplicity is gain'd."
Variation 1	A duet between the *oboe* and the *bassoon.* Other *woodwinds* and *brass* join in on the "simplicity" phrase. At the end of the variation, the *harp* and *piano* begin weaving a busy-sounding figure.
Variation 2	*Violas* and *trombones* play the melody first, then *violins* and *horns* enter in canon. The *bass* and *cello* add to the thickening texture. *Harp, piano,* and *woodwinds* continue the busy-sounding figure.
Interlude	Fragments of the theme are passed back and forth in the *woodwinds.* The *brass* and *strings* crescendo as they move up the scale.
Variation 3	The *brass* section plays the melody vigorously. *Trumpets* and *trombones* are chased by the *strings,* racing up and down the scale.
Interlude	A slower tempo, using just the last half of the theme. The *woodwinds* create a calmer mood.
Variation 4	The *entire orchestra* plays the theme in majestic, augmented rhythm. Lower *brass, string,* and *timpani* lines are heavy and slow.
The "Foil"	Each section takes a turn playing the theme as the register moves from low to high. Low *brasses* start, followed by *strings* and then the high *woodwinds. Harp* and *piano* provide steady chords throughout.

Play the theme and variations again to confirm the order of events. Discuss how composers work with a broad palette of musical possibilities when writing for orchestra.

Closing the lesson

7) *Just as a composer or designer can vary a basic idea to create interest, you can plan a theme and variations of your own.* As a practice run for future individual or small-group projects, do a quick class example. Sing an extremely simple, well-known melody, accompanying the singers with a very plain chordal accompaniment ("Hot Cross Buns" or the first verse of "Go Tell Aunt Rhody" would be good choices.) *Let's sing that melody four times, trying to perform the song in the same way each time just to show how tiresome the repetition becomes.* Generate musical choices on the board such as fast/slow, soft/loud, duple meter/triple meter, major/minor, and others the students suggest. *Let's make a plan to sing our melody simply the first time through but for each subsequent repetition suggest ways we can vary the singing to make the song more interesting for the listener.* List the suggestions of the students on the board for each numbered repetition to create a performance plan. Perform the class variations. *Do our variations "work"?* Ask for any modifications and perform again. Encourage students to begin to generate ideas for their own theme and variations form using voices, classroom instruments, band or orchestral instruments, or keyboard. This project would extend over several class periods, culminating in performance of the variations created by individuals or small groups of students.

Assessment

~ Note the level of detail and accuracy in students' descriptions of the Shaker chairs.

~ Through the discussion, note how students relate the visual appearance of the chairs to the Shaker aesthetic.

~ How readily can the students read the standard notation for "Simple Gifts"? Does their performance of the song change in style after listening to the recording of the adult Shaker singers?

~ Do students solve the task of ordering the descriptive strips by attending to the structure and elements in Copland's theme and variations?

~ Observe the fluency of ideas for varying the simple tune sung by the class. Are students ready to generate their own ideas for theme and variations?

Extending the lesson

~ Ask students to notate their plan for variations in some way and describe their decisions after performing their piece for the class. If students are interested in notation, find a full score of Copland's work so students can observe the way he notates the variations. Because the composition is so frequently performed, many recordings are available. Play various recordings of the work to demonstrate how conductors and performers differ in their interpretation of Copland's score.

~ Find other examples of Shaker music to perform. A particularly appropriate song for classroom use is "Turn to the Right" on the *Simple Gifts* recording. This song begins with a charming lyric, "Turn to the right, ye lovely band / Turn to the right, in heart and hand," followed by a section of wordless singing that is another characteristic trait of the Shaker vocal tradition. For additional information on the Shakers, see:

> Bial, R. (1994). *Shaker home.* New York: Houghton Mifflin.
>
> Bolick, N. O., & Randolph, S. G. (1993). *Shaker villages.* New York: Walker.
>
> Randolph, S. G., & Bolick, N. O. (1990). *Shaker inventions.* New York: Walker.
>
> Renwick Gallery of the National Collection of Fine Arts. (1973). *Shaker: Furniture and objects from the Faith and Edward Deming Andrews collections, commemorating the bicentenary of the American Shakers.* Washington, D.C.: Smithsonian Institution Press.
>
> Yolen, J. (1976). *Simple gifts: The story of the Shakers.* New York: Viking.

~ Encourage students to choose a visual theme to vary by using elements of their choice (shape, size, position, color quality, line, depth, movement) in a medium of their choice. Display the works and ask the artists to describe how they chose to design the pieces. Extend this study by asking students to find examples of artworks showing theme and variations.

~ Study the ballet *Appalachian Spring,* including Copland's music, the story of the ballet, and the 1945 performance with Martha Graham's brilliant dancing. The ballet can be seen on the videotape *Martha Graham in Performance* (Graham, 1980). Find photographs of Martha Graham.

The Facets Model: Leading from the Work Outward

This lesson plan on Copland's theme and variations on "Simple Gifts" also emphasizes the Shaker origin of the tune and the particular meaning of the text within that community, which adds an expanded dimension to the way we perform and perceive this well-known melody. The facets for "Simple Gifts" in its Shaker origins are provided in Figure 7.4. To perform the folklike tune and straightforward text in a way that honors the Shaker context, we could refer to Daniel Patterson's (1979) description of musical practices in the Shaker community:

> I cannot recall a single instance of the use of dynamic marking in any Shaker song manuscripts. In the first half of the nineteenth century Shaker singing was usually "strong, with a high pitch and a great volume." . . . The early Shaker singers—like those at Sabbathday Lake today—must have remained faithful to the traditions of Anglo-American folk singing, using neither vibrato nor covered tone, avoiding "expressive" devices such as ritards, diminuendos, or crescendos, and making no effort to play up winsomely to their listeners. (p. 27)

How would a member of the Shaker community respond to Copland's setting of "Simple Gifts" or the use of the tune for commercial purposes? Sister Frances Carr, one of the remaining Sabbathday Lake Shakers, writes: "Although the World has made the song famous, we feel troubled that, in its fame, it is taken so lightly. To Believers it holds a real message reminding us that we do have to come down to 'the place just right' in order to live out Mother's Gospel" (The Shaker Community of Sabbathday Lake & Cohen, 1995, p. 62).

Copland's setting of the tune can be studied by examining the theme and variations themselves and their relationship to the entire ballet, *Appalachian Spring*. The facets of the variations on "Simple Gifts" (see Figure 7.5) suggest how the study of a work can lead outward to the naturally related study of other subjects and themes. These connections offer satisfying ways to relate music to other art forms, history, and the social studies.

The additional perspective provided by the contextual facets is the subject of Chapter 8 as we address the historical and cultural content of musical works.

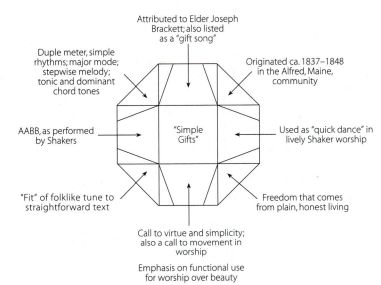

Figure 7.4 (left)
Facets of the Shaker Song "Simple Gifts"

Figure 7.5 (below)
Facets of "Simple Gifts" as Found in Variations on "Simple Gifts" from Copland's Appalachian Spring

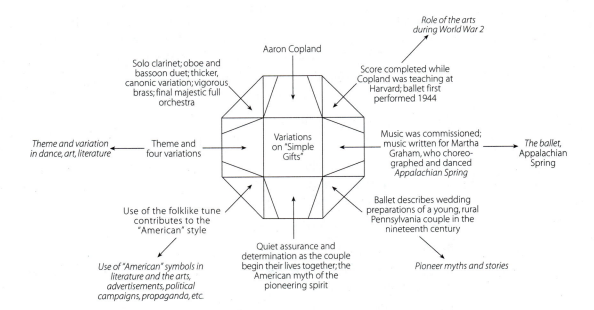

REFERENCES

Arbuthnot, M. R., & Root, S. L. (eds.). (1968). *Time for poetry.* Glenview, Ill.: Scott, Foresman.

Bach, J. S. (1985). *Two-part inventions BWV 772a–786; Three-part inventions BWV 780–810* [CD]. A. Schiff, pianist. New York: London.

Bial, R. (1994). *Shaker home.* New York: Houghton Mifflin.

Bolick, N. O., & Randolph, S. G. (1993). Shaker villages. New York: Walker.

Boston Camerata, Schola Cantorum of Boston, and The Shaker Community of Sabbathday Lake. (1995). *Simple gifts: Shaker chants and spirituals* [CD]. Germany: Erato.

Copland, A. (1983). *Appalachian Spring* [CD]. Los Angeles Philharmonic Orchestra, conducted by Leonard Bernstein. Hamburg: Polydor.

Davidson, L., & Scripp, L. (1989). Education and development in music from a cognitive perspective. In D. J. Hargreaves (ed.), *Children and the arts.* Philadelphia: Open University Press.

Fleischman, P. (1988). *Joyful noise: Poems for two voices.* New York: Harper & Row.

Graham, M. (1980). *Martha Graham in performance* [video]. W. Long Branch, N.J.: Kultur International Films.

Herman, J. L., Aschbacher, P. R., & Winters, L. (1992). *A practical guide to alternative assessment.* Alexandria, Va.: Association for Supervision and Curriculum Development.

Martin Jr., B. (1994). *The maestro plays.* New York: Henry Holt.

Parsons, M. (1987). *How we understand art: A cognitive developmental account of aesthetic experience.* Cambridge: Cambridge University Press.

Patterson, D. W. (1979). *The Shaker spiritual.* Princeton: Princeton University Press.

Randolph, S. G., & Bolick, N. O. (1990). *Shaker inventions.* New York: Walker.

Renwick Gallery of the National Collection of Fine Arts. (1973). *Shaker: Furniture and objects from the Faith and Edward Deming Andrews collections, commemorating the bicentenary of the American Shakers.* Washington, D.C.: Smithsonian Institution Press.

The Shaker Community of Sabbathday Lake & Cohen, J. (1995). Liner notes for Boston Camerata, Schola Cantorum of Boston, and The Shaker Community of Sabbathday Lake (Performers). (1995). *Simple gifts: Shaker chants and spirituals* [CD]. Germany: Erato.

Stiggins, R. J. (1994). *Student-centered classroom assessment.* New York: Merrill.

Wolf, D. P. (1989). Artistic learning as conversation. In D. J. Hargreaves (ed.), *Children and the arts.* Philadelphia: Open University Press.

Yolen, J. (1976). *Simple gifts: The story of the Shakers.* New York: Viking.

{ chapter 8 }

MUSIC IN CONTEXT

Even in our increasingly mobile and electronically networked society, birthplaces and life stories continue to fascinate us. When we meet someone new, the conversation often turns at some point to the subject of hometowns and the circumstances that brought us to that moment. During the exchange of autobiographies, we frequently discover shared experiences, affiliations, or mutual acquaintances. The process of recognizing some connection between individuals is gratifying and, at the same time, piques our interest because of all of the possible variants of life. We seek commonality and relish differences. The conversational search, far from idle chatter, functions as a powerful social act to establish who we are and how we are related in some fashion to the other.

So it is with music. New songs or works are not new for long as we relate what we hear or perform to music that we have heard or performed before by searching for stylistic categories, recognizable texts, and characteristic motives. Perceived similarities to and differences from the music we already know influence how deeply we respond to the new piece, how likely we are to seek it out for another hearing, or how expressively we perform it. Just as we seek to discover the personal history of a new acquaintance, we may be moved to investigate the particular musical history of a work of interest and the origins, transformed versions, and meanings of the work in varied times and places. The circumstances and settings of our own lives at the time of the encounter with the work may influence our interpretation of it. This search for context is a natural tendency that has implications for the way we choose, teach, and learn new music. These implications extend beyond a perfunctory mention of the origin of a musical work to central questions of curriculum and instruction, such as: How important is the context of musical examples to curriculum development? What knowledge about context enhances our understanding of music? How does a search for context suggest opportunities for meaningful work in classrooms—work that maintains and enhances the integrity of complementary disciplines?

Not long ago, a university supervisor was visiting a high school to observe the progress of a student teacher in a choral music classroom. When the supervisor arrived early, she struck up a conversation with one of the singers. "What music will you be rehearsing in choir today?" the supervisor asked the student. "We've been working on a piece called 'Gloria,'" replied the singer. "Which Gloria?" asked the supervisor, thinking of Vivaldi or Schubert or Haydn. "I'm not sure," replied the student. "It's the one with the purple cover."

What is lost when we study or perform music in a detached and impersonal manner without knowing its connection to composer, era, people, location, or influence on society? What is gained when we know more about the music's context? Connecting a work to a time and place strengthens our understanding, performance, and appreciation of the work. Knowing who composed it may demystify the artistic process of creation, thereby inviting us to respond to artworks by creating our own. Understanding the style of the music, a reflection of time and place, helps us to perform with sensitivity or to listen with understanding. We may not be able to infer from the scenario above that the student cannot sing her part in the Gloria with musicality just because she doesn't remember the name of the composer. But it calls our attention to potential misperceptions and misunderstandings that students may have about works if we fail to situate musical examples in related traditions to emphasize their contextual meaning.

Related facts, dates, and settings are building blocks for contextual knowledge, but the mortar of understanding is supplied by the meanings students bring to the instructional setting and the new insights gained through rich classroom experiences. Elliott (1995) defines context as "the total of ideas, associations, and circumstances that surround, shape, frame, and influence something and our understanding of that something" (p. 40). Attention to context can counteract curricular blandness by bringing what could be inert content to life. Attention to context also counteracts student detachment by asking students to investigate and consider multiple, ambiguous, messy, "real" meanings. Through this search for context, students are prompted to discover how musical works are connected to other forms of knowledge and school subjects in valid ways.

Music as a Window to History

Although it wasn't her usual practice, Elise Campbell drove by her elementary school late one Saturday afternoon so she could sit in her fifth-grade classroom alone for a while to sort out her thoughts. She had just returned from a two-day conference sponsored by the Alliance for Arts Education in her state; as a fifth-

grade classroom teacher, she had been invited to attend by her music teacher friend. Her thoughts were not that easy to sort because the excitement of the past two days had stretched her thinking in many new directions and produced intriguing ideas that were now tangled in a jumble of possibilities.

The conference had been well organized and the clinicians engaging, but what impressed Elise the most was the enthusiasm and curiosity of the students who had been invited to showcase their ideas. One group of children presented an original musical they wrote to dramatize the signing of the Declaration of Independence, complete with a contemporary epilogue to underscore the power of the document centuries later. Another group presented the results of the oral history project it had conducted with members of immigrant groups in the state, complete with photographs, interviews, and folk songs taught to the children by those they had interviewed. The students seemed energized, not just by the thrill of presenting their work to a group of teachers but also by their genuine curiosity and enthusiasm for the processes and ideas of history.

"My students could do that given the right conditions, access to resources, and some encouragement," thought Elise. "I could plan a project of a smaller scale for my own fifth graders, but I also think my ideas would be stronger if I worked with the music specialist and the other fifth-grade teachers in my team." As she considered this collaboration, she scanned the room, noticing the familiar arrangement of furniture, student work stapled to the bulletin boards, stacks of books, and plastic bins filled with papers. In her mind's eye, she began to see a transformation of the space into a hub of historical activity—small groups of students engaged in lively discussion, the rehearsal of music and dramatic vignettes, and the production of drawings and models built to scale. It was almost possible to hear the productive hum of the fifth graders engrossed in thinking. She pulled out a blank pad to record her ideas before the images and her enthusiasm had a chance to fade.

Elise began to generate a list of questions to think about and discuss with her colleagues. The social studies curriculum seemed like such a natural place to start because she felt a need for some innovative thinking in her own approach to the study of American history she taught every year. What areas of the social studies curriculum would be easiest to invigorate and revitalize with an expanded range of examples drawn from the arts? Could she successfully incorporate music into her curriculum with available resources and her own musical abilities along with her colleagues' help? What activities from previous years would be replaced or eliminated with this new focus? Where could she go to find more information and good examples of projects as guidelines for design? Most importantly, she wondered how the use of music would help to convey the fundamental ideas and feelings of the past in a way that might generate some of the same enthusiasm and liveliness she observed at the conference.

Why Study the Past through Music?

Music is a symbolic means of expression woven through the strands of human experience we label as history. Just as a knowledge base of dates, places, events, and figures can help us place crucial ideas in a chronological span of economic, political, technological, and social achievements, music can reveal the more cultural, personal, and expressive side of human development. Music can be a powerful tool in our quest to *experience* history rather than merely to *encounter* it. Through music, we can situate ourselves more vividly in the beliefs, values, and traditions of the past, thus building a richer representation of history and culture from an insider's perspective.

Frith (1987) discusses the power of music to mark present time, as our experiences in the here and now are made vibrant and intense: "One measure of good music is . . . its 'presence,' its ability to 'stop' time, to make us feel we are living within a moment, with no memory or anxiety about what has come before, what will come after" (p. 142). We may be carried along by the music through seconds, minutes, or longer periods of intense concentration and personal response to what is heard and felt. Perhaps the reverse is more descriptive, as individuals do the work of carrying the music along, perceiving, organizing, and evaluating the musical work. This complex engagement of mind, body, and spirit during musical experience affects performers, composers, and listeners in profound ways.

Music often directs our attention to the past, through recollection of music we have heard at certain times in our lives. People, places, or sensory impressions can be evoked through memories associated with particular music, such as romantic requests to play "our song." Such "blasts from the past" trigger varied thoughts and feelings, from nostalgic recollection to mild embarrassment at the musical tastes of our youth, or perhaps more unpleasant connotations. Although these musical references distinctly mark our personal histories, they are highly idiosyncratic; what leads us down memory lane may hold little meaning, or different meanings, for those around us.

Music also directs our attention to history through the association of musical styles with particular decades, generations, and eras; associations that are more commonly shared across individuals. When we hear a musical example, characteristic lyrics or elements arranged in recognizable patterns allow us to pinpoint or approximate its possible time of origin. One expression of musical literacy, then, may be the listener's ability to "stamp" an unfamiliar composition with its historical period, such as the Renaissance, the Baroque, or the 1940s, 1950s, or 1960s. Indeed, soundtracks for films or television programs often use this phenomenon to good effect as the historical setting of the dramatic action is established through music.

Not only can we knowledgeably situate music in particular time frames by perceiving the characteristics of the music itself, but we can sometimes attribute examples to the individuals or groups that most likely performed, created, or valued those examples. Study of the music leads to the consideration of the social conditions, practices, and beliefs of past eras and historical periods, often distinguished further by the individual's or group's ethnicity, gender, or socioeconomic status.

Certain musical works become symbols of (a) identity for membership as a citizen of a particular state, province, or country (officially sanctioned anthems of political bodies); (b) association with an educational institution (school songs); or (c) ethnicity (folk songs or anthems). The performance of these pieces becomes a ritual in the celebrations, ceremonies, and traditions of a group. We usually think about such rituals as occasions to express civic or social pride. Such expressions of shared belief and ideology are usually cast in a positive and socially beneficial light. The thoughtful educator may also unearth uses of music to deceive, suppress, or undermine identity (music as propaganda, music used to stereotype ethnic groups or satirize individuals). Public perception and opinion can be influenced by music used for artistic purposes (expressing ideas in sound, conveying musical or extramusical ideas) and nonartistic purposes (advertising products, calling people to attention, masking background noise). Understanding the functions of music is part of the challenge of becoming musically literate.

Consider how music has served or can serve as an active agent in historical events. Can music sharpen and give voice to deeply held beliefs that clarify or change social or political attitudes? Is it possible that music can have a direct impact on the events of a time? Where does this power come from—the musical example itself or what people do with the musical example? Seeger (1991) studied the culture of the Suyá tribe of central Brazil, examining societal structures and musical practices, and concluded: "History is the subjective understanding of the past from the perspective of the present. Events do not simply happen; they are interpreted and created. I argue that members of some social groups create their past(s), their present(s), and the vision(s) of the future partly through musical performances" (p. 23).

The expressive nature of music can bring crucial aesthetic dimensions to the social studies. By aesthetic dimensions, we refer to the capacity of the musical example to engage and challenge our perceptions, and to invite and deepen our feelingful responses. A song or instrumental composition may excite the imagination, stir emotions, or generate under-standing that can only be represented by the individual's aesthetic response to the sound. A student's capacity to perceive and respond is made stronger through contact with rich, multidimensional educational experiences. Retention is also strengthened through the webs of relation-ships and structures of ideas encoded in memory. Works of music, art, and literature can serve as "text" in a social studies classroom in addition to what we normally consider as the content of the curriculum represented by textbooks. Brady (1989) contends that historical narratives often fail to capture the imagination of students because "all of the characteristics which usually make a story appealing—the idiosyncrasies of the teller, the subjectivity, the undisguised speculation, the overstatement, the emotion-al peaks, the humor—are edited out" (p. 85). Music, art, and literature restore those very human dimensions to the center of the educational experience.

Eisner (1991) argues for the inclusion of art, music, and literature in social studies, not as mere entertaining adjuncts to more traditional stud-ies, but as curricular components necessary to understanding. This view is based on the assumption that students possess multiple forms of literacy:

> What students can learn about a culture, past or present, is both constrained and made possible by the forms of repre-sentation to which they have access and are able to "read." When social studies carries its messages to students mainly or solely through textbooks, it inevitably and severely limits what students are able to learn. Thus, attention to the arts, to music, and to literature in social studies programs is not a way to "gussy-up" the curriculum, it is a way to enlarge human understanding and to make experience in the social studies vivid. (p. 553)

A student-centered view of education also seems to warrant the devel-opment of educational experiences that address the preferences, needs, interests, and intelligences of diverse learners. Expanded views of mind, which include Howard Gardner's theory of multiple intelligences (1985) and the cognitive-developmental schools of thought in contemporary psychology, have had a profound impact on the way educators view dif-ferences in the ways students learn. Even the look and feel of classrooms reflects this change in thinking, as straight rows of desks facing the teacher have been rearranged as workstations, multimedia centers, and areas for small-group work. In light of these transformations, teachers are expanding their conceptions of what belongs in classrooms, and students are choosing new options to demonstrate their understanding and skill in a way more suited to individual talents and abilities. Eisner addresses this expansion in regard to the arts in social studies:

> One practical implication of these newly developing ideas about mind and intelligence is that social studies programs that constrain what they teach through a restricted array of tasks and highly limited forms of representation are unfair to those whose aptitudes reside in areas neglected in the curriculum. If the sole mediator of the message is the written word, not only will the meanings made available be constrained by what the word can reveal, but the opportunities to learn will be biased towards those whose proclivities reside in the processing of text. (p. 553)

Music draws students into the instructional setting by engaging the mind, voice, eye, hand, and heart, as well as the ear. Through projects that involve music, students can demonstrate the depth and breath of their understanding through skilled analyses, performances, and exhibitions.

A Call for Collaboration

In this chapter, we suggest that part of the challenge of studying the arts deeply includes connecting works to their time, place, and heritage, making it "essential that those who construct arts curricula attend to issues of ethnicity, national custom, tradition, religion, and gender, as well as to the artistic elements and aesthetic responses that transcend and universalize such particulars" (Consortium of National Arts Education Associations, 1994, p. 14). Teachers help students build a foundation of competence and understanding in music, from which they can branch out to make connections with related disciplines and topics.

Professional organizations support these connections by calling for interdisciplinary collaboration within the general curriculum. For example, the ninth content standard for music in the 1994 *National Standards for Arts Education* underscores the importance of "understanding music in relation to history and culture."[1] The standards for social studies (National Council for the Social Studies, 1994), which encompass the related disciplines of history, geography, government, economics, sociology, and anthropology, include 10 themes (see Table 8.1). These themes are illustrated with examples that intersect and overlap with the fundamental forms of experience in the arts.

Table 8.1

*Themes of the
Social Studies
Standards*

1. Culture
2. Time, continuity, and change
3. People, places, and environments
4. Individual development and identity
5. Individuals, groups, and institutions
6. Power, authority, and governance
7. Production, distribution, and consumption
8. Science, technology, and society
9. Global connections
10. Civic ideals and practices

Under the theme "culture," for example, elementary students are expect-ed to "describe ways in which language, stories, folktales, music, and artis-tic creations serve as expressions of culture and influence behavior of peo-ple living in a particular culture" (p. xiii). In the discipline of history as part of the theme of "time, continuity, and change," students are encour-aged to examine documents and narrative accounts that convey a sense of time situated within personal, academic, pluralist, and global views of human growth and progress. The creative teacher can see how documents and narrative accounts could be broadened to encompass works of art, dance, literature, drama, and music.

In all disciplines, the development of content and achievement stan-dards was conducted by teams of educators who engaged in careful delib-eration and extensive discussion of the merits and values of interdiscipli-nary curricula. The standards provide an eloquently stated framework to be used by individual teachers who select materials and design experi-ences to make attainment of these broad goals possible. Valid connections between and among subject areas depend upon the efforts and commit-ment of teachers who see the potential for connections and who exem-plify an interdisciplinary spirit and inquisitive orientation toward new forms of knowing and experience.

Selecting Music for Contextual Connections

Ellen, Peter, and Jeff meet in a conference room of the campus library to discuss plans for the curriculum project for their elementary/middle school music meth-ods class. The three members of the cooperative group have prepared for this planning meeting by bringing some interesting materials they have collected through library searches and a survey of their personal CD collections and favorite books. Peter, an enthusiastic blues guitarist, shares a selection, "Hard Times, Cotton Mill Girls," that he has learned to play by listening to a dusty album—Brown Lung Cotton Mill Blues—he found in the record bin. Ellen and Jeff are quite impressed. They agree that the repetitive chorus could be taught quickly and easily to the class during the limited time they have to present their ideas.

> *It's hard times, cotton mill girls*
> *It's hard times, cotton mill girls*
> *It's hard times, cotton mill girls*
> *It's hard times everywhere.*

Ellen, who has an interest in the labor movement in the early twentieth century, begins to imagine ways to introduce this historical period so the class will understand how the song symbolizes the frustrations and struggles of the workers. Although Jeff has never really thought about this topic before, he volunteers to do some background research on textile mills and the role women and children played in the labor force. By the time they start trading ideas, an idea forms in Ellen's mind to simulate the conditions of the cotton mill as much as possible in the classroom when they introduce the song. Things start to fall into place.

On the day of the presentation, they meet to check their materials. Jeff has reproduced some photos of children and women in the textile mills, which he displays on a series of overhead transparencies. Ellen asks the students to move their desks together in the middle of the room, so close that they can barely move. She places a jug of water on the table in front of the class and distributes small packets of yarn, directing the students to weave the strands back and forth between their fingers as they begin their lesson. Peter starts playing his guitar, softly at first, then all three of them join in singing the first verse and chorus of the song. The music stops while Ellen asks the group to imagine the conditions at the mill, the heat and thirst, long hours and fatigue, harsh supervisors and concern for the children working alongside the women. By the time she finishes her description, the class is transfixed. Peter, Ellen, and Jeff continue to sing the rest of the verses, subtly signaling the class to join in as the repetitive chorus takes on significance, meaning, and explanatory power.

Music intersects with social, cultural, and historical studies when it leads us to consider the hopes, dreams, aspirations, frustrations, and accomplishments of the people who brought the music to life. In that regard, interdisciplinary inquiry can start with a musical example as a springboard to the study of a cultural or historical setting. A symbiotic relationship results when our study leads us to a deeper appreciation of the music. The strength of the connection depends in large part on the thoughtful, deliberate selection of musical examples.

Although almost any form of music can point outward to sociological connections, song texts and tunes are especially useful vehicles to transport students to particular times and places. Texts carry literal and metaphorical meanings that are often enhanced by melodies, and rhythms, which sink deep into memory. In a classroom setting, the study of songs offers opportunities to be sensitive to the rhythms of language, vocabulary, and phrase structure. Students and teachers can engage in lively curriculum work by operating as text and tune detectives, using auxiliary sources of information to produce historically and culturally grounded performance.

Restoring Context to Familiar Songs

Many songs we can sing by heart or hear frequently have interesting origins and histories that may be worth studying. To test this idea, make a list of common and familiar songs (some interesting choices might be "Happy Birthday," "London Bridge Is Falling Down," or "The Star-Spangled Banner"). What do you know about the origins of these songs? After you have listed what you know, search for additional materials and references. You may also wish to trace the origins of songs found in music series texts, such as "Donkey Riding" or "Run, Children, Run."

What discoveries do you make in your search?

The questions posed by the expanded facets model (see Figure 8.1) are useful to guide study beyond the origins of a particular work to the other times and places in which it has meaning. This model suggests that music endures but also changes, depending upon how it is performed and, perhaps, altered by the cultures that value it.

A search for contextual meaning in songs begins by asking questions about (a) the song at its point of origin, (b) the song's path of transmission and the multiple meanings it acquires on its journey, (c) the inclusion of the song in the repertoire of individuals and groups, and (d) the song's relationship to contemporary experience.

Point of origin. When was the song created? Where was it created? Who created it? If a song was composed by a specific individual, we may be able to pinpoint its origin, like tracking down a birth certificate. If we are particularly fortunate, we may also find documentary evidence that points to the genesis of the piece, such as journals, sketchbooks, reviews, or the composer's notes on the manuscript. Were there particular inspirations or creative impulses that influenced the work, such as a collaboration or commission? When you listen to the song, can you hear stylistic influences or similarities with other works, composers, or traditions? It may be difficult to pinpoint the first performance of a song in a folk tra-

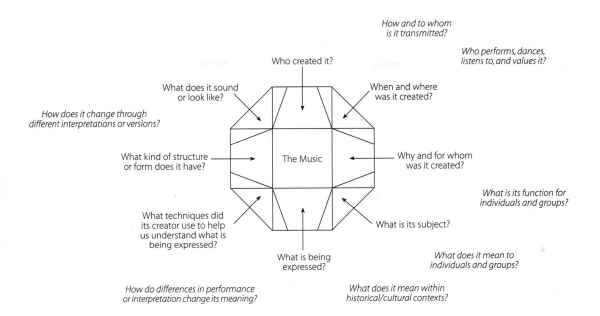

How and to whom
is it transmitted?

Who performs, dances,
listens to, and values it?

Who created it?

What does it sound
or look like?

When and where
was it created?

How does it change through
different interpretations or versions?

What kind of structure
or form does it have?

The Music

Why and for whom
was it created?

What is its function for
individuals and groups?

What techniques did
its creator use to help
us understand what is
being expressed?

What is its subject?

What is being
expressed?

What does it mean to
individuals and groups?

How do differences in performance
or interpretation change its meaning?

What does it mean within
historical/cultural contexts?

Figure 8.1
*Expanded Facets
Model with Focus
on Culture and
History*

dition where the creator is unknown, but patience and perseverance may lead you to trace the earliest versions of a folk song.

We often forget the origins of songs when performance of them becomes routine. The significance of the song may be lost as repetition lulls us into an unquestioning acceptance of the words forming on our lips as we sing. Well-planned and well-researched experiences can restore these connections. For example, we usually think of "Yankee Doodle" as a children's song, but few realize that the text was intended as a satirical mockery of Americans by the British. The tune was used as a spirited march and became a source of American identity and pride during the Revolutionary War (Sonneck, 1909/1972). Other texts, such as Francis Scott Key's "The Star-Spangled Banner" or Katherine Lee Bates's "America the Beautiful," need to have their meanings and origins refreshed. Much of the meaning can be renewed through the use of narrative historical accounts, anecdotes, maps, paintings, dances, plays, or poetry. These personal accounts and artifacts may lend insight into the feelings, concerns, expectations, and priorities of individuals and social groups. Nonmusical aspects of printed music can also connote the spirit of the time, such as sheet-music covers or advertisements for musical events.

Path of transmission and multiple meanings. Most of us have had the experience of singing a song learned in childhood for a friend, who recognizes the song but sings it with a slightly different tune or a variation on the text. Songs rarely stay fixed and stable, preserved and frozen in an original state. Swanwick (1994) explains: "Music travels and—like language—is continually begin refashioned, adapted, reinterpreted; creating 'new human values,' organizing thought and feeling, transcending the limits of local culture and the personal self. Every new composition or improvisation is an action capable of inflecting and regenerating cultural heritages" (p. 220). The preservation and alteration of culture through music becomes a continuous historical thread we can trace as we study the path of transmission.

Mobility and flux are particularly pertinent to songs in the oral tradition, in which the next singer adds and deletes according to the dictates of memory and flourishes of individual license. Some of the identity of the song is retained, some is lost, and some is added. These alterations can be fascinating to study, particularly as a window to changing sensibilities and attitudes. Where have alternate versions come from and how have they traveled from voice to voice or hand to hand? What changes have added to the meaning or transformed the meaning? How do transformations reveal the points of view of the transformers? Multiple versions of a work pique our curiosity as we compare and contrast X with Y and Y with Z. Conflicting points of view or curious twists of meaning in the texts may turn into interesting paradoxes and conundrums for further study.

The historical validity of the selections we choose is also a fruitful topic for classroom investigation. Consider, for example, the prevalent practice of altering traditional song texts that could easily be construed as offensive when viewed in the context of our diverse society. A quick survey of many song anthologies will yield song texts that are embedded with issues of race, class, and gender, and with political, religious, and moral beliefs. Who decides to alter these texts and what changes are justified without sacrificing authenticity?[2] What role does school culture play in deciding which examples are acceptable as subjects to study and which are not? These are difficult questions that raise issues of authenticity, diversity, democracy, and ownership. Controversy may arise as deeply held norms, beliefs, and values are brought to the surface for examination, discussion, and evaluation.

In today's world, the transmission of musical ideas is not bound by physical location and face-to-face contact between musicians. The rapid, global dissemination of musical ideas has resulted in some curious blends and seemingly improbable hybrids. For example, we recently studied an antebellum minstrel tune from the southern United States, "Cotton-Eyed Joe," that had found its way into the repertoire of a technopop band from Sweden (Veblen, McCoy, & Barrett, 1995). One of us ran across an advertisement for a CD of Elvis Presley tunes sung in Latin, recorded by a Finnish choir.

Finally, the way music is transmitted and represented in print can change or alter original meanings. Consider Woody Guthrie's widely sung "This Land Is Your Land," a perennial favorite often found in anthologies and music textbooks for children. Familiar verses as sung in public schools declaim a simple patriotic message, that "this land was made for you and me." Other verses, which are rarely heard and seldom printed in school songbooks, relate a more complex point of view:

> As I went walking, I saw a sign there
> And on the sign it said "No Trespassing."
> But on the other side it didn't say nothing,
> That side was made for you and me.
>
> In the shadows of the steeple I saw my people,
> By the Relief Office I seen my people;
> As they stood there hungry, I stood there asking
> Is this land made for you and me?
>
> Nobody living can ever stop me
> As I go walking that freedom highway;
> Nobody living can ever make me turn back,
> This land was made for you and me. (Schmid, 1991, p. 44)

Woody Guthrie wrote these words during his travels as a musician and union activist during the Great Depression in the 1930s. The "lost" verses restore their original charged meaning to this well-worn tune. Through the omission of problematic verses, "This Land Is Your Land" is rendered safe. And yet, these images may hold the most relevance for us today. Through the processes of oral and/or written transmission, we see how meanings of song texts can be lost, perverted, enhanced, or transformed.

The inclusion of the song in the repertoires of individuals and groups. People choose to perform music for many reasons, including a desire to strengthen identity and affiliation with others. The social and cultural history of reception leads us to ask why certain songs come to be associated strongly with certain individuals and groups and to consider how songs are used symbolically to refer to ideas that transcend original or literal meanings.

One of the ways to determine the strength of affiliation of a song with a particular time is to identify the number of times a song has been mentioned in texts or included in print or recorded anthologies. Some works almost seem to be welded or cemented to a particular time. As an example, think of "We Shall Overcome" as the anthem for the civil rights movement. How does a song come to signify extramusical ideas, movements, or eras? What other examples can you think of that refer specifically to individuals, groups, or historical periods? A "sound collage" of such distinctive works could serve as an aural time line through history.

A collection of the most familiar compositions or songs associated with particular eras, styles, or periods may tell only part of the story, however. Sometimes a group of works attains a privileged status as the canon of repertoire, music that reflects the beliefs, values, and identities of the historians, musicologists, or educators who have traditionally held the power to select knowledge and sanction it as an official topic for study. Those who write and preserve history may intentionally disregard music whose creators and performers do not align with the historian's values and beliefs. Other music may be inadvertently omitted from the historical records. As you search for potent examples to introduce to your students, keep in mind that what you *exclude* from your curriculum is just as significant as what you *include*. In other words, your choice of examples can challenge or perpetuate traditional beliefs about history.

This suggests that teachers who make a special effort to search for less common works for inclusion in the curriculum may find gems that seem to be hidden from view. A fortuitous discovery of intriguing material can lead to a host of provocative questions, including: How does music become "lost" in history and whose music tends to get lost? Why? How can we find "lost" music? Once we locate such treasures, how are they revived and reintroduced into the public arena? Music often comes packed with hidden messages as voices of the dominant culture vie with minority voices. We can uncover these messages and learn how to read them, often by comparing different versions.

Relationship to contemporary experience. Another crucial consideration is the power of the example to reveal a sense of history to contemporary students. How does the selection transfer across time to connect to present-day sensibilities, problems, and thoughts of students? Surely the arts, which expose commonalities of human experience and feeling, help build bridges across eras. The thoughtful teacher may also realize, however, that there are particularities and contextual meanings that are not so readily transposed; contemporary life influences the way we perceive the music of the past. Deep and comprehensive research may be crucial to avoid misrepresenting different cultural constraints, societal expectations, or worldviews of a historical period by too easily superimposing contemporary thoughts and perspectives on past traditions, a fallacy historians call "present-mindedness." For example, song texts that strike us as offensive because of what seem to be derogatory references to ethnicity, gender, or sexual preference may not have connoted the same meanings at the time of their creation. Yet reverberations of the past through the present compel us to stop and examine current personal experience, asking why a text suddenly makes sense to us at this particular moment when we've heard it so many times before. Current events, tragedies, triumphs, and societal problems are heard in counterpoint to past voices.

In musical examples using text (that is, songs rather than instrumental compositions), the transfer of understanding may be impeded by differences in the way language carries across time. The language of a particular time or region may have different or obscured meanings, or may have fallen from common use. Foreign-language texts in translation may provide similar challenges if the translation does not represent the original intent well.

What insights or distortions arise from viewing the old from the perspective of the new? How do new populations of listeners find fresh meaning in works seemingly fixed in the past? Recognizing our situated perspectives can be difficult, for insight often comes from distance. Consider, for example, the intergenerational surprise when parents hear their children singing golden oldies in slick, MTV manifestations or when children find out that stodgy parents know all of the words to the latest hits that are really covers of older tunes. How are these songs "owned" by father, mother, son, or daughter and affixed anew to the identity of a succeeding generation?

Enhancing the contextual understanding of a musical example. In our technologically enhanced environment, we have access to recordings of music performed with artistic sophistication and preserved with technical fidelity. Although few of us would turn our backs on these advances, some crucial aspects of music making can be lost in the perfection of the small, shiny CD. Attending a live performance adds to the quality of the listener's experience by allowing us to watch the performers, hear the occasional mistake, and contribute to the dialogue of performance through our presence as audience members. If you can arrange live musical performances, the students' experience will be heightened through direct contact with the performers who transform a composition into an interactive conversation in sound. Performing the music firsthand adds another dimension as students solve puzzles of performance using their vocal and instrumental skills to create an expressive performance of their own.

When it is not feasible, however, to bring a performing group into your classroom, the use of quality recordings can also shape students' performance toward more authentic and contextually appropriate sounds. As an example, we could describe an experience related to the "Simple Gifts" lesson presented in Chapter 7. After students in our classes sang the

Shaker tune first by reading it from notation, and then listened to the recording of the song by the Boston Camerata joined by the remaining Shakers of Sabbathday Lake, subsequent performances took on an entirely different character as students sang with more vigor and straightforward style. We have found comparing several recordings of the same work to be another fruitful strategy for studying context. Students can contrast obvious or subtle differences in the performances by any two soloists or ensembles under the baton of different conductors, for example. Many times this comparison leads to consideration of performance practices and the evaluation of one interpretation as more "authentic" than another.

The symbiotic approaches of using music to enhance the understanding of social studies and using cultural and historical context to strengthen performance and deepen the response to music are worthy considerations for teachers.

Examining the Contexts of "Dixie"

The expanded facets model (see Figure 8.1, page 145) provides useful questions related to the context of a song or instrumental composition. Sometimes a work is so rich and varied in its contextual associations that it offers musicologists, teachers, and students many avenues for study. One such example is the tune so closely associated with the Confederacy during the American Civil War, "Dixie." Sacks and Sacks (1993) wrote a fascinating account of this familiar but controversial song. In *Way Up North in Dixie: A Black Family's Claim to the Confederate Anthem,* they describe its disputed origin. For many years, the song was attributed to Daniel Decatur Emmett, a white musician who allegedly composed the song for performance in a minstrel show in New York City in 1859. Quite recently, however, a different attribution of the origin has emerged. Sacks and Sacks relate the story of two African American musicians from Ohio, Ben and Lew Snowden, who claimed to be the composers (an inscription on their tombstone in Ohio reads, "We taught 'Dixie' to Dan Emmett").

Sacks and Sacks also note how quickly the song was adopted as the Confederate anthem upon the South's secession in 1861. Numerous Civil War–era parodies based on the tune show the power music has to communicate, to influence opinion, and to mobilize people to action.[3] When Emmett's text is compared with a parody by General Pike, "Everybody's Dixie," we see how music was used as a way to recruit soldiers for the cause. Contrast Pike's text with the satirical tone of "Union Dixie" to get a feeling for the intense emotions on both sides of the conflict.

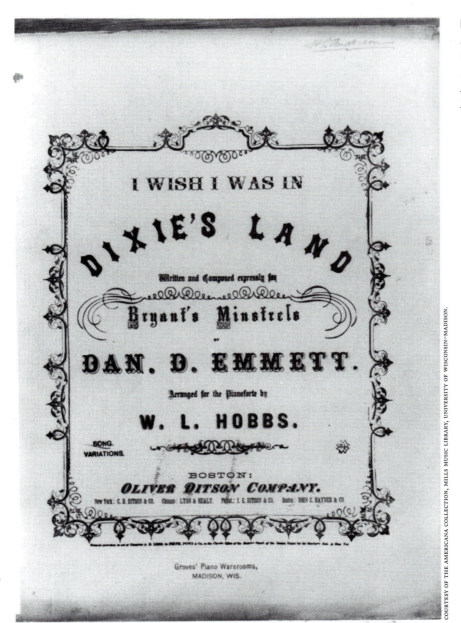

COURTESY OF THE AMERICANA COLLECTION, MILLS MUSIC LIBRARY, UNIVERSITY OF WISCONSIN–MADISON.

Figure 8.2

Sheet–Music Cover, "I Wish I Was in Dixie's Land," by Daniel D. Emmett

"Dixie's Land"
(Daniel Decatur Emmett)

I wish I was in de land ob cotton,
Old times dar am not forgotten,
Look away! Look away! Look away, Dixie Land.
In Dixie Land whar I was born in,
Early on one frosty mornin',
Look away! Look away! Look away, Dixie Land.

I wish I was in Dixie, Hooray! Hooray!
In Dixie Land, I'll take my stand,
To live and die in Dixie,
Away, Away, Away down south in Dixie,
Away, Away, Away down south in Dixie.

"Everybody's Dixie"
(General Pike's Parody)

Southrons, hear your country call you!
Up, lest worse than death befall you!
To arms! To arms! To arms in Dixie!
Lo the beacon fires lighted!
Let our hearts be now united
To arms! To arms! To arms in Dixie!

Advance the flag of Dixie! Hurrah! Hurrah!
To Dixie's Land, we'll take our stand,
To live and die for Dixie!
To arms! To arms! And conquer peace for Dixie!
To arms! To arms! And conquer peace for Dixie!

"Union Dixie"

Away down South in the the land of traitors,
Rattlesnakes and alligators,
Right away, come away, right away, come away.
Where cotton's king and men are chattels,
Union boys will win the battles,
Right away, come away, right away, come away.

Then we'll all go down to Dixie, away, away.
Each Dixie boy must understand
That he must mind his Uncle Sam,
Away, away, and we'll all go down to Dixie.
Away, away, and we'll all go down to Dixie.

To describe the meaning of the song in contemporary settings, Sacks and Sacks follow "Dixie" from the Civil War to the era of the civil rights movement, when its performance at the halftime shows of college football games provoked African American students to stage walkouts. For the students, this song was an embodiment of racism and oppression. Sacks and Sacks (1993) contend that "Dixie" still holds power over identity and opinion as it continues into its second century:

> For good or ill, "I Wish I Was in Dixie's Land" expresses something of America's changing character and consciousness. After more than a century and a quarter in the popular repertoire, "Dixie" thrills some and humiliates others. Largely because of its rich variety of meanings, "Dixie" refuses to lie peacefully in that trunk of Victorian sheet music forever consigned to the attic. It grabs at our popular culture in ways both subtle and overt, and it continues to shape the identity of the blacks and whites in its community of origin. (p. 5)

The search for context represents a valid form of curriculum inquiry in many classrooms and across many disciplines. Curricular materials can lose meaning through haphazard oral transmission or fade through cycles of publication, resulting in student disengagement, routine enactment of plans, and insipid performance. As an antidote, teachers can search for provocative musical problems to shape into vibrant educative experiences. Productive paradoxes of origin and transmission can be identified, alternate versions collected for comparison, and primary and secondary sources of information consulted to raise questions about the intersections of music, history, and culture. Although this work requires commitment of time, access to resources, and considerable intellectual energy, the benefits include satisfying, personal engagement for teachers and students, deeper connections of understanding, and a renewed sense of curricular ownership. When this grounding is omitted, mentioned only in passing, or trivialized in the curriculum, significant opportunities to represent music as an embodiment of human aspirations and as a reflection of historical and social meanings are compromised. Musical performance, listening, and arranging are informed by connections to the lives of individuals and communities who are represented in sound.

Marc Aronson (1995) calls for a reexamination of authenticity that recognizes the complexity of culture and the depth of historical lineage: "We came into this world two by two, and just as the wonderful mixture of our parents' genes made us, the incredible tapestry of world traditions lie beneath all of our songs and stories. Tracing those tangled lineages gives us our heritage" (p. 168). Just as we are unlikely to find every piece of the puzzle in a genealogical search, we are also unlikely to find purely authentic versions of works. But the process of resituating songs and tunes in historical and cultural contexts or tracing their transformations across regions or generations is challenging, thought provoking, and worthy work for teachers and students.

In Chapters 9 and 10, we continue this emphasis on contextual understanding by illustrating close relationships between music and history. The Renaissance, a period of great intellectual and artistic development, offers many opportunities for imaginative curriculum design. During the American Civil War, music often served as a way to express the political, social, and emotional tenor of the time. We provide lesson plans and outlines for all-school projects that engage students and teachers in historical research and musical analysis and performance, which lead to a fuller understanding of both disciplines.

REFERENCES

Aronson, M. (March/April 1995). A mess of stories. *The Horn Book Magazine,* pp. 163–168.

Brady, M. (1989). *What's worth teaching: Selecting, organizing, and integrating knowledge.* Albany: State University of New York Press.

Consortium of National Arts Education Associations (1994). *National standards for arts education: What every young American should know and be able to do in the arts.* Reston, Va.: Music Educators National Conference.

Eisner, E. W. (1991). Art, music, and literature within social studies. In J. P. Shaver (ed.), *Handbook of research on social studies teaching and learning* (pp. 551–558). New York: Macmillan.

Elliott, D. J. (1995). *Music matters: A new philosophy of music education.* New York: Oxford University Press.

Frith, S. (1987). Towards an aesthetic of popular music. In R. Leppert & S. McClary (eds.), *Music and society: The politics of composition, performance and reception* (pp. 133–149). Cambridge: Cambridge University Press.

Gardner, H. (1985). *Frames of mind: The theory of multiple intelligences.* New York: Basic Books.

National Council for the Social Studies. (1994). *Expectations of excellence: Curriculum standards for social studies.* Washington, D.C.: Author.

Sacks, H. L., & Sacks, J. R. (1993). *Way up North in Dixie: A black family's claim to the Confederate anthem.* Washington, D.C.: Smithsonian Institution Press.

Schmid, W. (1991). *A Tribute to Woody Guthrie & Leadbelly* [CD and booklet]. Reston, Va.: Music Educators National Conference.

Seeger, A. (1991). When music makes history. In S. Blum, P. V. Bohlman, & D. M. Neuman (eds.), *Ethnomusicology and modern music history.* Urbana: University of Illinois Press.

Silber, I., & Silverman, J. (1995). *Songs of the Civil War.* New York: Dover.

Sonneck, O. G. T. (1972). *Report on "The Star-Spangled Banner" "Hail Columbia" "America" "Yankee Doodle."* New York: Dover Books. (Original work published 1909.)

Swanwick, K. (1994). Authenticity and the reality of musical experience. In H. Lees (ed.), *Musical connections: Tradition and change.* Proceedings of the Twenty-First ISME Conference, Tampa, Fla., pp. 215–226.

Veblen, K. K., McCoy, C. W., & Barrett, J. R. (1995). Where did you come from? Where do you go? Searching for context in the music curriculum. *Quarterly Journal of Music Learning and Teaching* 6 (3): 46–56.

❋{ chapter 9 }❋

MUSIC AS AN EXPRESSION OF HISTORY: THE RENAISSANCE

The cleanup for the Ridgecrest Elementary PTA back-to-school luncheon had begun when Sarah Birney, a third-grade teacher, pulled up a chair next to Erik Olsen, the music specialist. "Erik, I just got a call from my brother, Nigel, from Colorado last night—you know, the one who's the lute maker. He's planning to come out for Thanksgiving to spend a week with us. While he's here, I'd love to have him come into my classroom, play his lute, and talk about what he does. I want to prepare my students for Nigel's visit and possibly find a way to tie his presentation in with my regular curriculum. But I don't know where to start because I don't know much about the music he plays. You're always full of good ideas. Can you help me?"

"Sure, but I'll have to think about it for a while. He'll probably be playing Renaissance music, and, you know, we really don't study much Renaissance music in my classes. I love Renaissance music, yet it always seems so far removed from kids' everyday experience that I just haven't tried to include it in the curriculum. Let me look through my CDs and resources to see if I can come up with something that would work for third grade."

The next week, as Erik was listening to public radio while driving home from school, his ears perked up at the sound of Renaissance music. "What is this they're playing?" he wondered. "It's definitely Renaissance music, but they're singing 'Three Blind Mice.' A Renaissance 'Three Blind Mice'? This is really fun! What a great way to introduce students to Renaissance music!"

Erik thought about juxtaposing the version of "Three Blind Mice" that most people know today with the version by Thomas Ravenscroft he had heard on the radio. It might be interesting to explore other contemporary objects and experiences that have their roots in the Renaissance— the guitar as the lute's modern-day relative, for example. What other things that are familiar to third graders have Renaissance ancestors? Could this be an effective way to prepare for Nigel's visit? Erik posed these questions to Sarah and her student teacher, Fran Ruiz, after he shared

Figure 9.1

"The Lutemaker," from The Book of Trades [Ständebuch], *1568.*

COURTESY OF DOVER BOOKS, 1973.

157

his discovery of the "Three Blind Mice" with them. Fran offered, "In art history we studied a painting by Brueghel called Children's Games. *It depicted children of the Renaissance period playing many of the same games children play on the playground these days."*

"What great ideas!" exclaimed Sarah. "We could contrast how things stay the same with how things change over time—that's a natural link with my social studies curriculum. That way when my brother visits, the students will have some sense of when and what the Renaissance was. Nigel's music and his instrument will have a context. Why don't we get together next week to plan some specific lessons?"

Lesson Plan I
Children's Songs and Games with Roots in the Renaissance

Rationale From generation to generation, children acquire a repertoire of songs and games—culturally transmitted activities that give hours of delight and pleasure. Children understandably know these songs and games in relation to the here and now, each generation feeling as if it owns these cultural treasures. Many of these robust traditions reach back decades or even centuries, but we may not know about their genesis. In this lesson, teachers collaborate to design complementary educational experiences for students that emphasize the historical roots of familiar works. In the first part of the two-part plan, the music specialist introduces the origins of "Three Blind Mice" as a natural entry point for an investigation of the times and music of the Renaissance. The classroom teacher or the art teacher can expand this theme through a focus on common children's games like hopscotch, leapfrog, or jacks in the second part. These favorite pastimes are traced to the Renaissance through a painting by Pieter Brueghel the Elder[1] and poetry based on the painting.

Grade Level Third and Fourth

Objectives for Part 1 (music specialist) Students will

- ~ situate the present date on a time line and work backward to the Renaissance beginnings of "Three Blinde Mice" as published by Ravenscroft in 1609.
- ~ compare and contrast the modern notation of "Three Blind Mice" with notation in a Renaissance manuscript.

~ compare and contrast the musical characteristics of the Renaissance version with the modern version of the song and use those characteristics as a basis for making decisions about performance.

Materials

~ Recording: "Three Blinde Mice" from Consort of Musicke (performers), (1991), *There were three ravens* [CD], London: Virgin Classics.

~ Prepared transparency with three notated versions of "Three Blind Mice": (a) the traditional (Example 9.1), (b) the Renaissance version in modern notation (Example 9.2), and (c) the Renaissance version as reproduced from Ravenscroft's *Deuteromelia* (1609/1971) (Example 9.3).

Example 9.1
"Three Blind Mice," traditional version

Example 9.2
"Three Blinde Mice," by Thomas Ravenscroft

Example 9.3
*"Three Blinde
Mice" as Printed
in* Deuteromelia

COURTESY OF DA CAPO PRESS, 1971.

thou the knife.

**Introducing
the lesson**

1) Draw a time line on the board, from 1400 to the present, dividing the centuries into 50-year increments. Place students' birth years on the time line. *Can you think of a song that only you and your friends know, perhaps one that is also very new?* Write titles on the time line under the current year's date. *Do you know any songs that your parents sang when they were growing up? Do you know when they sang those songs? What about a song that your grandparents sang as children?* Write titles in approximate locations. *What is the oldest song you can think of? I'll name several familiar songs; vote for the one that you think is the oldest.* Name or sing examples like "Row, Row, Row Your Boat," "Three Blind Mice," and "Yankee Doodle." Tally responses. *Today we'll find out that one of these songs has been sung for hundreds of years. We may not realize it as we sing the song, but our performance links us to people who lived very long ago. The song comes from a very important period of time in the world's history.*

**Developing
the lesson**

2) *I'm going to play a recording made in 1991 of this song that is hundreds of years old. It won't take you long to recognize the words. After you recognize it, start to listen for ways that the song is the same as the version you know, and also how it is different.* Play the recording of "Three Blinde Mice" from *There Were Three Ravens. What is the tune? Is it the one you voted for as the oldest tune? Tell your neighbor one way that the song was different from the way you know the song.*

3) *This music comes from the fascinating time in history called the Renaissance.* Bracket the approximate dates from 1430 to 1600 on the time line. Provide title (with the Renaissance spelling, "Three Blinde Mice"), date of publication (1609), and place (England) for this piece.

4) *Can you figure out what this transparency shows?* Display the transparency of the three notated versions. Guide students to pick out similarities and differences in the notation of the music and the text. *The third version shows us the way this song was published in 1609 by Thomas Ravenscroft, who collected interesting songs and rounds for people to sing and wrote them down.* Draw attention to the shape of the note heads, the ornamented first letter, and the different shapes for the letter *s* as in "she scraped her tripe." *What is the same in the Renaissance manuscript as in the notation for the modern version?* (The five-line staff, the shape of the melody.)

5) Sing the traditional version as a class. Teach the Renaissance version, using the text to explain some of the contextual background.

Origins and Significance of "Three Blind Mice"

"Three Blind Mice," possibly the most popular round in the world, has a fascinating pedigree extending back in time more than 400 years. Sung by adults for entertainment before its inclusion in the earliest printed collections of rounds,* "Three Blind Mice" was eventually relegated to the nursery.

The earliest published collections of rounds were Thomas Ravenscroft's *Pammelia* (1609/1961) and David Melvill's *Buik of Roundels,* published in 1612. Their collections were published almost simultaneously, but Ravenscroft was in England and Melvill in Scotland, and there is no indication that they knew of each other. The collections contain so much of the same information that it is an inescapable conclusion that rounds had been around for a long time and handed down orally.

What is the meaning of this round? Even a literal interpretation raises more questions than it answers. Why three mice? How did they become blind? Who is Dame Julian? Why are they preparing tripe (cow's stomach) for cooking? One fanciful attempt to read historical significance into this round identifies the miller's wife as Queen Mary I of England and the mice as her courtiers who were burned at the stake. In certain circles, this song was considered unlucky. If the tune was played during a circus performance, for instance, performers refused to do their tricks for fear of dreaded results.

Although it would be impossible to substantiate, another possible theory links superstitions concerning mice to the Black Death in Europe. Rats and mice have long been considered ominous portents, perhaps springing from an ancient belief that mice are sometimes visible manifestations of the soul. It was thought that a mouse running over a person or one squeaking behind a sickbed were infallible signs of death. Faith in the curative properties of mice was also common in Britain until recently. This may have come from a notion that some diseases like measles or whooping cough were caused by mice and could be healed by them. Only 50 years ago, elderly people were interviewed who remembered eating fried, roasted, baked, or stewed mice in their youth as a tonic or cure.

SOURCES: Baring-Gould & Baring-Gould, 1962; Opie & Opie, 1955; Opie & Tatem, 1989; Radford & Radford, 1948/1961; Scholes, 1970.

6) *How could we perform the traditional version to contrast with the Renaissance version on the recording? Let's listen again to the recording to describe the style of the sound.* Gather information in the form of a chart, such as the following:

Table 9.1

	"Three Blinde Mice" in the Style of the Renaissance	"Three Blind Mice" in the Style of Today
Timbre of singing	Men's voices	Children's voices
Quality of singing	Dark and heavy	Light and clear
Tempo	Slow	Fast and lively
Mode	Minor	Major
Accompaniment	Unaccompanied	Guitar chords
Texture	Polyphonic (round)	Voices in unison

Closing the lesson

7) When students learn the Renaissance version and can sing it with confidence, perform it as a round. Invite the students to suggest other ideas for varied performance, such as an instrumental introduction or interlude (students might play the descending F-E-D of "Three Blinde Mice," for example). It may also be effective to imitate a lute-like string sound by tuning the guitar to D-A-D-F-A-D and encouraging students to pluck the strings rather than strum.

Assessment

~ Can students compare and contrast versions of "Three Blind Mice," both in aural and in notated form?

~ Do they make stylistically appropriate suggestions for their own performance?

~ As they perform either version as a round, are the parts accurate, balanced, and expressive?

Objectives for Part 2 (teacher or art specialist): Students will

- pantomime common playground games and activities played with simple equipment or no equipment at all.
- search for Brueghel's inclusion of those games in his painting Children's Games.
- choose poems to accompany the painting and perform those poems expressively.

Materials

- Print or slide of Children's Games by Pieter Brueghel the Elder
- Book: Fraser, K. (1968), *Stilts, somersaults, and headstands: Game poems based on a painting by Peter Breughel,* New York: Atheneum

Introducing the Lesson

1) Prepare slips of paper upon which are written names of familiar children's games. Include these in particular—follow the leader, tug of war, which hand? jacks, scissors/paper/rock, leapfrog, and tag. Ask for volunteers to draw these slips of paper from a hat, and then pantomime the action of the game for other students to guess. *Do you remember when you learned to play these games? Who showed you how to play them?*

2) Draw a time line on the board, similar to the one drawn in Part 1 of this lesson. *How old are these games? When did children first play them? Which games are the oldest?* Challenge the students to think about a historical puzzle. *We know that people sang "Three Blinde Mice" in the Renaissance because we have what is called an artifact, or a record of what happened and when: Ravenscroft's notation. How would we know which games were played by children during the Renaissance? Who would keep a record? What kind of record could it be?*

Developing the lesson

3) *Pieter Brueghel the Elder was a painter who lived in Belgium from around 1525–1569* (put these dates on the time line). *He especially loved to show all of the detail and activity in large scenes of people doing everyday activities. One of his most famous paintings shows children who fill the street of a Flemish town, playing all sorts of wonderful games. Take a minute to soak up as much as you can in Brueghel's painting.* Display a large print of the painting or a slide and provide sufficient time for a period of observation and concentration before asking questions: *What catches your eye when you first*

Figure 9.2
*Pieter Bruegel the
Elder.* Children's
Games.

COURTESY OF THE KUNSTHISTORISCHES MUSEUM, VIENNA.

*see the painting? What games do you see? Can you estimate the number of
games Brueghel has shown in this painting?* Encourage students to name
any familiar games such as follow the leader, tug of war, which hand? jacks,
blindman's buff, marbles, stilts, and wrestling. Make a list of the games that
you can find in the painting that are still played today. *How does Brueghel
show the delight and movement of the children? When you look at the entire
painting, how does Brueghel tie everything together so we aren't overwhelmed
by all of the activity?*

4) *Sometimes people are so moved by paintings that they are inspired to create
    new ideas of their own. A modern-day woman was traveling in Europe with her
    husband when they visited a museum in Vienna, where Brueghel's painting is
    displayed. She was so fascinated to recognize all of the games from her own
    childhood in this Renaissance painting that she created a book of poetry based
    on her experience. In her book, she also helps us with the work of looking by
    dividing the painting into smaller sections and labeling the games in each part.*
    Read a selection of poems, such as "Turn Yourself Around" and "Follow the
    Leader" from Fraser's book, helping students see where the sections fit in
    the whole painting.

Closing the lesson

5) *Like the pantomime actions that we performed at the beginning of class, some of Fraser's poetry gives us the feeling that we are playing the games along with the Flemish children in the painting. In small groups, choose a poem, decide how you will read it, and add movement to the reading if you wish to show how the game feels. What do you have in common with children who lived in the Renaissance?*

Assessment

~ Do students understand how a painting can serve as a historical artifact?

~ Are they drawn into finding the games in Brueghel's painting?

~ Notice the children's descriptions of the overall composition and elements found in the painting.

~ As they read Fraser's poems, do they vary the style of reading to match the feeling of the game or activity?

Extending the lesson

~ Listen to a recording of "The Marriage of the Frogge and the Mouse" from *There Were Three Ravens* (Consort of Musicke, 1991). What other versions of this song do the students know? Is the story the same? Discuss how folk songs can have many versions. Sing the chorus. If the class is younger, act out the parts of frog, mouse, and other characters. Another appealing song for younger children is "Tomorrow the Fox Will Come to Towne," from the same recording. See also *Mr. Frog Went A-Courting* (Chalk, 1994).

~ Read about Brueghel's style and other paintings in *What Makes a Brueghel a Brueghel?* (Muhlberger, 1993).

In the scenario and lesson above, Erik's discovery of "Three Blinde Mice" became the pivotal piece of the puzzle that he needed to introduce the Renaissance to children in a meaningful way. Through the process of exploring the song's musical elements and structure, its historical and cultural context, and its expressive content (see Figure 9.3), new ideas for how to teach the song emerged and interdisciplinary collaborations were launched.

Figure 9.3
Facets of "Three Blinde Mice"

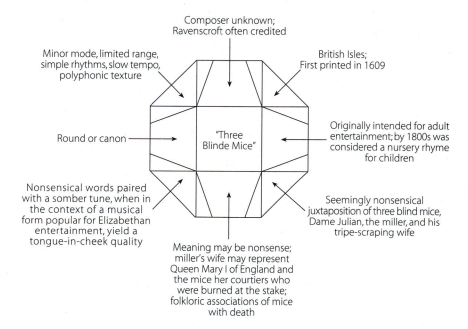

Erik was excited about the experiences that he, Sarah, and Fran had planned for their third-grade students to help them construct some meaning about a time as far removed as the Renaissance. As he observed the students' engagement and interest during the lessons and their mounting anticipation of Nigel's visit, he began to wish that other students could also have a similar opportunity. He was struck by the realization that every year he taught his fourth graders to play the recorder—an instrument that was extremely popular during the Renaissance— but he had never helped his students understand the historical significance of the instruments they were playing. He had used recorder playing as a vehicle for teaching the students to read music; the music the students had played on their instruments consisted mostly of folk songs and popular tunes. He had not helped his students make a conscious connection between their recorder performances and the recorder's Renaissance roots. "Wouldn't it be a wonderful experience," he thought, "for the fourth graders to learn some Renaissance music on their recorders so that they could perform with Nigel when he visits?"

Lesson Plan II
Playing a Renaissance Dance on Recorder

Rationale   Students usually relish playing instruments such as the recorder, a seven-hole woodwind instrument with a whistle mouthpiece that was very popular in Renaissance times. Because it is relatively inexpensive and easy to learn, recorder instruction is often included in elementary and middle school music curricula.

The first reference to a recorder was made in the household accounts of King Henry IV of England in 1388. It became an instrument of choice for play in consorts or ensembles during the Renaissance. Music was written for sets of recorders (in a range of sizes from sopranino to descant, treble, tenor, and bass) or for recorder with other instruments.

There are many Renaissance pieces for recorder that older elementary and middle school students could play well. In this lesson it is assumed that students can play the pitches G, A, B, C^1, D^1, and E^1. Small percussion instruments such as finger cymbals and hand drums add zest to a simple tune.

Grade Level   Fourth through Seventh

Objectives   Students will

- ~ analyze a simple dance form.
- ~ play a Renaissance dance on recorders.
- ~ create an accompaniment with percussion instruments.

Materials
- ~ Recording: Calliope (performers), (1990), *Diversions* [CD], Tempe, Ariz.: Summit Records
- ~ Music for "Bouffons" by Thoinot Arbeau (Example 9.4)
- ~ A recorder for each student
- ~ Percussion instruments such as finger cymbals or a small hand drum

Introducing the lesson
1) *Can you identify a familiar instrument in this performance?* Play "Bransle" from the CD *Diversions*. *If you heard a recorder, you're right! In fact, there are two recorders playing a duet along with some type of drum and a lute.* Write the name of the composer (Tielman Susato) and the date the music was published (ca. 1550) on the board or transparency. *Susato's music was printed by a new invention of the time: the printing press. Before the printing press was invented, all books and music had to be copied by hand, so not many people had access to books or music. In Susato's time, amateur musicians were eagerly buying the first sheet music ever printed.*

2) *In the Renaissance, composers were not considered geniuses but rather crafts-people who wrote music on demand. Composers and other musicians were hired by noble patrons and the church to provide music for courtly entertainment and for church services. When a composer's music was printed, the printer, not the composer, received the money people paid for the music. How does this compare with today?* (Current copyright laws give composers legal rights to their works until 50 years after their death. Contemporary composers may write for their own artistic and personal satisfaction—sometimes with the hope of commercial success—or they may be commissioned by an individual or group to write a new work. The shift from royal and church patronage to free enterprise began in the Renaissance along with other changes in social structure.)

Example 9.4
"Bouffons," by
Thoinot Arbeau

**Developing
the lesson**

3) *Today we're going to play a dance from the Renaissance by a composer named Thoinot Arbeau, who was an expert on dancing. As I play it for you, imagine how you might dance to it.* Teacher performs "Bouffons" on the recorder. *As I play it again, tap your fingers in your palm to show how you think the dancers' feet would move. The dance that would have been done to this music involved swords.[2] Do you think the dancers' swordplay would have been angry or more lighthearted? The mood of the music and the title might give us a hint. This dance is called "Bouffons."* Write the title on the board. *This French word is very similar to its English translation,* buffoon. *Does anyone know what a buffoon is? A buffoon* is another word for clown.

4) Distribute copies of "Bouffons." *Study this music and tell me what you notice. How many phrases are there? Do any of the phrases repeat? What is the form? What pitches are used? What meter is it in? How does it move?* To prepare students to play the piece, consider these strategies: (a) speaking the rhythm, (b) singing the pitches, and (c) singing while practicing fingering. Students practice the piece until they can play it accurately.

Closing the lesson

5) *Because this is a piece for dancing, we want it to sound dance-like. Listen again to Susato's "Bransle" to think of ways we can make our performance match the style in the recording.* Guide students to notice the tempo, articulation, and added percussion and lute. Record student suggestions on the board. *Let's play "Bouffons" several times, experimenting with these suggestions.* The teacher can add a plucked chordal accompaniment on the guitar to simulate the lute. An accompaniment of finger cymbals and a small hand drum would be stylistically appropriate. Another approach to the accompaniment would be to recreate the sounds that would have been made by dancers who wore bells on their legs and clashed their swords as part of the dance. Small bells could be played in the rhythm of the dancers' feet and rhythm sticks could recreate the sound of the swords (see Example 9.5).

Example 9.5
Accompaniment Patterns for "Bouffons"

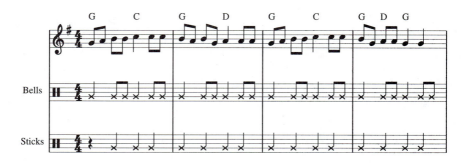

Assessment

~ Can students analyze the form of "Bouffons"?

~ Are students' performances accurate?

~ Can students perceive the stylistic characteristics of Susato's "Bransle" and apply them to their performance of "Bouffons"?

~ Are the instrumental accompaniments appropriate to the dance?

**Extending
the lesson**

~ In Renaissance times, wealthy people often kept full sets of recorders for company. After dinner, the guests and hosts would retire to the music room to play music all evening. Special music folios were printed with parts facing different directions so that people around the table could all play at once. The video *James Galway's Music in Time. Part 4: The Golden Age* (1982) features recorder consorts playing from one of these four-sided folios.

~ Contact local colleges or universities or a local chapter of the American Recorder Society to find volunteer recorder groups, Renaissance ensembles, or teachers. (American Recorder Society, Inc., P. O. Box 631, Littleton, Colo. 80160; telephone (303) 347–1120; e-mail: 74363.3365@compuserve.com.)

Nigel packed up his lute and headed back to Sarah's house after an intense session of demonstrating how a lute is made, answering innumerable questions, playing several Renaissance lute pieces, and accompanying the fourth graders in a performance of "Bouffons." Sarah, Fran, and Erik flopped down on the well-worn couches in the teacher's lounge, exhausted, but exhilarated. "I couldn't believe how attentive the students were! And they asked Nigel such interesting questions!" Erik exclaimed. Sarah nodded in agreement.

"Thanks, Fran," Sarah added, "for suggesting that the third graders give a presentation to the fourth-grade classes on what they had learned about the Renaissance. I could tell they were very proud of what they had learned."

"Do you think your brother will visit again next year?" Erik asked. "I'd like to think about expanding our Renaissance lessons to include more grades, or maybe even the whole school. Do you think the other teachers would be interested in collaborating in a schoolwide study of the Renaissance?"

Why Study the Renaissance?

The Renaissance, literally "rebirth," signaled the flowering of European culture. During this creative period, which spanned the fourteenth through the sixteenth centuries, there seemed to be an explosion of information and discovery.[3] We study the Renaissance in schools today because many important ideas were born during that time. Another compelling reason to study the Renaissance is for the mirror it holds up to view our contemporary lives. Vaclav Havel, playwright and human rights activist who has served as president of the Czech Republic, commented:

> Today, many things indicate that we are going through a transitional period, when it seems that something is on the way out and something else is painfully being born. . . . Periods of history when values undergo a fundamental shift are certainly not unprecedented.... It happened during the Renaissance, which opened the way to the modern era. The distinguishing features of such transitional periods are a mixing and blending of cultures, and a plurality or parallelism of intellectual and spiritual worlds. These are periods when all consistent value systems collapse, when cultures distant in time and space are discovered or rediscovered. New meaning is gradually born from the encounter, or the intersection, of many different elements. (1994, p. 45)

By exploring the riddles of the Renaissance, we may better solve those of our own time. Both the Renaissance and modern times are marked by rapidly expanding frontiers, which further demand heightened abilities to synthesize new knowledge. In the Renaissance, a person who excelled in many disciplines and art forms was the ideal; in our modern age, a person must understand multiple perspectives and respond to new realms of human thought and feeling. Maxine Greene (1991) speaks to the centrality of experiences in the arts in this rapidly changing landscape, which leads individuals to "unexpectedly perceive patterns and structures they never knew existed in the surrounding world." These changes result in the discovery of "new perspectives as the curtains of inattentiveness pull apart" (pp. 28–29).

One of the thematic strands woven through the fabric of the Renaissance is the exploration of space. This was the age when Magellan sailed around the world, Columbus landed on American shores, and Copernicus hypothesized a heliocentric system. Space was also explored in the realm of art: The use of perspective found in works of Michelangelo and Leonardo da Vinci provided the illusion of three-dimensional space absent in flat medieval renderings of the world.

Change in forms of communication is another important theme of the Renaissance. During the Middle Ages, the arts—stained glass, architecture, sculpture, legends, and songs—were powerful modes of communication and education. Indeed, they were the main modes of communication by necessity because most people could not read nor write. With the advent of the printing press, there was a shift in attention from oral communication to print literacy.

The move from visual to print literacy in the Renaissance may find a parallel in the twentieth-century shift from the printed page to the computer screen. Perhaps we are experiencing the beginnings of a general shift in modes of communication, this time from print back to icons, in the form of music video and computer graphics. Before the Renaissance, communications were limited to an individual's vicinity and, for the most part, to face-to-face contact. Just as the printing press facilitated communication, current technology is dramatically opening up possibilities for instant and global connection.

Other possible parallels between the Renaissance and the present day include the Black Death, which wiped out a third of Europe's population, and the AIDS epidemic and possible resurgence of plague in India.[4] Explorers such as Columbus and Magellan have modern counterparts in astronauts. Modern discoveries in scientific fields parallel great Renaissance advances in medicine, physics, chemistry, biology, and mathematics.

The broad canvas of time from 1430 to 1600 presents a challenge as we seek to find representative and engaging materials and teaching strategies to help students understand the significance of the Renaissance and make connections between the Renaissance and contemporary life. It could be said that there is nothing so new as the distant past because it is constantly being reinvented. By reenacting elements of a time period so long ago, we offer students both real and imagined worlds to explore. The music and the arts of the Renaissance, because they engage the imagination as well as the intellect, offer rich possibilities for connecting with those who have lived before.

Music is a way of communicating, in this case, across centuries. We cannot know the world as did the people living in earlier times. We can recognize, however, the individuality of those people and their connection to us as humans. Music can help evoke the imaginative and emotional aspects of another era. Just as students need logical and factual tools, they also need the intuitive and expressive tools the arts provide to learn and grow.

Because Sarah Birney and Erik Olsen's enthusiasm for their Renaissance collaboration had piqued the interest of so many of their colleagues, the staff at Ridgecrest Elementary decided to plan a schoolwide interdisciplinary project around the Renaissance. The teachers met in the media center for an hour of brainstorming. Broad questions about history were written on a large pad of paper, with newly generated ideas radiating out like spokes of a wheel. The first rush of ideas came thick and fast, producing numerous topics that neatly aligned with the goals of the social studies curriculum. Then connections to other subject areas and class settings at Ridgecrest began to emerge.

Valerie Nguyen, a sixth-grade teacher, studied the board. "We forgot to record the idea of linking science lessons with the Renaissance—the golden mean, Galileo, Leonardo da Vinci's scientific observations, for example."

"And a big time line. We forgot the big time line," volunteered Lisa Strander, the art teacher.

Chester Mortenson looked glum. "I don't want to be a wet blanket. I mean, this all sounds fine. But it's a lot of extra work. And my class is way behind in science. You know I've got those new kids, who need a lot of drill with the basics. I just don't have the hours to develop new lessons right now. I don't have any time to do anything!"

"You're right that this project will be more work," said Sarah. "But Erik and I found that it really paid off for our students. This project might give your new students a chance to show their interests and give them some reasons to acquire new skills. Besides, everyone here will contribute to the project in different ways. Maybe you can find a small way to be involved."

Valerie chimed in, "You know, we might think about displaying student work at a parents' night. That would be a good way to bring those new students and their parents into our school community."

"A feast—we could have a feast!" Erik blurted out. Chester raised an eyebrow and shook his head. "Just hear me out," Erik continued. "When I was doing research on the Renaissance in preparation for Nigel's visit, I read about an incredible event called the 'Feast of the Pheasant.' The feast is well docu-

mented, and we even have a record of the music that was performed. Perhaps we could use the feast as a focal point for our interdisciplinary planning. The feast could be a vehicle for students to share what they have been learning about the Renaissance."

After lively debate, the Ridgecrest Elementary staff agreed to develop a schoolwide interdisciplinary project around the Feast of the Pheasant. "We'll need to have plenty of resources to help us in our planning," said Valerie, casting an imploring look to the media specialist.

Sara added, "We'll also need to find resources for our students to use in their own research. I think everybody needs to be on the lookout for books, music, videos, paintings, and anything else we can use in our classrooms."

Developing a Schoolwide Project around the Renaissance

The grand sweep of the Renaissance suggests a grand and inspiring curriculum, perhaps a schoolwide interdisciplinary project. Although planning and coordinating schoolwide efforts requires teachers to demonstrate organization, commitment, and sustained effort, students can develop similar intellectual habits as a result of cohesive, stimulating, and memorable experiences. Creating an interdisciplinary curriculum can help students synthesize knowledge by bridging subject areas. An interdisciplinary project based on the Renaissance can incorporate study in separate subject areas while emphasizing the relationships between and among disciplines.

As the preceding scenario suggests, large-scale curriculum projects bring challenges, opportunities, and rewards. Each school is unique, with different configurations of power and autonomy, influence and initiative. Logistical issues of time, coordination, and resources tend to emerge during planning. Successfully solving these logistical challenges can help build camaraderie among teachers and result in benefits for students.

The Ridgecrest Elementary planning team is trying to find the right focus for their interdisciplinary project to provide educationally significant experiences while, at the same time, addressing the multiple priorities of teachers, administrators, parents, and students. There are many ways to approach such a project so that the process of inquiry and thematic content makes sense to the participants. For projects centered on historical periods, a useful organizing technique can be to focus on a pivotal date, placing it in the context of events that came before and after that date. This technique may help students place events within a flow of time (Young, 1994).

The year 1454 is an interesting and pivotal date because it allows comparisons between the medieval and Renaissance periods in Europe. This was the year Gutenberg invented the printing press, which allowed new scientific, political, and cultural ideas to spread more quickly. During this time, people explored and rediscovered the arts and writings of ancient Greece and Rome. All aspects of life were infused with a heightened spirit of inquiry. People began to question doctrine of the Roman Catholic Church. The middle of the fifteenth century marked a time of great exploration and expansion, bringing people from different continents into direct contact.

Table 9.2 outlines the events of the Middle Ages that precede 1454, as well as events of the Renaissance that follow this pivotal date. In this chart, historical events are cast from a European perspective. For example, although gunpowder had long been used in China, it was first discovered in Europe by the German Grey Friar Berthold Schwarz in 1313 (Grun, 1991).

Table 9.2

Flow of Historical Events in Europe Using 1454 as a Pivotal Date

800–1453	1454	1454–1650
a Charlemagne	**b** Gutenberg uses movable type	**a** Spanish Inquisition
b neumes in musical notation	**a** Hundred Years' War ends	**a** Spanish Jews exiled
a Vikings discover Greenland	**a** Fall of Byzantine Empire	**a** Columbus
b chess, paper introduced from China	**b** Feast of the Pheasant	**a** Henry VIII
a El Cid		**b** madrigals
a Battle of Hastings		**b** Michelangelo
c sugar		**a** Martin Luther
b the Sorbonne, University of Oxford		**b** present day violin
a Marco Polo		**c** Copernicus
a Crusades, Children's Crusade		**a** Spanish Armada
c gunpowder		**a** Africans enslaved
a Inquisition		**b** Shakespeare
a Magna Carta		**c** tobacco, tulips
a Hundred Years' War		**a** Sikhs in India
a Jacquerie Revolt, Peasants' Revolt		**a** Magellan
c Black Death		**b** "Greensleeves"
a Henry the Navigator		**c** plague
a St. Joan of Arc		**a** New World

Key: a = significant political and religious events
      b = significant events in cultural life
      c = significant events in science, health, and food

The Feast of the Pheasant or *Le Banquet du Voeu,* 1454

One of the events that occurred in 1454 was *Le Banquet du Voeu*[5] (The Feast of the Pheasant), which was notable even in a time of elaborate feasts, and was chronicled in detail by several observers.[6] You may know the nursery rhyme that some think commemorates this banquet:

Sing a song of sixpence, a pocketful of rye
Four and twenty blackbirds baked in a pie
When the pie was opened, the birds began to sing
Wasn't that a dainty dish to set before the King?

It's likely that the blackbirds in the verse not only sang but flew out at the guests because they were living birds contained in a prebaked pastry shell (Purdy, 1984). "Animated pyes," containing live animals and people, were popular entertainments at ostentatious banquets held in the fifteenth through the seventeenth centuries.

Renaissance feasts engaged the eyes as well as the tongue. Feast givers vied to create spectacles and culinary creations disguised as illusions, such as salmon masquerading as a boar's head. Unusual animals were created by stitching the front half of one animal, such as a pig, to the back half of another animal, such as a chicken, and vice versa. Showy birds, such as peacocks, were made to appear live by reassembling the carcass and refeathering it after cooking.

At this time, most people were poor and ate what they could find. Feasts were the province of the wealthy. Feasts were a political statement, a display of wealth, and a challenge to all appetites (Riley, 1993). Banquets at noble courts were put on for guests from near and far. They lasted for hours, even days. Between the courses, guests listened to elaborate musical entertainments, danced, or rested in their own rooms.

The Burgundian court under the dukes of Burgundy (1364–1477) became the most powerful political force in western Europe. These celebrated dukes of the house of Valois displayed their wealth through a lavish, resplendent court. For more than 100 years, the Burgundian court was a center of French language and culture.

The dukes involved themselves in music making and patronized music in grand style. They maintained two separate retinues of musicians, one for the chapel and one for entertainments. Minstrels of the court and chapel accompanied their lord everywhere, even in battle.

Le Banquet du Voeu was given for the French Burgundian Court by Duke Philip the Good of Burgundy. It took place on February 17, 1454, at Lille after two minor feasts and a jousting tournament. Although the dinner guests did not know it beforehand, the banquet was a political event designed to raise support for a mighty crusade. Constantinople had fallen to the Turks the year before. This meant that the Holy Lands were under Muslim rule. Deeply troubled, the pope invited the Duke of Burgundy to lead a new crusade against the Turkish forces.

Duke Philip's reply took place in the form of an elaborate pageant. Although many people planned and took part in the feast, all prepara-

Figure 9.4
The Garden of Love at the Court of Philip the Good (1432)

COURTESY OF RÉUNION DES MUSÉES NATIONAUX.

tions were kept a close secret. On the night of the feast, guests passed through five barred doors to a hall ablaze with lights from candles and torches. Servants wore liveries of gray and black, which served as a backdrop to the brilliant gold and scarlet brocades and other fancy costumes worn by the guests. As the ladies walked into the huge room, their rubies, pearls, and golden jewelry glittered in the candlelight. Magnificent banners hung about the hall.

Three enormous dining tables occupied the center. Duke Philip the Good sat at the head table with the most honored guests. One end of the table held a model church with a belfry, stained glass windows, an organ, and four singers inside. Other representations on the duke's table included a rose-water fountain, a chained woman, and a ship with sails and crew.

Tableaux at the other tables included animals prowling in jungles, a mermaid, a castle, a fool riding a bear through a wintry landscape, and people acting out proverbs. One table had a huge pie filled with 28 minstrels dressed as blackbirds. Minstrels in the pie played a trumpet, a bagpipe, a crumhorn, tambourines, lutes, flutes, vielles, and other instruments. The conductor of the pie was Charles, count of Charolais, who later became Duke Charles the Bold (1467–1477). He was known for his expertise as a conductor, harpist, and composer.

Figure 9.5
Illustration of Dance Positions for "Bouffons" from Thoinot Arbeau's Orchesography.

COURTESY OF DOVER BOOKS.

Before the food was served, guests strolled around the room, marveling at the displays. Onlookers sat in the galleries above the hall, invited to witness the wonderful meal but not to eat.

Finally the food came. One guest wrote that the number of dishes seemed infinite in number. There was so much food, so elaborately prepared that no one thought to write down a menu. Carriages containing food were lowered from the roof. Each meat course had more than 40 different dishes, and each carriage contained 82 pieces of meat. Because it is impossible to reconstruct the menu, the first course (of seven) from another feast provides an idea of what might have been served (see Table 9.3).

Table 9.3

First Course of the 1586 Wedding Feast of Wilhelm of Bavaria and René of Lorraine (Fisher, 1994, p. 10)

Crab	Fried goat
Peacock gravy	120 quail
Almond sauce	15 Rovig cakes
15 peacocks in broth	Yellow Kaiser soup
15 breast of lamb and goat	Fried lamprey in egg sauce
Wild boar with dark French gravy	Venison in dark broth with almond mincemeat
15 baked rabbits and 15 roast hare with pepper	Beef in puff paste with sweet green sauce
15 capon in dough with sausage quarters and bread slices	120 baked liver sausages in addition to capon liverwurst
15 hazel hen and 15 rock partridge with 25 wild pigeon in yellow Kaiser soup	Trout cooked in sweet wine with parsley and pepper
45 roast pheasants with lemon slices and orange pieces	

Musical entertainments were performed between courses of the feast. Fanfares from the hall played by "loud minstrels" were followed by secular songs and instrumental music performed by musicians encased in the pie. After the secular music, the musicians in the church performed sacred music with organ, bells, and voices. Two musicians with their backs to each other, mounted on a steed festooned with pink silks, trumpeted fanfares. A young boy and a white stag sang a duet, the stag's part provided by an offstage singer.

In addition to these musical interludes, giants, horses, jugglers, and jesters entertained the feasters. A trained falcon hunted live birds in the hall. A series of skits mimed the story of Jason, with reference to Duke Philip's chivalric Order of the Golden Fleece.

All of these diversions built toward the climax and real purpose for this feast. All eyes stared in amazement at the final spectacle. A giant dressed in green and striped silk to look like a Turk, holding a battle-ax in one hand, entered the hall leading an elephant. The elephant's back supported a tower holding a woman dressed in mourning who sang a pitiful dirge. This spectacle was an allegory. The woman, who represented the Holy Church, begged the feasters to save her from the Turkish enemy (signified by the giant) who held her captive. The elephant represented exotic lands and the tower stood for the strong faith of the Christians.

Brilliantly clad heralds appeared, including the golden fleece king-at-arms carrying a live pheasant. The pheasant's collar was made of gold, gems, and pearls. This referred to the custom of knights swearing a vow while eating birds thought to be noble, such as peacock, heron, or pheasant. All the knights present swore solemn vows to fight in a crusade led by Duke Philip the Good. Ladies of the court dressed as the Virtues made speeches in praise of the event. Then dancing, jousts, and other extravagances filled out the evening.

Soon after this fabulous feast, the pope died. Although everyone had the best of intentions, the crusade was never mounted.

Interdisciplinary Project
The Feast of the Pheasant

Rationale   The Feast of the Pheasant was an event of such spectacular proportions that its re-creation could capture the imagination of an entire school community. The surviving narratives, music, and other arts that document the feast help us understand this particular occasion at the Burgundian court and also give us insights into Renaissance society in general.

Staging the Feast of the Pheasant could include some of the music that was heard at the original feast. The sophisticated intertwining melodies and French lyrics of the composer Binchois may, however, be too difficult for students to perform. Through contemporary recordings of music known to have been performed at the feast, students can sample the authentic sounds that would have been heard in 1454. If recordings of this specific music cannot be located, comparable selections can be substituted.

Unlike the scripted lesson plans for single lessons found in previous chapters, this plan provides a menu of ideas that can be adapted to fit student interests and abilities. The ideas in "Avenues for Student Research" illustrate but a few of the ways teachers can orchestrate learning and research opportunities for students to guide them in finding answers to the essential questions below.

Project goals
- ~ To encourage individual student research and investigation using various types of sources, including examples from the arts
- ~ To bring content and processes from various disciplines together in the study of the Renaissance
- ~ To coordinate the efforts of teachers and students in planning and presenting the results of their inquiry in the context of a reenactment of a Renaissance feast

Essential questions
- ~ What was the Renaissance?
- ~ Why is the Renaissance an important time for study?
- ~ How does life during the Renaissance compare with modern life?
- ~ How do we know what life was like in the Renaissance?
- ~ What does the Feast of the Pheasant tell us about Renaissance life?

Social studies themes
Depending on the research topics the students choose to pursue, these themes may be addressed through this project (National Council for the Social Studies, 1994):

- ~ Culture
- ~ Time, continuity, and change
- ~ Individuals, groups, and institutions
- ~ Production, distribution, and consumption
- ~ Science, technology, and society

Resources for student and teacher research
- ~ Textbooks; atlases; globes; encyclopedias; illustrated histories; photographs of buildings, paintings, costumes, and musical instruments from the Renaissance period
- ~ Age-appropriate nonfiction and fictional accounts of the Renaissance
- ~ Recordings of Renaissance music, specifically the music from the Feast of the Pheasant: Ensemble Gilles Binchois (performers), (1991), *Le Banquet du Voeu 1454* [CD], London: Virgin Classics
- ~ Videos about the Renaissance

~ Narrative of the feast (provided earlier in this chapter)

~ Event resources, books for students, and other suggestions at the end of this chapter

Teacher planning and preparation

In addition to gathering resources, teachers will want to arrange their classrooms so that students have ready access to materials for their research. A listening area, with recordings of music from the feast, should be set up so that students can decide which music fits with the style and character suggested by their scripts.

Teachers will want to preview the materials included in the resource list to determine the materials' suitability and utility for their classrooms. They will also want to consider the sources of information, the variety of types of information, and points of view provided by the resources. Students may identify with differing points of view, which in itself brings up interesting points for discussion.

CONTROVERSY IN THE CURRICULUM

Reading the Records

When students read about the Renaissance, they may assume that the materials portray the Renaissance accurately and completely. Just as contemporary media often convey stories from a dominant cultural perspective with little reference to alternate minority viewpoints, the records of the past may emphasize certain points of view over others. It is tempting to take what we want to see and disregard the inequalities or unpleasant aspects of another time. Such selective telling may be packaged as media sound bites or oversimplified synopses. Encyclopedias and history texts will likely tell of triumphant military maneuvers, wealthy people, and stories of the most powerful individuals and groups. Our vision may also be clouded with stereotypes that we bring to the reading—imagined feasts, Robin Hood àla Hollywood, contemporary Renaissance fairs, and idealized peasant life. But if one squints a little at the spectacle of the aristocratic great feast, one might see the shadow of the beggars who wait, hopeful for meat-soaked trenchers or plates of bread. The full story of the Feast of the Pheasant contains echoes of the Black Death, peasant uprisings, and hunger in addition to the courtly music and fantastic displays.

Therefore, when surveying any historical period, it is essential for teachers to consult a wide range of resources that represent the period as fully and authentically as possible. It may be possible to construct several plausible but contradictory interpretations from the same materials. Thorough immersion in these sources provides a wealth of knowledge that allows us to study the period from many points of view.

The past contains many stories. Who is speaking to us through the records? Whose voices are *not* heard? What point of view guides the historian's hand? Attempts to discover the answers to these questions can lead to a fuller, more authentic, and more vivid sense of history.

Introducing the Feast of the Pheasant

Here is a menu of ideas designed to pique student interest in the Feast of the Pheasant:

~ Perform "Sing a Song of Sixpence." Although the nursery song may not specifically commemorate the Feast of the Pheasant, its familiarity helps students identify with this period in time.

~ Read *A Medieval Feast* by Aliki (1983), which describes a feast that is very similar to the Feast of the Pheasant. The book provides a richly illustrated account of the preparations necessary to prepare such a feast.

~ Retell the account of the feast, noting unfamiliar vocabulary or references.

~ Listen to an instrumental piece, "Et c'est Assez," composed by Jacques Vide, chamber musician at the Burgundian court in the 1420s (track 1 of *Le Banquet du Voeu 1454* [Ensemble Gilles Binchois, 1991]). After listening to the high, intertwining reed instruments, introduce this piece as a fanfare that signaled the start of an entertainment between courses of the Feast of the Pheasant. Listen a second time, inviting students to imagine what events might come next in the feast.

~ Invite students to imagine a conversation that might take place during the feast. Have them generate a list of persons who might have been present, such as a young noble woman from the Burgundian court, a dancer, a serving boy who washes dishes and peels carrots, one of the blackbird minstrels from the pie, or an old beggar woman. Ask students what role each of these people plays in the evening's entertainment. What part of the great feast would they eat? What clothes would each wear? What was their favorite part of the feast? How did they interact? What was regular life like for these guests? Compile a list of questions the class would like to research and discuss possible strategies for finding the information.

Avenues for Student Research

The products of student research, which can take many forms, can be incorporated into the reenactment of the Feast of the Pheasant. Students may generate scripts portraying conversations between guests at the event. Small ensembles may perform music or dances of the period. Student interpretations of artwork from the Renaissance could provide important information to guide choices of costumes and decorations for the feast. Students may wish to research and prepare some of the festive foods of the time (see *To the King's Taste*, Sass, 1975). As a group, decide upon the sequence of events to be included in the reenactment. Plan the props, scenery, costumes, entertainments, and food that will enhance the presentation. The ideas that follow are samples of the kinds of research the students might undertake.

~ The study of a new historical period is bound to bring with it new vocabulary. Students can develop a Renaissance vocabulary list for the new terms and new ideas they encounter. Often terms will lead to broader questions and topics that students may wish to pursue in greater depth.

~ The study of musical instruments involves explorations of both history and culture. Many early instruments look exotic yet familiar because they are forerunners of modern orchestral instruments. The guitar, lute, dulcimer, and oboe, which have their origins in the Middle East, were brought back from the Islamic world by crusaders. Our modern violin developed from medieval *fidels, vielles,* and *fitheles*. Students may wish to research the origins of instruments that they play or enjoy. The CD-ROM *Musical Instruments* (1994) can be a good starting point for their research. The Internet is also a source for information. There is, for example, a home page for the Lute Society of America (http://www.cs.dartmouth.edu/~wbc/lsa/lsa.html); a lute page with photographs of lutes, examples of lutes in paintings, and a sound file with a lute performance (http://www.cs.dartmouth.edu/~wbc/new/new_lute.html); and a recorder home page (http://iinet.net.au/~nickl/recorder.html). For books with instrument illustrations, see Blackwood (1991), Diagram Group (1976), and Montagu (1976).

~ European experiences from the fourteenth through sixteenth centuries are represented in both fictional and nonfictional accounts. Wood's picture book *The Renaissance* (1993) highlights a Florentine townhouse, Columbus's ship, St. Peter's in Rome, and a printer's workshop with see-through overlays to show both interior details and exterior structures. Tapestries and visual arts convey the poverty and violence as well as the expansion of knowledge and expression in *The Renaissance: The Living Past* (Goodenough, 1979). *A Florentine Merchant* (Caselli, 1986) tells the story of a rich merchant's household in the fourteenth century from the viewpoint of a slave. *Renaissance Places* and *Renaissance People* (Howarth, 1992a, 1992b) contain engaging illustrations suitable for readers in elementary and middle schools.

~ The contrast between aristocratic and common life in the Renaissance can be seen in artwork from the time. *October,* by the Limbourg Brothers (Janson, 1969), shows peasants harvesting crops in the shadow of a castle. Brueghel's *Peasant Dance* (Gardner, 1970) and *Peasant Wedding* (Janson, 1969) can be contrasted with portraits of noble life such as Holbein's *Henry VIII* (Janson, 1969). Celebrations from this period also show the differences between social classes. *Merry Ever After: The Story of Two Medieval Weddings* (Lasker, 1976) contrasts the nuptial ceremony of a peasant with that of an aristocrat. The book describes the origins of many wedding customs that continued into the Renaissance and beyond to the present day. Poortvliet's compelling *Daily Life in Holland in the Year 1566* (1992) may interest older students who wish to investigate class distinctions in the Renaissance. Costumes of the period can be found on the World Wide Web at http://www.siue.edu/COSTUME/history.html.

~ If one of your curricular goals is to expand the study of the Renaissance period from Europe to a more global perspective, you may wish to consult histories and atlases such as *Datelines of World History* (Arnold & Trease, 1983) and *Timetables of History* (Grun, 1991). *Exploration and Empire* (Kramer & Adams, 1990) includes graphics for all continents covering events from the Renaissance to the Industrial Revolution. *The World in 1492* (Fritz, Paterson, Mahy, McKissack, McKissack, & Highwater, 1992) introduces events throughout the world through beautiful illustrations. *Old Worlds to New* (Podell & Anzovin, 1993) offers more text for older readers. The Middle Eastern perspective can be explored through *The Rise of Islam* (Powell, 1980). Two books from the same series, *Umm El Madayan: An Islamic City through the Ages* (Ayoub, Binous, Gragueb, Mtimet, & Silm, 1994) and *Lebek: A City of Northern Europe through the Ages* (Hernandez & Ballonga, 1991), trace the growth of these fictional cities from the Middle Ages to the present. The McKissacks provide an engaging account of thriving African empires during the Renaissance period in *The Royal Kingdoms of Ghana, Mali, and Songhay* (1994).

Sarah Birney entered Ridgecrest Elementary on the night of the reenactment of the Feast of the Pheasant. The air was feverish with excitement, with sounds of last-minute recorder rehearsals and bright red crepe-paper streamers wafting in the currents of rushing students.

Families arrived with steaming dishes for the potluck, video cameras slung around shoulders. As the Robinson family passed the displays mounted on the cafeteria wall, Josiah Robinson seemed about to explode. "That's my project!" he exclaimed, pointing to a poster of how a printing press works.

A fifth grader ran up to Sarah, asking for help with her wimple. As Sarah pinned the cone hat into place, Chester Mortenson wheeled a papier-mâché *elephant past on the AV cart. Chester gave Sarah the thumbs-up sign, then disappeared down the corridor, steadying the elephant with one hand.*

References

Aliki. (1983). *A medieval feast.* New York: Thomas Y. Crowell.

Amman, J., & Sachs, H. (1973). *The book of trades [Ständebuch].* New York: Dover. (Original work published 1568.)

Arbeau, T. (1967). *Orchesography* (M. S. Evans, trans.). New York: Dover. (Original work published 1588.)

Arnold, G., & Trease, G. (1983). *Datelines of world history.* New York: Warwick.

Ayoub, A., Binous, J., Gragueb, A., Mtimet, A., & Silm, H. (1994). *Umm El Madayan: An Islamic city through the ages.* Boston: Houghton Mifflin.

Baring-Gould, W. S., & Baring-Gould, C. (1962). *The annotated Mother Goose.* New York: Crown.

Blackwood, A. (1991). *Music: The illustrated guide to music around the world from its origins to the present day.* New York: Mallard.

Calliope (performers). (1990). *Diversions* [CD]. Tempe, Ariz.: Summit Records.

Cartellieri, O. (1929). *The court of Burgundy.* London: Kegan Paul.

Caselli, G. (1986). *A Florentine merchant.* New York: Peter Bedrick.

Chalk, G. (1994). *Mr. Frog went a-courting.* London: Dorling Kindersley.

Chamberlin, E. R. (1969). *Everyday life in Renaissance times.* London: B. T. Batsford.

Consort of Musicke (performers). (1991). *There were three ravens* [CD]. London: Virgin Classics.

Diagram Group. (1976). *Musical instruments of the world.* Amsterdam: Smeets Offset.

Ensemble Gilles Binchois (performers). (1991). *Le banquet du voeu 1454* [CD]. London: Virgin Classics.

Fallows, D. (1991). Liner notes to Ensemble Gilles Binchois (performers) *Le banquet du voeu 1454* [CD]. London: Virgin Classics.

Fisher, G. (1994). The use of voices and instruments at a sixteenth-century wedding feast, *Choral Journal* 35 (1): 9–12.

Fraser, K. (1968). *Stilts, somersaults, and headstands: Game poems based on a painting by Peter Breughel.* New York: Atheneum.

Fritz, J., Paterson, K., Mahy, M., McKissack, F., McKissack, P., & Highwater, J. (1992). *The world in 1492.* New York: Henry Holt.

Gardner, H. (1970). *Gardner's art through the ages* (5th ed.). Revised by H. de la Croix & R. G. Tansey. New York: Harcourt, Brace & World.

Goodenough, S. (ed.). (1979). *The Renaissance: The living past.* New York: Arco.

Greene, M. (1991). Texts and margins. *Harvard Educational Review* 61 (1): 27–39.

Grun, B. (1991). *The timetables of history: A horizontal linkage of people and events.* New York: Simon & Schuster.

Havel, V. (1994). What the world needs now, *New Age Journal* 11 (5): 45–48, 161–162.

Hernandez, X., & Ballonga, J. (1991). *Lebek: A city of northern Europe through the ages.* Boston: Houghton Mifflin.

Howarth, S. (1992a). *Renaissance people.* Brookfield, Conn.: Millbrook.

Howarth, S. (1992b). *Renaissance places.* Brookfield, Conn.: Millbrook.

James Galway's music in time. Part 4: The golden age [video]. (1982). Princeton, N.J.: Films for the Humanities.

Janson, H. W. (ed.). (1969). *History of art.* New York: Harry N. Abrams.

Kramer, A., & Adams, S. (1990). *Exploration and empire: Empire-builders, European expansion and the development of science.* New York: Warwick.

Lafortune-Martel, A. (1984). *Fête noble en Bourgogne au XVe Siécle: Le banquet du faisan (1454): Aspects politiques, sociaux et culturels.* Montréal, Canada: Institut d'Études Médiévales Université de Montréal.

Lasker, J. (1976). *Merry ever after: The story of two medieval weddings.* New York: Viking.

Lockwood, L. (1980). Renaissance. In *The new Grove dictionary of music and musicians.* Vol. 15, pp. 736–741. London: Macmillan.

Mann, W. (1982). *James Galway's music in time.* Englewood Cliffs, N.J.: Prentice-Hall.

McKissack, P., & McKissack, F. (1994). *The royal kingdoms of Ghana, Mali, and Songhay: Life in medieval Africa.* New York: Henry Holt.

Montagu, J. (1976). *The world of medieval and Renaissance musical instruments.* Woodstock, N.Y.: Overlook.

Muhlberger, R. (1993). *What makes a Brueghel a Brueghel?* New York: Viking.

Musical instruments [CD-ROM]. (1994). U.S.A.: Microsoft/Dorling Kindersley.

National Council for the Social Studies. (1994). *Expectations of excellence: Curriculum standards for social studies.* Washington, D.C.

Opie, I., & Opie, P. (1955). *The Oxford nursery rhyme book.* London: Oxford University Press.

Opie, I., & Tatem, M. (1989). *A dictionary of superstitions.* Oxford: Oxford University Press.

Podell, J., & Anzovin, S. (1993). *Old worlds to new: The age of exploration and discovery.* New York: H. W. Wilson.

Poortvliet, R. (1992). *Daily life in Holland in the year 1566 and the story of my ancestor's treasure chest.* Kampen, The Netherlands: Harry N. Abrams.

Powell, A. (1980) *The rise of Islam.* New York: Warwick.

Purdy, S. G. (1984). *As easy as pie.* New York: Collier.

Radford, E., & Radford, M. A. (1961). *Encyclopaedia of superstitions.* London: Hutchinson & Co. (Original work published 1948.)

Ravenscroft, T. (1971). *Deuteromelia.* Amsterdam: Da Capo Press. (Original work published 1523.)

Richardson, S. (1995). The return of the plague. *Discover* 16 (1): 69–70.

Riley, G. (1993). *Renaissance recipes.* San Francisco: Pomegranate Artbooks.

Sass, L. J. (1975). *To the king's taste: Richard II's book of feasts and recipes.* New York: The Metropolitan Museum of Art.

Scholes, P. A. (1970). *The Oxford companion to music.* Oxford, England: Oxford University Press.

Vaughan, R. (1970). *Philip the good.* New York: Barnes & Noble.

Wood, T. (1993). *The Renaissance.* New York: Viking.

Wright, C. (1979). *Music at the Court of Burgundy 1364–1419: A documentary history.* Ottawa, Canada: Institute of Mediaeval Music.

Wright, C. (1980). Burgundy. In *The new Grove dictionary of music and musicians.* Vol. 3, pp. 464–468. London: Macmillan.

Young, K. A. (1994). *Constructing buildings, bridges and minds: Building an integrated curriculum through social studies.* Portsmouth, N.H.: Heinemann.

Resources for Teachers and Students

RESOURCES FOR THE FEAST OF THE PHEASANT

Ashelford, J. (1983). *A visual history of costume: The sixteenth century.* London: B. T. Batsford.

Austern, L. P. (1992). *Music in English children's drama of the later Renaissance.* Philadelphia: Gordon & Breach.

Brooke, I., & Landes, W. (1993). *Western European costume: Thirteenth to seventeenth century*. Studio City, Calif.: Players.

Conté, P. (1974). *Danses anciennes de cour et de théatre en France*. Paris: Dessain et Tolra.

Desmond, K. (1986). *The timetables of invention and discoveries from pre-history to the present day*. New York: M. Evans.

Grun, B. (1991). *The timetables of history: A horizontal linkage of people and events*. New York: Simon & Schuster.

Hellemans, A., & Bunch, B. (1991). *The timetables of science*. New York: Simon & Schuster.

Riley, G. (1993). *Renaissance recipes*. San Francisco: Pomegranate Artbooks.

Sass, L. J. (1975). *To the king's taste: Richard II's book of feasts and recipes*. New York: The Metropolitan Museum of Art.

Scott, M. (1986). *A visual history of costume: The fourteenth and fifteenth centuries*. London: B. T. Batsford.

Wood, M. (1964). *Historical dances twelfth to nineteenth century*. London: Lowe & Brydone.

AUDIO RECORDINGS

Calliope (performers). (1990). *Diversions* [CD]. Tempe, Ariz.: Summit.

Consort of Musicke (performers). (1991). *There were three ravens* [CD]. London: Virgin Classics.

Early Music Consort of London (performers) & Munrow, D. (director). (1976). *The pleasures of the royal courts* [CD]. New York: Elektra Asylum Nonesuch.

Ensemble Gilles Binchois (performers). (1991). *Le banquet du voeu 1454* [CD]. London: Virgin Classics.

Grupo de Música "Alfonso X El Sabio" (performers). (1992). *Music in the time of Columbus* [CD]. London: Decca.

The Hilliard Ensemble (performers). (1990). *Sacred and secular music from six centuries* [CD]. London: Hyperion.

Hespérion XX (performers) & Savall, J. (director). (1992). *El cancionero de palacio 1474–1516* [CD]. France: Astrée Auvidis.

Kalenda Maya (performers). (1985). *Medieval and Renaissance music.* [CD]. Oslo, Norway: Simax.

Kirby, E. (soprano), & Rooley, A. (lute). (1989). *John Dowland: The English Orpheus* [CD]. London: Virgin Classics.

Partridge, I. (tenor), & Ragossnig, K. (lutenist). (1990). *A gardin for delights: English lutesong from the Renaissance* [CD] Heidelberg, Germany: Bayer.

Pilpot, M., Rumsey, S., & Wilson, C. (performers). (1992). *From a Spanish palace songbook: Music from the time of Christopher Columbus* [CD]. London: Hyperion.

VIDEO RECORDINGS

The Boast of Kings. (1986). Chicago: Home Vision.

James Galway's music in time. Part 3: The Renaissance. (1982). Princeton, N.J.: Films for the Humanities.

James Galway's music in time. Part 4: The Golden Age. (1982). Princeton, N.J.: Films for the Humanities.

Sutton, J. (1991). *Il ballarino* (The dancing master): *The art of Renaissance dance.* Pennington, N.J.: Dance Horizons.

NONFICTION BOOKS FOR STUDENTS

Arnold, G., & Trease, G. (1983). *Datelines of world history.* New York: Warwick.

Byam, M. (1988). *Arms and armor.* New York: Alfred A. Knopf.

Caselli, G. (1986). *The Renaissance and the new world.* New York: Peter Bedrick.

Chrisp, P. (1993). *The search for the East: Exploration & encounters, 1450–1550.* New York: Thomson Learning.

Fritz, J., Paterson, K., Mahy, M., McKissack, F., McKissack, P., & Highwater, J. (1992). *The world in 1492.* New York: Henry Holt.

Gail, M. (1968). *Life in the Renaissance.* New York: Random House.

Goodenough, S. (ed.). (1979). *The Renaissance: The living past.* New York: Arco.

Howarth, S. (1992). *Renaissance people.* Brookfield, Conn.: Millbrook.

Howarth, S. (1992). *Renaissance places.* Brookfield, Conn.: Millbrook.

Kramer, A., & Adams, S. (1990). *Exploration and empire: Empire-builders, European expansion and the development of science.* New York: Warwick.

Muhlberger, R. (1993). *What makes a Brueghel a Brueghel?* New York: Viking.

McKissack, P., & McKissack, F. (1994). *The royal kingdoms of Ghana, Mali, and Songhay: Life in medieval Africa.* New York: Henry Holt.

Podell, J., & Anzovin, S. (1993). *Old worlds to new: The age of exploration and discovery.* New York: H. W. Wilson.

Shapiro, I. (ed.). (1962). *The golden book of the Renaissance.* New York: Golden.

FICTION BOOKS FOR STUDENTS

Aliki. (1983). *A medieval feast.* New York: Thomas Y. Crowell.

Ayoub, A., Binous, J., Gragueb, A., Mtimet, A., & Silm, H. (1994). *Umm El Madayan: An Islamic city through the ages.* Boston: Houghton Mifflin.

Caselli, G. (1986). *A Florentine merchant.* New York: Peter Bedrick.

Hernandez, X., & Ballonga, J. (1991). Lebek: A city of northern Europe through the ages. Boston: Houghton Mifflin.

Lasker, J. (1976). *Merry ever after: The story of two medieval weddings.* New York: Viking.

Macaulay, D. (1973). *Castle.* Boston: Houghton Mifflin.

Macaulay, D. (1973). *Cathedral.* Boston: Houghton Mifflin.

Ventura, P. (1986). *There once was a time.* New York: G. P. Putnam's Sons.

{ chapter 10 }

MUSIC AS AN EXPRESSION OF HISTORY:
THE AMERICAN CIVIL WAR

When Ken Lee sauntered into the teachers' lunch room whistling the tune of "Bonnie Blue Flag," Beth Humphry, the seventh-grade general music teacher, put down her tuna sandwich and remarked, "You're in an awfully good mood today. What's that tune you're whistling?"

"It's 'Bonnie Blue Flag.' I guess it's also 'The Homespun Dress,' because they have the same tune. It was on the sound track for the Civil War video I was showing in social studies today. I've heard it so many times that it's stuck in my head and I can't get it out."

"I'm embarrassed to admit it, but my knowledge of Civil War music is limited to 'The Battle Hymn of the Republic,' 'Dixie,' and 'When Johnny Comes Marching Home,'" Beth said. "We didn't spend much time on American music in our music history class at the university. How is it that you know these songs?"

"Oh, I'm a Civil War buff. I've collected lots of books and recordings. I also hear some of these songs when I attend reenactments of Civil War battles."

"I'd be interested in learning some more about Civil War music so I could incorporate it in the American music unit in my general music classes," Beth said. "Say—what would you think about planning some lessons together that focus on music from the Civil War?"

"That sounds like a great idea. You know, even though I'm familiar with this music and the students hear it in the video sound tracks, I've never really consciously incorporated it into my classes. Would you like me to bring you some of my books and recordings?

"Great! It might not be a bad idea for me to watch those Civil War videos, too. Why don't we get together next week to brainstorm some ideas?"

Music and the American Civil War

The Civil War was a defining moment in American history; on its outcome hinged the ideals of nationhood laid out in the Declaration of Independence and the Constitution. Because of its great importance, the Civil War has a prominent place in the curriculum of nearly every school in the United States.

The Civil War was fought over the issue of Southern states removing themselves from the Union. The Southern states, with their agricultural economy, depended on the institution of slavery to survive. Northern states had a primarily industrial economy and did not practice slavery. The South, fearing that the North would exert its power to limit or abolish slavery, chose to secede from the Union and form the Confederate States of America. Because the North had no intention of abandoning the idea of a united nation that had been established less than a century before, war became inevitable.

Some of the major events related to the Civil War are summarized in Table 10.1.

Table 10.1 *Major Events of the Civil War*		
	October 17, 1859	Abolitionist John Brown and followers captured the U. S. arsenal at Harper's Ferry, Virginia.
	April 12, 1861	Confederate troops attacked Fort Sumter.
	April 15, 1861	Lincoln issued a call for troops.
	July 21, 1861	Northern troops retreated after the first battle of Bull Run.
	August 27–30, 1862	South was victorious in second battle of Bull Run under the leadership of Jackson and Lee.
	September 17, 1862	Confederate forces defeated in Battle of Antietam.
	December 13, 1862	Union forces defeated at Fredericksburg.
	January 1, 1863	Lincoln issued the Emanicipation Proclamation.
	July 1–3, 1863	Northern victory at Gettysburg marked a turning point in the war.
	July 4, 1863	Vicksburg fell to Union troops led by U. S. Grant.
	September 2, 1864	General Sherman captured Atlanta.
	April 9, 1865	Lee surrendered to Grant at Appomattox.

Would simply learning these facts, names, and dates give students a real understanding of that pivotal time in our nation's history? Surely not. Students must come to know who the people involved in the conflict were and why they were willing to fight and die for beliefs that divided the country. Music provides a powerful vehicle for understanding the aspirations, emotions, hardships, and politics of the people who lived through that tumultuous time. In the music we can hear the voices of the soldiers, the family members left behind, and the African Americans in slavery who yearned for freedom.

Much of the music from the Civil War period remains firmly woven in the American cultural fabric. "The Battle Hymn of the Republic," "When Johnny Comes Marching Home," and "Dixie" are readily recognized by many Americans; spirituals such as "Wade in the Water" and "Steal Away" can be heard in churches and concert halls. The spiritual "Oh Freedom" was revived with new meaning in the 1960s as the words *no more segregation* were sung to the tune. These songs evoke a strong emotional response, which accounts, in part, for their great longevity.

CONTROVERSY IN THE CURRICULUM

Should You Sing Dixie?

"Dixie" can arouse very different emotional responses in different people. While "Dixie" symbolizes regional pride to some, to others the song is offensive as a symbol of racial oppression (Sacks & Sacks, 1993). Because of this, teachers must be sensitive in the way they use this song in the class-room. While it is appropriate to listen to the song and learn about it as an important cultural artifact of the Civil War period, it may be less appropriate to sing it as a quasi-patriotic song or use it solely for entertainment purposes.

A factor contributing to the proliferation and preservation of Civil War music from the white culture was the rapid growth of the young music publishing industry in the United States. During the mid-1800s, many middle class homes had a piano in the parlor; people played and sang songs for their own entertainment. Civilians quickly snapped up sheet music of songs written about the latest events of the war or sentimental songs about the soldier's yearning for home and family. Sheet music, along with newspaper accounts, photographs, and soldiers' and civilians' journals, gives us a good idea of the kind of music that was being heard at the time.

Figure 10.1
Illustration from Little Women: *The March Family Gathered around the Piano*

The Role of Musicians in the Civil War

Musicians, both military and civilian, played an integral role in the Civil War. Music was used to rouse patriotic fervor, to convey political messages, to relieve the loneliness and boredom of soldiers far from home, and to comfort the families left behind.

ILLUSTRATION BY FRANK T. MERRILL FROM LITTLE WOMEN:
"THE MARCH FAMILY GATHERED AROUND THE PIANO" (ALCOTT, 1880, P. 13)

Music was often used for practical purposes. Fife and drum corps and bands helped keep the soldiers in step as they marched. Notice in Figure 10.2 that the bells of the brass instruments point backward. This allowed the sound to be directed back to the soldiers the musicians were leading.

Figure 10.2

Members of a Wisconsin Band during the Civil War Era

COPY OF A COMPOSITE TINTYPE OF THE 1ST BRIGADE, 3RD DIVISION, 15TH ARMY CORPS BAND, WIS., CIVIL WAR. ORIGINALS DONATED BY BAND LEADER KIMBERLY IN 1918. STATE HISTORICAL SOCIETY OF WISCONSIN, WHI (X3) 35083, LOT 2947.

In the camps, buglers signaled the major events of the day from rising for morning roll call (reveille), to dinner call, to the final roll call (tattoo), then, finally, to bed (taps)[1] (Billings, 1993). Although musicians called troops to battle, they usually did not participate in the battle themselves. More often than not, musicians were given the grim task of assisting with the dead and wounded. This did not mean, however, that musicians were exempt from danger: Many were killed or wounded while carrying out their duties.

Music, provided either by regimental bands or soldiers in camp, helped the troops pass the time as they waited for the next round of fighting. Soldiers who could sing or play a guitar, harmonica, or violin treated their comrades to such favorites as "Tenting Tonight," "Just Before the Battle, Mother," "John Brown's Body," "The Battle Hymn of the Republic," "The Girl I Left Behind Me," and "The Battle Cry of Freedom" (Wilkinson, 1990).

Sometimes, when the Union and Confederate troops were camped near each other, they could hear each other's music. Leo Faller, a Union soldier camped at the Chickahominy River across from a Confederate camp, wrote to his sister on June 19, 1862: "A few minuets [*sic*] ago we could hear one of their Bands playing very distinctly and last evening one of their bands played Yankee-Doodle" (Flower, 1963, p. 77). When there was no other music to be heard, even the enemy's music was welcomed. Faller later wrote: "We are not allowed to have any music here at all and I have not heard the Tap of a Drum since we have been here, except the Rebels Drums and I tell you it is a little dry soldering [*sic*] without music" (Flower, 1963, p. 78). Even though each side had tunes that were expressly identified with their respective causes, such as "Dixie" and "Bonnie Blue Flag" for the South and "Battle Cry of Freedom" and "The Battle Hymn of the Republic" for the North, many songs were known and loved by soldiers on both sides. "Lorena," a sentimental song about the beloved left behind, and "Tenting Tonight," a song expressing the soldiers' sadness and weariness as the war dragged on, spoke to the human condition that transcended political divisions. One evening when the Blue and the Gray soldiers were camped on either side of the Rappahannock River, soldiers on both sides listened as the Northern musicians played a concert of Union tunes, then some Confederate tunes, then ended with a song expressing a shared sentiment, "Home, Sweet Home" (Lord & Wise, 1966, p. 205). This event's testimony to the power of music to unite the soldiers, if even momentarily, is captured in John Thompson's poem, "Music in Camp" (Miles, 1911).

Music in Camp

Two armies covered hill and plain,
    Where Rappahannock's waters
Ran deeply crimsoned with the stain
    Of battle's recent slaughters.

The summer clouds lay pitched like tents
    In meads of heavenly azure;
And each dread gun of the elements
    Slept in its hid embrasure.

The breeze so softly blew it made
    No forest leaf to quiver,
And the smoke of the random cannonade
    Rolled slowly from the river.

And now where circling hills looked down
    with cannon grimly planted,
O'er listless camp and silent town,
    The golden sunset slanted.

When on the fervid air there came
    A strain, now rich, now tender,
The music seemed itself aflame,
    With day's departing splendor.

A Federal band, which eve and morn
    Played measures brave and nimble,
Had just struck up with flute and horn
    And lively clash of cymbal.

Down flocked the soldiers to the banks
    Till, margined by its pebbles,
One wooded shore was blue with "Yanks,"
    And one was gray with "Rebels."

Then all was still, and then the band
    With movements light and tricksy,
Made stream and forest, hill and strand,
    Reverberate with "Dixie."

The conscious stream, with burnished glow,
    Went proudly o'er its pebbles,
But thrilled throughout its deepest flow
    With yelling of the Rebels.

Again a pause, and then again
    The trumpet pealed sonorous,
And "Yankee Doodle" was the strain
    To which the shore gave chorus.

The laughing ripple shoreward flew
    To kiss the shining pebbles,
Loud shrieked the crowding Boys in Blue
    Defiance to the Rebels.

And yet once more the bugle sang
    Above the stormy riot;
No shout upon the evening rang,
    There reigned a holy quiet.

The sad slow stream its noiseless flood
    Poured o'er the glistening pebbles;
All silent now the Yankee stood,
    And silent stood the Rebels.

No unresponsive soul had heard
    That plaintive note's appealing,
So deeply "Home, Sweet Home," had stirred
    The hidden founts of feeling.

Or Blue or Gray the soldier sees,
    As by the wand of fairy,
The cottage 'neath the live-oak trees,
    The cabin by the prairie.

Or cold or warm his native skies
    Bend in their beauty o'er him;
Seen through the tear-mist in his eyes,
    His loved ones stand before him.

As fades the iris after rain
    In April's tearful weather,
The vision vanished as the strain
    And daylight died together.

But Memory, waked by Music's art,
    Expressed in simplest numbers,
Subdued the sternest Yankee's heart,
    Made light the Rebel's slumbers.

And fair the form of Music shines,
That bright, celestial creature,
Who still 'mid War's embattled lines
Gave this one touch of Nature.

John Thompson

Much of the soldiers' lives was characterized by too much or too little. Northern soldiers too often had hardtack and rancid bacon to eat and too rarely had fresh meat and vegetables. Both sides often waited too long in the camps or trenches for the next major battle, but when the action came, it was nearly always too furious and awful. Just as the soldiers yearned for music when they didn't have a chance to hear any, they found out what happened when the music didn't stop:

> As the weeks passed with little tactical activity other than an occasional raiding party the problem of boredom became more acute in the ranks, and General Ledlie ordered the superb band of the 56th Massachusetts, alternating with those of the other regiments of the division, to play for the men at his headquarters in the rear, morning, noon, and night.... In the beginning, the playing soothed and cheered the tattered and depressed combat soldiers. But, as usual, the general made a poor decision, this time in allowing too much of a good thing. The continual music began to have the opposite effect on the soldiers' morale, and the men soon became exasperated hearing the same repertoire over and over and over, until they could not stand to listen to one more note. Even the Confederates, who could hear the music clearly in their close-by trenches, had had enough, and they countered with threats and insults and tried to drown out the repetitious Northern songs with patriotic Southern airs played by their own bandsmen. (Wilkinson, 1990, p. 196)

Recycled Tunes and Parodies

Many songs that were popular in the Civil War borrowed tunes that were associated with other songs. "The Star-Spangled Banner," for example, originated as a text written by Francis Scott Key in 1814 that was set to the tune of a British drinking song, "To Anacreon in Heav'n." The technique of creating new songs by writing new words to existing tunes was popular for several reasons. First, new songs could be created more quickly if the author had only to write the words. Printing music was an expensive and time-consuming process. If a new song used an existing melody, the music-printing process could be bypassed and the lyrics could be printed easily on a single sheet of paper called a **broadside.** This was a quick method of circulating songs; sometimes people received news of the war by way of broadsides before they were able to read it in a newspaper. Another reason that songs using previously composed melodies were so popular is that anyone, regardless of their ability to read music, could learn to sing them quickly and could pass them on to other people.

The tune of one of the most celebrated songs of the Civil War, "The Battle Hymn of the Republic," has had many uses. It was originally a hymn tune that later was borrowed for "John Brown's Body," which was sung to celebrate the memory of the abolitionist, John Brown. Julia Ward Howe, herself an abolitionist, knew the tune well. When she wrote the poem, "Mine Eyes Have Seen the Glory of the Coming of the Lord," to be sung to the tune of "John Brown's Body," she raised the song to a new level of sophistication and meaning. Additional lyrics to the tune kept appearing throughout the Civil War; among the many versions was one celebrating the first regiment of African American soldiers to fight in the war. (See Example 10.1.)

As the war dragged on, life in the South became increasingly difficult. The cost of raising and arming the Confederate troops, the loss of so many young men as workers, the impact of Northern blockades, and damage to cities and farms all took their toll on the Southern economy. The willingness of Southern women to make sacrifices for the cause of the Confederacy was expressed in the song "The Homespun Dress." This song was sung to the tune of "Bonnie Blue Flag," which itself originated as an Irish melody.

"When Johnny Comes Marching Home" is one of the songs of the Civil War that has endured in popularity. An Irish song known as "Johnny, I Hardly Knew Ye" shares the same tune. (See Lesson Plan IIa for music and lyrics for these songs.) There is uncertainty about which song came first, but the two songs make for interesting contrasts. Patrick Gilmore's "When Johnny Comes Marching Home" represents wishful thinking by those who waited at home that their loved ones would return in glory. "Johnny, I Hardly Knew Ye" presents a bleaker, if more realistic, picture of the outcome of war for thousands of soldiers.

Bringing the Music of the Civil War Period into the Classroom

Beth Humphry and Ken Lee, after doing their own research about the Civil War period and the music associated with it, sat down to compare notes and begin

Example 10.1
"Battle Hymn of the Republic"
(Alternate Lyrics on Page 204)

brainstorming about teaching strategies. "I'd really like for my students to see history as a story of people rather than just a long list of names and dates," Ken said.

Beth nodded. "I think I've done a good job of teaching the students about the elements of music when we sing Civil War music in my class, but I'd like to work more with the historical and emotional aspects of music. How can we pull this together?"

Before plunging into lesson planning, they looked at existing social studies and music curricula to see what was taught. They then listed essential questions about the Civil War era:

~ *What was the Civil War?*

~ *Who was involved in the war?*

~ *What were the immediate effects of the Civil War on American society?*

~ *What were the long-term effects of the war on American society?*[22]

John Brown's Body
(sung to the tune of "Battle Hymn of the Republic")

John Brown's body lies a-mouldering in the grave
John Brown's body lies a-mouldering in the grave
John Brown's body lies a-mouldering in the grave
His soul is marching on.

Chorus:
Glory, glory hallelujah,
Glory, glory hallelujah,
Glory, glory hallelujah,
His soul is marching on.

Marching Song of the First Arkansas Regiment
(sung to the tune of "Battle Hymn of the Republic";
words ascribed to Capt. Lindley Miller)

See, there above the center, where the flag is waving bright,
We are going out of slavery; we're bound for freedom's light;
We mean to show Jeff Davis how the Africans can fight,
As we go marching on!

Chorus:
Glory, glory hallelujah,
Glory, glory hallelujah,
Glory, glory hallelujah,
As we go marching on.

Lyrics for "Bonnie Blue Flag"
(sung to the tune of "The Homespun Dress")

We are a band of brothers, and native to the soil,
Fighting for the property we gained by honest toil;
And when our rights were threatened, the cry rose near and far:
"Hurrah for the Bonnie Blue Flag that bears a single star!"
Hurrah! Hurrah! For Southern rights, hurrah!
Hurrah for the Bonnie Blue Flag that bears a single star!

Example 10.2
"The Homespun Dress" (Alternate Lyrics on Page 204)

Oh, yes, I am a South-ern girl, And glo-ry in the name, ___ And boast it with far great-er pride Than glitt'-ring wealth or fame. ___ We en-vy not the North-ern girl, Her robes of beau-ty rare, ___ Though dia-monds grace her snow-y neck, And pearls be-deck her hair. ___ Hur-rah! ___ Hur-rah! ___ For the sun-ny South so dear; ___ Three cheers for the home-spun dress The South-ern la-dies wear. ___

The following series of lesson plans builds on the essential questions about the Civil War posed in the scenario by adding questions such as, What would the lives of people living in the 1860s have been like? How would historical events have affected them? and, What was the role of music in the Civil War? They were designed to address two of the performance expectations for middle grades outlined in the Curriculum Standards for Social Studies:[3]

~ identify and use processes important to reconstructing and reinterpreting the past, such as using a variety of sources, providing, validating, and weighing evidence for claims, checking credibility of sources, and searching for causality

~ develop critical sensitivities such as empathy and skepticism regarding attitudes, values, and behaviors of people in different historical contexts.

They also address these middle school achievement standards in music:[4]

~ sing music representing diverse genres and cultures, with expression appropriate for the work being performed

~ describe specific music events in a given aural example, using appropriate terminology

~ compare in two or more arts how the characteristic material of each art (that is, sound in music, visual stimuli in visual arts, movement in dance, human interrelationships in theatre) can be used to transform similar events, scenes, emotions, or ideas into works of art

~ compare functions music serves, roles of musicians, and conditions under which music is typically performed.

The first lesson launches students on their own inquiry into the American Civil War by using music as one of several sources of information and motivation. Students are encouraged to put themselves in the place of people who lived during the Civil War. The "You Are There" scenarios, one from the point of view of a Northern boy and the other from the point of view of a Southern girl, include references to music that would have been a part of their lives.

Because Lesson Plan I focuses primarily on social studies content and because it requires students to pursue independent research over time, it might most appropriately be undertaken within the context of the social studies class. Lesson Plans IIa and IIb are meant to be taught by two teachers, a social studies teacher and a music specialist. Both lessons are centered on the songs "When Johnny Comes Marching Home" and "Johnny, I Hardly Knew Ye." Lesson Plan IIa uses these songs, a poem, and visual media to contrast the heroic aspects of the Civil War with the human suffering it engendered. Lesson Plan IIb explores the relationship of musical elements and the text to the songs' meanings and traces the use of the tune in a contemporary composition, *American Salute*. Figure 10.3 indicates how the various facets of Civil War music are addressed in the lessons.

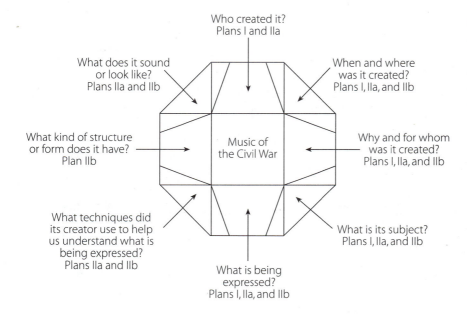

Figure 10.3
Facets of Civil War Music Addressed in Lesson Plans I, IIa, and IIb

---

Lesson Plan I
How the Civil War Affected the Lives of People in the North and South

Grade Level   Fifth through Eighth

Objectives   Students will research and formulate answers relating to these essential questions:

~ What was the Civil War?

~ Who was involved in the war?

~ What effect did the Civil War have on American society in the late nineteenth century?

~ What would the lives of people living in the 1860s have been like?

~ How would historical events have affected them?

~ What was the role of music in the Civil War?

Materials

~ Primary source materials from the Civil War including newspaper accounts, diaries, letters, copies of songs, photographs, drawings, and paintings

~ Nonfiction accounts of the Civil War written for young readers

~ Historical fiction

~ Recordings of music from the Civil War (see "Resources" list at end of chapter)

~ Collections of music from the Civil War such as Glass, P., & Singer, L. C. (1968), *Singing soldiers: The spirit of the sixties,* New York: Grosset & Dunlap; and Crawford, R. (ed.), (1977), *The Civil War songbook,* New York: Dover

~ Videos about the Civil War

~ Other reference sources such as *Apple pie music: Music of American history, history of American music* [CD-ROM] (1994), Blacksburg, Va.: Lintronics Software

Introducing the lesson

1) Have students read the following scenarios, either aloud or silently. Sing the songs referred to in the "You Are There" scenarios.

You Are There

The year is 1862. You are a 12-year-old boy living in Massachusetts. Any time you see a group of adults gathered on street corners, in the dry-goods store, or outside the church, you can guess what they are talking about—the war! Your uncle says that when the war began with Confederate soldiers firing on Union soldiers at Fort Sumter, almost everyone thought that it would be short. Now, it's a more than year later and it looks as if the war is going to be bigger and longer than expected. You see posters tacked up all around the town square advertising a "Great War Meeting" next Friday night to recruit more soldiers for the Union army. It's sure to be an exciting event.

On Friday night it seems as if the whole town is gathered in the square. Red, white, and blue banners are hung in store windows, and flags are flying everywhere. The town band is playing "The Star-Spangled Banner," "Yankee Doodle," and a stirring new song, "The Battle Cry of Freedom." You pay special attention to the drummer because your father had been teaching you how to play the drum before he died. A woman starts singing the tune of "John Brown's Body," but with some new words: "Mine eyes have seen the glory of the coming of the Lord." When she gets to the chorus, everybody joins in singing, "Glory, glory, hallelujah." Rousing speakers proclaim that now is the time for able-bodied young men to join their brothers on the battlefield to preserve the Union.

Your head is spinning! If it is a young man's duty to protect the Union, you want to do your part. Besides, going to war would be exciting. You'd give anything for the chance to see far-off states like Virginia, Pennsylvania, and Tennessee when as far as you've ever traveled is to the next town. Your aunt and uncle, with whom you have been living since your parents died, wouldn't miss you. You decide to enlist!

Back home, your 18-year-old cousin tells the family that he's decided to join the army. Your uncle and aunt look worried, but they say that it's the right thing to do. Should you say what you're thinking? Your heart is pounding so loudly that you're sure everyone in the room can hear it. You take a deep breath and blurt out, "I'm going to enlist, too." At first your uncle and aunt laugh, but when they see how serious you are, their smiles disappear. "You're too young to serve in the army," they say. "No, he's not," your cousin chimes in. "He can join as a drummer boy."

You Are There

Although it's hard to knit by the light of one lonely candle, you keep working at the pair of stockings you're making for your father. The creak of the door and your mother's deep sigh tell you that Mother has closed the store for the day. Since Father joined the Confederate army to fight the Yankee invaders, Mother has had to take over his work.

Your mother has fewer and fewer things to sell in the store because the Yankees are preventing goods from being shipped to the South. People don't have much money anyway, and prices for the things you can buy keep going up and up.

You get up to put out tonight's supper. It's potatoes and bacon, the same thing you had last night and the same thing you'll have tomorrow night. Everything is scarce because of the war—food especially. Being hungry can make people do crazy things. Last April, 1,000 women rioted and stole bread from bakeries in Richmond. Your mother says that no Southern woman should behave that way, but your hungry stomach helps you understand why those women stole the bread.

A lot of women are doing things these days that they would never have considered doing before the war started. Your Aunt Verina took care of soldiers in her house after they were wounded in a battle not far from her home. The description of the soldiers in her letters sent chills up your spine. You try not to imagine your father in the same condition as these men—filthy, half-starved, missing arms and legs. She begged you and your mother to rip up any bedsheets you could spare and roll the strips to be used as bandages. You sent her what you could, but cloth is also getting scarce.

In the days before the war, women would come to your father's store to buy fine fabrics for their dresses. Now women are learning to spin and weave their own cloth to make dresses. In fact, homespun dresses have become a kind of badge of honor to show the sacrifices you are willing to make for the sake of the Confederacy.

After supper you return to your knitting. A snippet of the song "The Homespun Dress" goes around and around in your head. You smile because you are doing your best to help support your father and the Southern cause.

Developing the lesson

2) The "You are There" scenarios are designed to pique students' interest in the Civil War. Find out what else your students would like to know about these fictional characters and situations in which they found themselves. Students may generate a list of questions to begin their research. Here are some questions that might be generated by the drummer boy scenario:

~ What happened to the boy in the story?

~ What were the duties of drummer boys in the Civil War?

~ What was army life like for the drummer boys and other soldiers?

~ Why were musicians important in the Civil War?

~ Why did soldiers on either side join the army to fight in the Civil War?

The Southern girl scenario could generate questions such as these:

~ Why did Southerners who did not own slaves fight for the Confederacy?

~ How did Southern women feel about sending their men off to war?

~ How did the war affect the families left behind?

~ What kinds of responsibilities did women take on in response to the war?

~ What new career opportunities were opened to women?

~ How did women feel about the changes in their lives brought about by the war?

Provide a variety of resources to help your students find the answers to their questions. Primary source materials from the Civil War, including newspaper accounts, diaries, letters, photographs, drawings, paintings, and political cartoons, are invaluable in leading students to a more authentic experience of history.

3) Many excellent nonfiction books about the Civil War have been written for young readers. General discussions of the Civil War and its origins can be found in *A Nation Torn: The Story of How the Civil War Began* (Ray, 1990), *Slavery to Civil War 1812–1865* (Katz, 1974), and *The Coming of the Civil War* (Goldston, 1972). The role of musicians and drummer boys is highlighted in *Music in the Civil War* (Currie, 1992), *The Boys' War* (Murphy, 1990), and *Behind the Blue and Gray: The Soldier's Life in the Civil War* (Ray, 1991). The role of women is discussed in *A Separate Battle: Women and the Civil War* (Chang, 1991). The extensive Civil War film series by Ken Burns (1989) is also a good source of information on these topics.

4) Historical fiction is a useful tool for helping students put distant events in human terms. *Red Cap* (Wisler, 1991) tells the story of a drummer boy who spent time in Andersonville Prison. *Across Five Aprils* (Hunt, 1964) and *Little Women* (Alcott, 1880) tell the story of Northern families with loved ones fighting in the war. *Turn Homeward, Hannalee* (Beatty, 1984) recounts the changes that the war made in the life of a 12-year-old Southern girl. In *Bull Run,* Paul Fleischman (1993) provides a multifaceted account of the first great battle of the war through fictional journal entries of 16 characters including a drummer boy, a slave woman, a sketch artist, and a general, among others.

5) Provide opportunities to sing and hear music of the Civil War, especially the songs referred to in the scenarios. In addition to group singing and listening, you might provide a listening station with headphones for students' independent exploration of the music. The CD-ROM *Apple Pie Music* (1994) can also be helpful to students' independent research. Sources for printed music, recorded music, and videos are included at the end of this chapter.

Assessment   Because this approach to the study of the Civil War encourages students to ask their own questions, students should have options for demonstrating their understanding of the central issues of what the Civil War was, who was involved in the war, and how the war affected the society of that time. The product of the students' research could take a number of forms. You might provide some suggestions but also encourage students to generate their own ideas. Here are some ways that students might demonstrate what they have learned:

~ Write a continuation of one of the "You Are There" stories in either story or play form.

~ Work cooperatively with several other students to create a radio drama from the perspective of a reporter on the battlefield, of a family member waiting for a soldier's return from the war, or of a musician in the army. Include music that played an important role in the war.

~ Write journal entries or a series of letters to family back home that tell of a soldier's experiences in the war.

~ Compose and perform a parody of a Civil War song that tells a story of the war from a point of view different from that of the original song.

In evaluating students' products, teachers should consider the following questions:

~ Do the products include accurate information?

~ Do the products convey an understanding of the human experience of the Civil War?

~ Do the products demonstrate a synthesis of information from several sources?

~ Does the student use his or her chosen form of expression skillfully? Are the stories well written? Do the lyrics of the parody fit the original tune? Does the play or radio drama capture the audience's interest?

Lesson Plan IIa
War: The Promise of Glory, the Painful Reality

Grade Level   Fifth through Eighth

Objectives   Students will

- analyze data to determine the Civil War's cost in terms of human lives.
- understand that war, though often portrayed as glorious and heroic, has negative consequences for all involved.
- find portrayals of both positive and negative aspects of war in songs, poems, photographs, and artwork of the Civil War period.

Materials

- Music and lyrics of "When Johnny Comes Marching Home" and "Johnny, I Hardly Knew Ye" (see Example 10.3)
- Recordings: McNeil, K., & McNeil, R. (performers), (1989), *Civil War songs* [audiocassette], Riverside, Calif.: WEM Records; Burns, K. (producer), (1990), *The Civil War: Original soundtrack recording* [CD], Beverly Hills, Calif.: Elektra Entertainment
- Copies of the poem "Driving Home the Cows" by Kate Putnam Osgood
- Photographs, paintings, or sketches of the Civil War (see Figure 10.4)

Introducing the lesson

1) Hum or play an instrumental recording of the tune "When Johnny Comes Marching Home." *Does anyone recall the name of this tune?* Students respond. *You're right, we usually sing the words "When Johnny comes marching home" to this tune. Today we're going to sing that song, but we're also going to learn another song that uses the same tune as "When Johnny Comes Marching Home."*

Developing the lesson

2) Provide students with a copy of "When Johnny Comes Marching Home." Sing the song together. You may need to explain the meaning of *Jubilee* as a celebration, *three times three* as the cheer "Hip, hip, hip, hooray!" and *laurel wreath* as an ancient Greek sign of honor given to the winner of a contest.

3) Next, introduce "Johnny, I Hardly Knew Ye," a song about an Irish soldier returning from fighting a war for Great Britain in East India. Sing the first verse and chorus of the song so the students can hear the subtle changes in word rhythms compared with "When Johnny Comes Marching Home," then sing it together as a group. *The chorus tells us that the woman thinks Johnny looks strange. Why does he look strange? Let's look at the other verses*

Example 10.3
"When Johnny Comes Marching Home" with additional verses and lyrics for "Johnny, I Hardly Knew Ye"

When Johnny Comes Marching Home

2.   The old church bell will peal with joy, Hurrah, Hurrah!
     To welcome home our darling boy, Hurrah, Hurrah!
     The village lads and lassies say
     With roses they will strew the way,
     And we'll all feel gay
     When Johnny comes marching home.

3.   Get ready for the Jubilee, Hurrah, Hurrah!
     We'll give the hero three times three, Hurrah, Hurrah!
     The laurel wreath is ready now
     To place upon his loyal brow,
     And we'll all feel gay
     When Johnny comes marching home.

4. Let love and friendship on that day, Hurrah, Hurrah!
    Their choicest treasures then display, Hurrah, Hurrah!
    And let each one perform some part,
    To fill with joy the warrior's heart,
    And we'll all feel gay
    When Johnny comes marching home.

Johnny, I Hardly Knew Ye

(sung to the tune of "When Johnny Comes Marching Home")

1. When goin' the road to sweet Athy, hoo-roo, hoo-roo,
    When goin' the road to sweet Athy, hoo-roo, hoo-roo,
    When goin' the road to sweet Athy,
    A stick in my hand and a drop in my eye,
    A doleful damsel I heard cry:
    "Johnny, I hardly knew ye."

Chorus:
    "With your guns an' drums, an' drums an' guns, hoo-roo,
        hoo-roo,
    With your guns an' drums, an' drums an' guns, hoo-roo, hoo-roo,
    With your guns an' drums, an' drums an' guns,
    The enemy nearly slew ye.
    Oh, my darlin' dear, ye look so queer;
    Johnny, I hardly knew ye."

2. "Where are the eyes that looked so mild, hoo-roo, hoo-roo,
    Where are the eyes that looked so mild, hoo-roo, hoo-roo,
    Where are the eyes that looked so mild,
    When my poor heart you first beguiled?
    Why did ye skidaddle from me an' the child?
    Johnny, I hardly knew ye."

Chorus

3. "Where are the legs with which you run, hoo-roo, hoo-roo,
    Where are the legs with which you run, hoo-roo, hoo-roo,
    Where are the legs with which you run,
    When first you went to carry a gun?
    Indeed your dancing days are done.
    Johnny, I hardly knew ye."

Figure 10.4
Winslow Homer.
News from the
War *(from
Harper's Weekly,
June 14, 1862).
Wood engraving.*

COURTESY OF THE METROPOLITAN MUSEUM OF ART, HARRIS BRISBANE DICK FUND, 1929.

Chorus

4. "You haven't an arm, you haven't a leg, hoo-roo, hoo-roo,
    You haven't an arm, you haven't a leg, hoo-roo, hoo-roo,
    You haven't an arm, you haven't a leg,
    You haven't an arm, you haven't a leg,
    You're an eyeless, boneless, chickenless egg.
    Johnny, I hardly knew ye."

Chorus

5. I'm happy for to see you home, hoo-roo, hoo-roo,
    I'm happy for to see you home, hoo-roo, hoo-roo,
    I'm happy for to see you home,
    All from the island of Ceylon,
    So long of flesh, so pale of bone.
    Johnny, I hardly knew ye."

Chorus

to see if we can find the answer. Read the words carefully and write down in your own words what the song tells you about what has happened to Johnny. Students may need some clarification about the meaning of the words *beguiled* and *skidaddle.* If students are puzzled by the meaning of *eyeless, boneless, chickenless egg,* ask them what remains of an egg when the chicken is gone—the shell. The lyrics are trying to convey that all that remains of Johnny is the shell of a man. Discuss how the images of war differ in "When Johnny Comes Marching Home" and "Johnny, I Hardly Knew Ye."

Continuing the lesson   The remaining activities described below could be conducted over a series of days. The entire class could engage in each activity, or particular activities could be assigned to groups who would then present their findings to the entire class.

4) Have the students find out how many soldiers fought in the Civil War. How many were killed or died of disease? How many were wounded? Calculate the proportion of the soldiers who died or were wounded in relation to the total number of soldiers who fought. Compare the number of soldiers killed or wounded in the Civil War with the number of people who live in your town or city today. Using this information, write a paragraph that supports your choice of "When Johnny Comes Marching Home" or "Johnny, I Hardly Knew Ye" as the most realistic portrayal of the results of war.

5) Read the poem "Driving Home the Cows" by Kate Putnam Osgood aloud. *Does the homecoming described in the poem more closely resemble the homecoming in "When Johnny Comes Marching Home" or "Johnny, I Hardly Knew Ye"? Why?*

Driving Home the Cows

Out of the clover and blue-eyed grass
        He turned them into the river-lane;
One after another he let them pass,
        Then fastened the meadow-bars again.

Under the willows, and over the hill,
        He patiently followed their sober pace;
The merry whistle for once was still,
        And something shadowed the sunny face.

Only a boy! and his father had said
        He never could let his youngest go;
Two already were lying dead
        Under the feet of the trampling foe.

But after the evening work was done,
　And the frogs were loud in the meadow-swamp,
Over his shoulder he slung his gun,
　And stealthily followed the foot-path damp,

Across the clover, and through the wheat,
　With resolute heart and purpose grim,
Though cold was the dew on his hurrying feet,
　And the blind bat's flitting startled him.

Thrice since then had the lanes been white,
　And the orchards sweet with apple-bloom;
And now, when the cows came back at night,
　The feeble father drove them home.

For news had come to the lonely farm
　That three were lying where two had lain;
And the old man's tremulous, palsied arm
　Could never lean on a son's again.

The summer day grew cool and late.
　He went for the cows when the work was done;
But down the lane, as he opened the gate,
　He saw them coming one by one,—

Brindle, Ebony, Speckle, and Bess,
　Shaking their horns in the evening wind;
Cropping the buttercups out of the grass,—
　But who was it following close behind?

Loosely swung in the idle air
　The empty sleeve of army blue;
And worn and pale, from the crisping hair,
　Looked out a face that the father knew.

For Southern prisons will sometimes yawn,
　And yield their dead unto life again;
And the day that comes with a cloudy dawn
　In golden glory at last may wane.

The great tears sprang to their meeting eyes;
        For the heart must speak when the lips are dumb:
And under the silent evening skies
        Together they followed the cattle home.

Kate Putnam Osgood

6) Listen to recordings of "Battle Cry of Freedom," "Bonnie Blue Flag," and "Tenting on the Old Camp Ground." Compare the tempo, mood, and the lyrics of these three songs. *Can you guess which two of these songs were written early in the war and which one was written later? What clues do the words and the music itself give you?*

7) Find illustrations of both triumph and devastation in the photographs by Civil War photographer Matthew Brady (Brady & Gardner, 1907) or in the paintings of Winslow Homer (Grossman, 1974). (See Figure 10.4.) Explain your choices of photographs or paintings.

Assessment

~ Can students analyze and contrast the meaning of the lyrics of "When Johnny Comes Marching Home" and "Johnny, I Hardly Knew Ye"?

~ Can students sing the songs accurately and with appropriate expression?

~ Did students find portrayals of both positive and negative aspects of war in songs, poems, photographs, and paintings of the Civil War period?

~ Were the conclusions in students' written reports or discussions supported by specific evidence?

Introducing and Leading a Song

There are many ways to teach a song. Often we teach songs by rote whereby students learn by imitating us. This process works well when the songs are simple or the students do not have access to printed music. For songs with many verses, copies of the lyrics are helpful. Even if students are not independent music readers, notation can still be helpful for providing cues about whether the pitches of the song go up, down, or stay the same. Music specialists work with students to develop skill in reading music notation. Classroom teachers should consult with the music specialist to see what kinds of music-reading skills can be expected of students at their particular grade level.

~ Simple songs can be taught by rote by simply singing or playing a recording of the song several times for students until they feel comfortable joining in. Longer songs are better taught phrase by phrase whereby the teacher sings a phrase and the students echo it back. Then phrases can be combined into larger sections until the entire song is learned.

~ Make sure that the key of the song is appropriate. Most children in fourth grade or above with unchanged voices can comfortably sing songs that fall within the following pitch range:

~ When starting a song for group singing, always indicate the starting pitch, the tempo of the song, and when the singers should begin. This is most easily accomplished with a sung introduction. An introduction for "When Johnny Comes Marching Home" might sound like this:

One,   two,   read - y sing.   When John - ny comes march - ing

This song is in the key of F minor, but begins on C. The first pitches of the introduction indicate the key note or **tonic** of the song, whereas the pitches on "ready sing" indicate the actual starting pitch.

~ The rhythms of successive song verses may differ slightly to accommodate the words. It can be helpful to demonstrate how the tune fits with the text in less-familiar verses.

Lesson Plan IIb
The Role of Mode and Tempo in the Mood of Music

Grade Level   Fifth through Eighth

Objectives   Students will

~ analyze the emotional content of song lyrics

~ discover how the interaction of music's mode and tempo influences the listener's emotional reaction

~ convey contrasting moods in performance

~ describe the variations on "When Johnny Comes Marching Home" in *American Salute* by Morton Gould

Materials   ~ Music and lyrics of "When Johnny Comes Marching Home" and "Johnny, I Hardly Knew Ye"

~ Recording of *American Salute* by Morton Gould. Sources include: Slatkin, L. (conductor) & St. Louis Symphony (performers), (1991), *The American album* [CD], New York: RCA Victor Red Seal; and Kunzel, E. (conductor), & Cincinnati Pops (performers), (1988), *American Salute* [CD], Cleveland: Telarc

Introducing the lesson   1) *Listen carefully to the words of these two songs. Write down some adjectives you could use to describe the mood of each of the songs.* Provide a copy of the lyrics for students, then sing or play a recording of this verse of "When Johnny Comes Marching Home":

> Get ready for the Jubilee, hurrah, hurrah.
> We'll give the heroes three times three, hurrah, hurrah.
> The laurel wreath is ready now to place upon his loyal brow,
> And we'll all feel gay when Johnny comes marching home.

Then sing or play a recording of this verse of "Johnny, I Hardly Knew Ye":

> Where are the legs with which you run, hoo-roo, hoo-roo,
> Where are the legs with which you run, hoo-roo, hoo-roo,
> Where are the legs with which you run,
> When first you went to carry a gun?
> Indeed your dancing days are done.
> Johnny, I hardly knew ye.

Solicit a sampling of student responses. The words students use to describe the mood will probably be related to happiness for the first song and sadness for the second. *Which words or ideas in the first song suggested that mood to you?* As described in Lesson IIa, you may need to explain the meaning of *Jubilee, three times three,* and *laurel wreath. Which words or ideas in the second song made you think it was sad?* Students should recognize that the song is talking about a soldier who has lost his legs in a war. *What did you notice about the melodies of the two songs?* Students should recognize that the melodies were basically the same although the words were different.

Developing the lesson

2) *Listen to these two versions of a song. What words can you think of to describe the difference you hear between the two songs?* Play "Twinkle, Twinkle, Little Star," first in its original major mode, then again in the altered version in minor mode.

Example 10.6
"Twinkle, Twinkle, Little Star" in Major Mode

Example 10.7
"Twinkle, Twinkle, Little Star" in Minor Mode

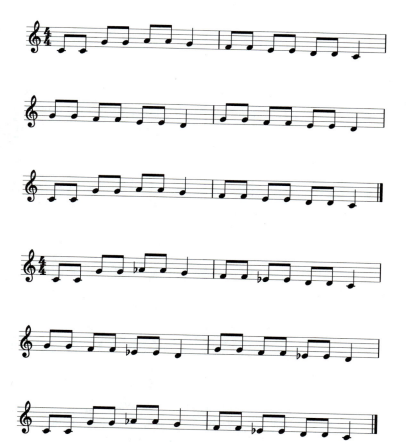

Students may respond, "The first one is good and the second one is messed up," or, "One is happy and the other is sad." Some students may also note that the first version is in major mode while the second is in minor mode. If no one volunteers those labels, supply them yourself. *A song can sound very different when it is played or sung in a major mode than it does when it is played or sung in a minor mode. We have learned to associate different moods with major and minor mode. The speed of the beat, called the tempo, can also influence our idea of the song's mood.*

3) *Copy the chart in Table 10.2.*

Table 10.2

	Fast	**Slow**
Major		
Minor		

Find the blank box that is in the column marked "Fast" and the row marked "Major." Imagine that you are hearing a piece of music that is both fast and in major mode. What word or words would best describe the mood of the piece you are imagining? Write your word choice in the blank box. Now do the same for "Slow-Major," "Fast-Minor," and "Slow-Minor."

4) After students have had adequate time to fill in their charts, compile a list of students' responses for each cell of the chart. You will probably find that responses for "Fast-Major" tend to relate to happiness while those for "Slow-Minor" tend to relate to sadness. You may notice less clear trends for the responses for "Fast-Minor" and "Slow-Major" because the mood associations with these combinations are more ambiguous.

5) *Listen again to the tune of the songs I sang at the beginning of class. Make a check mark in the box on the chart that best describes the combination of mode and tempo of this song.* Play the tune of "When Johnny Comes Marching Home" or sing it without words, using a neutral syllable such as *loo.* Note student responses. *I see that many of you hear that it is both fast and in minor mode. You'll remember that we had many different ideas about what mood a song that is fast and in a minor mode would convey. I wonder if singing words to the tune can help us clear up the confusion.* Sing "When Johnny Comes Marching Home." *Write the title "When Johnny Comes Marching Home" on your paper underneath the chart. Next to the title, write the word that best describes the mood of the song.* Students respond. *Now let's use the very same tune to sing the words of "Johnny, I Hardly Knew Ye."* Sing the song. *Write the title "Johnny, I Hardly Knew Ye" below "When Johnny Comes Marching Home." Next to the title write the word that best describes the mood of the song. Let's record your responses for each version of the song.* The responses will probably be very similar to those given to the lyrics alone at the beginning of the lesson. *How can "When Johnny Comes Marching Home" convey a*

happy mood and "Johnny, I Hardly Knew Ye" convey a sad mood when they have the very same melody? Students should make the connection that for melodies that are fast and in minor mode, the mood associations are less clear and strong than they are for melodies that are fast-major or slow-minor; therefore, the fast-minor melody is chameleon-like, taking on different moods when used with contrasting lyrics. *How might we show the difference in the meaning and mood of these two songs through our performance?* Incorporate student suggestions as you sing the songs again.

6) *Pass in your papers while I give you a listening guide. We are going to hear the tune we've been singing today in a composition called* American Salute. *Sometimes the guide will describe the music for you and other times it will ask you to make decisions about what you're hearing. Read through the guide to see what you will be asked to do as you listen to the music. Raise your hand if you see any terms or words that are new to you.* Students read through the guide. *I'll call out the numbers on the chart so you'll know where we are in the music. Let's begin.* Because the composition is only four minutes long, allow the students to listen to it twice before collecting or discussing the listening guide. To maximize learning, allow students to check their answers against yours as they listen to the music again.

LISTENING GUIDE

American Salute by Morton Gould

Introduction of the Theme
Read the descriptions as you listen to the music.

1. Fanfare introduction; full orchestra featuring brass and percussion.
2. Theme: Tune of "When Johnny Comes Marching Home" played by bassoons in low register.
3. Theme played by oboes and English horn.
4. Theme played by strings.

Brief Transition

Variations
Draw a line to match the variation with the best description.

5. Variation I   Brass featured in a march with syncopated "jazzy" rhythms.

6. Variation II   Trumpets and trombones play a "stretched-out" version of the tune for a somber effect.

7. Variation III   Tune resembles a lively Irish dance played by woodwinds.

Transition

Return of the Theme

   8. Check the box beside each word that best describes the music when the theme returns.

       ☐ simple   ☐ complex   ☐ driving

       ☐ faster   ☐ slower   ☐ calm

In two or three sentences describe the overall mood of *American Salute*. What did you hear in the music that contributed to the mood?

Assessment

~ Do students' responses on the tempo/mode charts and listening guide provide evidence of perceptive listening?

~ Do students' performances convey the contrasting moods of the songs?

~ Do students' justifications for their characterization of the mood of *American Salute* include references to tempo and mode?

CONTROVERSY IN THE CURRICULUM

Old Words with New Meanings

"When Johnny Comes Marching Home" and "Johnny, I Hardly Knew Ye" both contain words whose nineteenth-century meanings differ from their twentieth-century meanings. Some teachers may wish to change "And we'll all feel gay when Johnny comes marching home" to "And we'll all feel glad when Johnny comes marching home." Likewise, "Oh, my darlin' dear, ye look so queer" can be modified to "Oh my darlin' dear, I sadly fear." Such alterations may forestall inappropriate and insensitive reactions as students apply twentieth-century vernacular meanings to the words. Altering the words, however, censors a part of history and deprives students of an opportunity to learn that the meanings of words can change over time. Teachers must take into account the level of maturity and sophistication of their students in making the decision to alter the lyrics or to present them with historical authenticity.

Ken was pleased with the way his students responded to the inclusion of music in their study of the Civil War. Their projects and discussions showed empathy with the struggles and aspirations of people on both sides of the conflict. Some of the students who had never seemed to get excited about social studies before became engrossed in the music projects. As he walked down the hall to congratulate Beth on the success of their collaborative planning, he realized that their teaching strategies had focused primarily on the Civil War as it was experienced by Americans of European descent. Would it be possible to use music to help students understand the war and the events leading up to it from the African American perspective as well? "Hmmm," he thought, "perhaps Beth and I can work on this together, too."

Slavery and the Civil War

Although states' rights and preservation of the Union were ostensibly the issues over which the Civil War began, many contend that slavery was the underlying issue. Abraham Lincoln initially did not want to make slavery an issue in the war, but with the Emancipation Proclamation, the issue was on the table.

The issue of slavery troubled many Americans who believed in Thomas Jefferson's words that "all men are created equal." Jefferson, like some other Southerners, had personally opposed slavery but continued to own slaves partly out of perceived economic necessity and partly out of a paternalistic motivation to "protect" the slaves. The institution of slavery was referred to as a "necessary evil."

Abolitionists fiercely believed that owning another human being was immoral, no matter how well the slave was treated. To them it was clear that the Civil War was being fought over the issue of freedom for the slaves.

African American Spirituals

More than 100 years after the abolition of slavery in America, how can we understand the impact of slavery on a people? One way is to read oral histories compiled before and after the Civil War or autobiographical accounts written by slaves who had learned to read and write. Another extremely important resource for understanding the response of a people to the experience of slavery is the large body of spiritual songs that evolved within the African American community. Some of these songs reflect the bitter reality of life in slavery, whereas others reflect incredible optimism that this unjust and inhumane way of life could be transcended.

Africans who were brought by force to the Americas as slave laborers had their own tribal languages, customs, religion, and music. Once in America, they began to adopt and adapt the language, religion, and music of their masters. When slaves were given religious instruction, white preachers often emphasized scripture passages that exhorted slaves to obey their masters. The slaves, however, gravitated toward the biblical stories of Jesus, Moses, Daniel, and Joshua who triumphed over their oppressors. Slaves were exposed to hymn tunes in churches and camp meetings, but they developed their own songs that reflected their African musical traditions and their own experiences and religious values. Lovell (1972) describes these songs as "religious and spiritual because they tried, with inspired artistry, to pose the root questions of life, of before life, and of beyond life" (p. 17). Although spirituals include biblical and religious references, they are not exclusively expressions of religious faith—they are also deep expressions of the desire for justice and a better life on earth, as well as beyond.

African American spirituals often speak of a heavenly existence that is quite different from the slaves' earthly experience. One of the many painful aspects of slavery was the effect it had on the family life of African Americans. Slave marriages were rarely recognized and families were routinely separated by way of the auction block. Josia Henson (1962) described his own experience:

> My brothers and sisters were bid off first, and one by one, while my mother, paralyzed with grief, held me by the hand. Her turn came, and she was bought by Isaac Riley of Montgomery county. Then I was offered to the assembled purchasers. My mother, half distracted with the thought of parting forever from all her children, pushed through the crowd, while the bidding for me was going on to the spot where Riley was standing. She fell at his feet, and clung to his knees, entreating him in tones that only a mother could com-

mand, to buy her *baby* as well as herself, and spare to her one, at least, of her little ones. Will it, can it be believed that this man, thus appealed to, was capable not merely of turning a deaf ear to her supplication, but of disengaging himself from her with such violent blows and kicks, as to reduce her to the necessity of creeping out of his reach, and mingling the groan of bodily suffering with the sob of a breaking heart?... I must have been then between five and six years old. (pp. 12–13)

The experience of Henson and his family and countless other slave families is poignantly expressed in the song "Sometimes I Feel Like a Motherless Child." The haunting melody communicates the emptiness and pain of separation in a way that transcends words alone.

Spirituals can be taken at face value simply as religious songs, but the deep meaning of these songs for African Americans was the expression of a desire for deliverance from slavery. Many slaves risked death or severe beating to escape; the spiritual "Oh Freedom" gives voice to their feeling that death is preferable to lifelong bondage.

A number of spirituals have been associated with the Underground Railroad, a system of trails and safe houses that led to freedom in the North. Harriet Tubman, an escaped slave and organizer of the Underground Railroad, was sometimes referred to as "Moses" for her role in liberating other slaves. "Go Down Moses" was used by Tubman to call up potential freedom seekers. In the spiritual "Steal Away," the singer is ostensibly going to steal away to Jesus, but certainly is singing about physical escape from slavery (Lovell, 1972). Some spirituals were used to convey information about how to escape successfully. "Wade in the Water" told slaves how to keep the bloodhounds from following their scent. "Follow the Drinking Gourd" gave detailed information about finding the way North. The "drinking gourd" to which the song refers is the Big Dipper, which points the way to the North Star.

African American spirituals come from a folk tradition, that is, they were transmitted orally many years before they were written down or recorded. These songs remained almost exclusively within the African American community until after the Civil War when a group of singers from Fisk College began touring the United States in 1871, singing the songs that they had learned in slavery. Many of the modern-day recordings of spirituals would probably seem strange to the people who first sang them. When efforts were made to notate the songs, many of the subtle complexities of rhythm, intonation, and texture were lost due to the inability of standard Western music notation to record them precisely. Thus, when the songs are learned from notation exclusively rather than through the oral tradition, some of the wonderful expressive qualities of the songs can be lost. When African Americans trained in the European music tradition began to arrange spirituals, the songs began to take on more of the characteristic harmonies and textures of Western music. Today we often hear spirituals arranged either for a solo singer with piano or orchestral accompaniment, or for a choir without accompaniment.

Beth had lent Ken several collections and recordings of spirituals when he expressed interest in including African American music in the study of the Civil War era. He found several spirituals in the written collections with particularly intriguing texts that he wanted to use in a lesson, but he could not find a recording of them. He did not feel comfortable singing and playing them himself, so he asked Beth if the middle school chorus could learn them and perform them for the class. "I'm sorry, Ken," Beth replied, "but the chorus is in the midst of preparing for the concert at the end of the month. Would some of the students in your class be willing to come in before school to learn some of the songs? I'd be happy to teach them. If that doesn't work out, I could record myself singing the songs. I have an even better idea: I know some people in the community who might be willing to come to your class to perform these spirituals and teach them to your students."

Lesson Plan III
Layers of Meaning in Spirituals

Rationale In this lesson students examine spirituals as a source for understanding the realities, hopes, and visions of people who lived through the experience of slavery. The lyrics of spirituals, which usually contain religious references, can also be read for their symbolic content. Because students' previous misconceptions and misinterpretations may be revealed as they engage in the suggested activities, teachers should be prepared to address the sensitive nature of the content and to confront narrow views. For example, one of the spirituals in this lesson is presented in dialect. Teachers would be well advised to reflect on the discussion of dialect presented later in this chapter in the section "Controversy in the Curriculum: The Use of Dialect." A second element in the lesson that requires sensitive treatment is the comparison of contemporary life for African American students with the ideals expressed in spirituals.

Grade Level Fifth through Eighth

Objectives Students will

- sing spirituals and analyze their lyrics for symbolic and metaphorical content.
- contrast the vision of heavenly life expressed in African American spirituals with the reality of slave life.

~ reflect on progress that been made toward fulfilling the aspirations of African Americans as expressed in spirituals.

Materials
~ Music and lyrics of "Follow the Drinkin' Gourd" (Example 10.8), "All God's Chillun Got Wings" (Example 10.9), and "In Bright Mansions Above" (Example 10.10)

~ Books: Winter, J. (1988), *Follow the drinking gourd,* New York: Knopf; Cosner, S. (1991), *The underground railroad,* New York: Franklin Watts; Lester, J. (1968), *To be a slave,* New York: Dial Books for Young Readers; Katz, W. L. (1974), *Slavery to Civil War 1812–1865,* New York: Franklin Watts; and Hamilton, V. (1993), *Many thousand gone,* New York: Knopf

~ Optional: Recording of "Follow the drinking gourd," in Brown, J., & Burns, K. (producers), (1991), *Songs of the Civil War* [video], New York: Ginger Group Productions and American Documentaries; "All God's Chillun Got Wings," in Robeson, P. (voice) & Brown, L. (voice & piano), (1991), *Paul Robeson: The power and the glory* [CD], New York: Columbia; and "In Bright Mansions Above," in Battle, K. (soprano), Hendricks, B. (soprano), & Quivar, F. (mezzo-soprano), (1994), *Great American spirituals,* Ocean, N.J.: Musical Heritage Society.

~ Photographs or drawings of African Americans in slavery

Introducing the lesson
1) *Suppose you want to get a drink of water from a bucket and you don't have a straw, a glass, or a cup available. The bucket is too heavy to pick up. You can't put your face down into the bucket and drink directly from it. What might you use to get a drink of water?* Display a dipper or ladle. *Before the days of indoor plumbing, this was the way many people got a drink of water. If you were rich, you might have a dipper that was made out of metal. If you weren't, your dipper might have been made out of a gourd—a drinking gourd.*

Developing the lesson
2) *Listen to this song.* Sing or play a recording of "Follow the Drinking Gourd." *What does the song ask you to do? Why would someone want you to follow the drinking gourd? In this song, the drinking gourd is a symbol for something else. I'll give you a hint.* Draw a picture of the Big Dipper constellation on the board. *What does the drinking gourd symbolize? What special star does the Big Dipper point to? You're right, the North Star. If you were a slave wanting to escape to the North, it would be very important for you to know how to find the North Star.*

3) *Sometimes spirituals, such as "Follow the Drinkin' Gourd," contained coded messages that gave directions to slaves who were seeking freedom. Let's learn this song and see if we can decode the messages in it.* (Explanations of the meanings of the text can be found in *Follow the Drinking Gourd* [Winter, 1988] and *The Underground Railroad* [Cosner, 1991].)

Example 10.8

"Follow the Drinkin' Gourd"

Fol - low _____ the drink - in' gourd! _ Fol - low _____ the

drink - in' gourd. _ For the old man is a - wait - in for to

car - ry you to free-dom if you fol - low the drink - in' gourd. When the

sun comes up and the first quail calls, _____ Fol - low _____ the

drink - in' gourd, _ For the old man is a - wait - in' for to

car - ry you to free-dom if you fol - low the drink - in' gourd.

4) *Music was particularly useful in transmitting messages because several layers of meaning could be hidden in the lyrics. Simply humming a song could convey meaning to others who knew its significance.* Invite the students to work in small groups to analyze the lyrics of spirituals such as "Wade in the Water," "Go Down Moses," "Steal Away," and "Swing Low, Sweet Chariot." *What meanings might these songs have had for slaves that might not have been apparent to slave owners? Some spirituals, such as the ones we've analyzed, contained messages that pertained to immediate deliverance. Other spirituals contained a message that conveyed hope for justice and deliverance that might be realized beyond an individual's lifetime.*

5) *Sometimes when something absolutely wonderful happens, people have been heard to say, "I thought I'd died and gone to heaven." Think about three or four things that could make you that happy and write them down.* Solicit students' responses. *Now listen carefully to this song to see what made the singer that happy.* Sing or play a recording of the spiritual "All God's Chillun Got Wings."

Example 10.9
*"All God's
Chillun Got
Wings"*

I got a robe, you got a robe, All o' God's Chil-lun got a robe.

When I get to heab'n I'm goin' to put on my robe, I'm goin' to

shout all ov - ah God's Hea - b'n, _____ Hea - b'n, _____ Hea - b'n, _____

Ev - 'ry - bo - dy talk - in' 'bout heab'n ain't goin' _ dere; Hea - b'n, _____

Hea - b'n, _____ I'm goin' to shout all ov - ah God's Hea - b'n. _____

2. I got-a wings, you got-a wings,
    All o' God's Chillun got-a wings.
    When I get to heab'n I'm goin' to put on my wings,
    I'm goin' to fly all ovah God's Heab'n, Heab'n, Heab'n,
    Ev'rybody talkin' 'bout heab'n ain't goin' dere;
    Heab'n, Heab'n,
    I'm goin' to fly all ovah God's Heab'n.

3. I got a harp, you got a harp,
    All o' God's Chillun got a harp.
    When I get to heab'n I'm goin' to take up my harp,
    I'm goin' to play all ovah God's Heab'n, Heab'n, Heab'n,
    Ev'rybody talkin' 'bout heab'n ain't goin' dere;
    Heab'n, Heab'n,
    I'm goin' to play all ovah God's Heab'n.

(Johnson, 1962, pp. 71–73)

Example 10.10

*"In Bright
Mansions Above"*

In bright man - sions a-bove, In bright man - sions a-bove, Lord, I

want to live up yon - der, In bright man - sions a - bove.

1. My fa - ther's gone to glo - ry; I want to live there too, Lord, I

want to live up yon - der, In bright man - sions a - bove.

Fine

D.C. al Fine

Refrain:

> In bright mansions above,
> In bright mansions above,
> Lord, I want to live up yonder,
> In bright mansions above.

Verses:

1. My father's gone to glory,
   I want to live there, too, Lord,
   I want to live up yonder,
   In bright mansions above.

2. My brother's gone to glory,
   I want to live there, too, Lord,
   I want to live up yonder,
   In bright mansions above.

3. The Christian's gone to glory,
   I want to live there, too, Lord,
   I want to live up yonder,
   In bright mansions above.

(Marsh, 1876, p.198)

Why do you think the singer is so excited about putting on shoes when he or she gets to heaven?

6) *African American slaves often sang about the life that they would have when they were no longer in slavery. The spirituals "All God's Chillun Got Wings" and "In Bright Mansions Above" are two such songs. Examine the lyrics of these songs carefully to find out what kind of housing, clothes, shoes, head wear, and musical instruments the singers envisioned would await them in heaven. Also describe the kind of personal freedom and the relationship with their families they hoped they would have in heaven. Sometimes these things are clearly mentioned in the songs, and sometimes you will have to "read between the lines" to find the answer. Copy the chart in Table 10.3[5] and list the descriptions under the column "Heavenly Life." (This may be done individually or cooperatively in small groups.)*

Table 10.3

Item	Heavenly Life	Slave Life
freedom		
family		
housing		
clothes		
shoes		
head wear		
instruments		

Think back to what you know about the real life of slaves from the photographs you have looked at and the books you have been reading. On the chart under the column of "Slave Life" describe the freedom, family, housing, and so on they really had, based on the records of the time that we have available to us now. Discuss how the entries in the "Heavenly Life" column compare with the entries for "Slave Life." Refer to the discussion of African American spirituals earlier in this chapter to help students understand how spirituals used the language of religion to convey hope and yearning for deliverance and justice. Why is music an especially powerful way to convey these ideas and feelings?

Closing the lesson

7) *In what ways does the heavenly life described in spirituals differ from slaves' earthly lives? Now let's think about modern times. If a slave could see his or her great-great-great-great-great-great-grandchild living in this day and age, would they think that grandchild had crossed over into the promised land? Give specific reasons for your answer.[6] What kinds of changes have occurred in our society since the time of slavery? What kinds of changes still need to occur?*

Assessment

~ Do students' analyses of the lyrics show understanding of the symbolic and metaphorical content of the spirituals?

~ Do students' charts and discussions show evidence that they were able to derive sufficient information from the songs, books, photographs, newspaper articles, and other sources of information to contrast the reality of slave life with their dreams of a better life?

~ Can students articulate how changes in society since the time of slavery have fulfilled some of the aspirations for deliverance and justice expressed in spirituals?

CONTROVERSY IN THE CURRICULUM

The Use of Dialect

It is not unusual to find versions of spirituals in dialect as well as standard English. The version of "All God's Chillun Got Wings" in this chapter appears in dialect while "In Bright Mansions Above" appears in standard English. Each of these songs could be found elsewhere in another version. Why do these two different versions exist? When musicians started to transcribe spirituals, they attempted to capture African American dialect. Because English had some sounds that were foreign to African languages, the slaves substituted more familiar sounds; sometimes consonant sounds were softened or eliminated entirely. Thus the "th" sound in "there" became "dere" and the "d" in "children" was dropped. Over the years, however, there began to be changes in how the songs were sung, as well as in how they appeared in print. After the Civil War, when spirituals began to be sung by choirs from African American colleges, the pronunciation of the words began to reflect the formal education of the singers (Reagon, 1994). Some publishers became more interested in presenting the lyrics so that they conformed to contemporary literary standards than they were in preserving the speech patterns of the songs' originators.

The issue of the use of dialect in spirituals can be troubling for teachers and musicians. Which version should be presented? Some find the use of dialect demeaning. On the other hand, dialect and nonstandard grammar of spirituals can remind listeners that even under the wretched conditions of slavery, and with little or no formal education, African Americans were able to create wonderful works of art in their songs. When one looks to African American scholars and performers for the answer, there is no single point of view. In comparing scholarly discussions of spirituals, one sees Lovell (1972) presenting lyrics in dialect and Peters (1989) presenting lyrics in standard English. African American musicians Marvin Curtis and Lee Cloud (1991) echo James Weldon Johnson's contention that dialect is part of the performance practice of spirituals and that singers should not attempt to change the dialect to reflect standard English (Johnson & Johnson, 1962). However, performances by some African American singers trained in the tradition of Western art music conform more closely to standard English diction than to dialect.

Singing spirituals with very crisp consonants and perfectly formed vowels sounds can sound as artificial as singing spirituals with exaggerated dialect. Bernice Johnson Reagon, in a presentation for music educators about the music of African Americans (Music Educators National Conference, 1991) contrasted a performance of "All God's Chillun Got Wings" using crisp English diction with a more relaxed version in which the consonant sounds were softened, some to the point of being inaudible. She cautioned singers not to exaggerate the dialect by singing "chillun" but to find a middle ground for a more authentic sound.

Just as scholars and performers have different opinions about the use of dialect in singing spirituals, so too may there be different opinions in the communities in which we teach. As a teacher, you would be well advised to confer with parents and members of the African American community to determine what would be considered appropriate within your school culture.

Extending the lesson

~ Listen to "A Spiritual Reflection," a narrative about the origin and meaning of spirituals on *Choral and Vocal Arrangements of Moses Hogan,* Vol. 1 (Moses Hogan Chorale, 1995).

~ Listen to Maya Angelou explain her use of symbols derived from African American spirituals in the poem "On the Pulse of Morning," which was written for President Clinton's inauguration.

~ Listen to *Lincoln Portrait* (Copland, 1987), a powerful composition in which Aaron Copland weaves Lincoln's own words about slavery and the Civil War with a musical portrait.

~ Explore the role of music in other wars and social movements, such as World War II, Vietnam, the labor movement, and the civil rights movement.

REFERENCES

Alcott, L. M. (1880). *Little women.* Boston: Alfred Mudge & Son.

Angelou, M. (1993). *On the pulse of morning* [audiocassette]. New York: Random House.

Apple pie music: Music of American history, history of American music [CD-ROM]. (1994). Blacksburg, Va.: Lintronics Software.

Battle, K. (soprano), Hendricks, B. (soprano), & Quivar, F. (mezzo-soprano). (1994). *Great American spirituals* [CD]. Ocean, N.J.: Musical Heritage Society.

Beatty, P. (1984). *Turn homeward, Hannalee.* New York: William Morrow.

Billings, J. D. (1993). *Hardtack and coffee: The unwritten story of army life.* Lincoln: University of Nebraska Press.

Brady, M. B., & Gardner, A. (1907). *Original photographs taken on the battlefields during the Civil War of the United States.* Hartford, Conn.: Edward B. Eaton.

Brown, J., & Burns, K. (producers). (1991). *Songs of the Civil War* [video]. New York: Ginger Group Productions & American Documentaries.

Burns, K. (producer). (1990). *The Civil War: Original soundtrack recording* [CD]. Beverly Hills, Calif.: Elektra Entertainment.

Burns, K. L. (producer). (1989). *The Civil War* [video]. Alexandria, Va.: PBS Video.

Chang, I. (1991). *A separate battle: Women and the Civil War.* New York: Lodestar.

Consortium of National Arts Education Associations (1994). *National standards for arts education: What every young American should know and be able to do in the arts.* Reston, Va.: Music Educators National Conference.

Copland, A. (1987). *Lincoln portrait and other works* [CD]. Cleveland: Telarc.

Cosner, S. (1991). *The underground railroad.* New York: Franklin Watts.

Crawford, R. (ed.). (1977). *The Civil War songbook.* New York: Dover.

Currie, S. (1992). *Music in the Civil War.* Cincinnati: Betterway.

Curtis, M. V., & Cloud, L. V. (1991). The African American spiritual: Traditions and performance practice. *Choral Journal* 32 (4): 15–22.

Eastman Wind Ensemble (performers). (1990). *The Civil War: Its music and its sounds* [CD]. New York: Philips Classics.

Fleischman, P. (1993). *Bull Run.* New York: HarperCollins.

Flower, M. E. (ed.). (1963). *Dear folks at home: The Civil War letters of Leo W. and John I. Faller with an account of Andersonville.* Carlisle, Pa.: Cumberland County Historical Society and Hamilton Library Association.

Glascock, R. O., & Mitchell, E. H. (1990). *A curriculum connections model for the middle grades.* Baltimore: Maryland State Department of Education.

Glass, P., & Singer, L. C. (1968). *Singing soldiers: The spirit of the sixties.* New York: Grosset & Dunlap.

Goldston, R. (1972). *The coming of the Civil War.* New York: Macmillan.

Grossman, J. (1974). *Echo of a distant drum: Winslow Homer and the Civil War.* New York: Harry N. Abrams.

Hamilton, V. (1993). *Many thousand gone.* New York: Knopf.

Henson, J. (1962). *Father Henson's story of his own life.* New York: Corinth.

Hunt, I. (1964). *Across five Aprils.* Chicago: Follett.

Johnson, J. W., & Johnson, J. R. (eds.). (1962). *The books of American Negro spirituals.* New York: Viking.

Katz, W. L. (1974). *Slavery to Civil War 1812–1865.* New York: Franklin Watts.

Kunzel, E. (conductor). (1988). *American salute* [CD]. Cincinnati Pops. Cleveland: Telarc.

Lester, J. (1968). *To be a slave.* New York: Dial Books for Young Readers.

Lord, F. A., & Wise, A. (1966). *Bands and drummer boys of the Civil War.* South Brunswick, N.J.: Thomas Yoseloff.

Lovell, J. J. (1972). *Black song: The forge and the flame.* New York: Macmillan.

Marsh, J. B. T. (1876). *Story of the Jubilee Singers with their songs* (3rd ed.). London: Hodder & Stoughton.

McNeil, K., & McNeil, R. (performers). (1989). *Civil War songs* [audiocassette]. Riverside, Calif.: WEM Records.

Miles, D. H. (ed.). (1911). *Poetry and eloquence of blue and gray.* New York: The Review of Reviews.

Moses Hogan Chorale (performers). (1995). *Choral and vocal arrangements of Moses Hogan* (vol. 1). [CD]. New Orleans: MGH Records.

Murphy, J. (1990). *The boys' war.* New York: Clarion.

Music Educators National Conference. (1991). *Teaching the music of African Americans.* [video]. Reston, Va.: Author.

National Council for the Social Studies. (1994). *Expectations of excellence: Curriculum standards for social studies.* Washington, D.C.: Author.

Peters, E. (1989). The poetics of the Afro-American spiritual. *Black American Literature Forum* 23 (3): 559–578.

Ray, D. (1990). *A nation torn: The story of how the Civil War began.* New York: Lodestar.

Ray, D. (1991). *Behind the blue and gray: The soldier's life in the Civil War.* New York: Lodestar.

Reagon, B. J. (compiler & annotator). (1994). *African American spirituals: The concert tradition* [CD]. Washington D.C.: Smithsonian/Folkways Records.

Sacks, H. L., & Sacks, J. R. (1993). *Way up North in Dixie: A black family's claim to the Confederate anthem.* Washington D.C.: Smithsonian Institution Press.

Slatkin, L. (conductor). (1991). *The American album* [CD]. St. Louis Symphony. New York: RCA Victor Red Seal.

Wilkinson, W. (1990). *Mother, may you never see the sights I have seen: The Fifty-seventh Massachusetts Veteran Volunteers in the last year of the Civil War.* New York: Harper and Row.

Winter, J. (1988). *Follow the drinking gourd.* New York: Knopf.

Wisler, G. C. (1991). *Red cap.* New York: Lodestar.

Rᴇsᴏᴜʀᴄᴇs ғᴏʀ Tᴇᴀᴄʜᴇʀs ᴀɴᴅ Sᴛᴜᴅᴇɴᴛs

AUDIO RECORDINGS

Battle, K. (soprano), Hendricks, B. (soprano), & Quivar, F. (mezzo-soprano). (1994). *Great American spirituals* [CD]. Ocean, N.J.: Musical Heritage Society.

Battle, K. (Soprano), Norman, J. (Soprano), & Levine, J. (conductor). (1991). *Spirituals in concert* [CD]. Hamburg, Germany: Deutsche Grammophon.

Burns, K. L. (producer). (1990). *The Civil War: Original soundtrack recording* [CD]. Beverly Hills, Calif.: Elektra Entertainment.

Classical Brass (performers). (1981). *Honor to our soldiers: Music of the Civil War* [CD]. Ocean, N.J.: Musical Heritage Society.

Copland, A. (1987). *Lincoln portrait and other works* [CD]. Cleveland: Telarc.

Eastman Wind Ensemble (performers). (1990). *The Civil War: Its music and its sounds* [CD]. New York: Philips Classics.

Kunzel, E. (conductor), & Cincinnati Pops (performers). (1988). *American salute.* [CD]. Cleveland: Telarc.

McNeil, K., & McNeil, R. (performers). (1989). *Civil War songs* [audiocassette]. Riverside, Calif.: WEM Records.

Reagon, B. J. (compiler & annotator). (1994). *African American spirituals: The concert tradition* [CD]. Washington D.C.: Smithsonian/Folkways Records.

Robeson, P. (voice), & Brown, L. (voice & piano). (1991). *Paul Robeson: The power and the glory* [CD]. New York: Columbia.

Slatkin, L. (conductor), & St. Louis Symphony (performers). (1991). *The American album* [CD]. New York: RCA Victor Red Seal.

Southern Lace (performers). (1992). *Jackets of grey: Songs of the North and South from the Civil War era* [audiocassette]. Atlanta: Southern Lace.

Sweet Honey in the Rock (performers). (1994). *I got shoes* [CD]. Redway, Calif.: Music for Little People.

VIDEO RECORDINGS

Brown, J., & Burns, K. (producers). (1991). *Songs of the Civil War* [video]. New York: Ginger Group Productions & American Documentaries.

Burns, K. L. (producer). (1989). *The Civil War* [video]. Alexandria, Va.: PBS Video.

CD-ROMS

Apple pie music: Music of American history, history of American music [CD-ROM]. (1994). Blacksburg, Va.: Lintronics Software.

NONFICTION BOOKS FOR STUDENTS

Bircher, W. (1995). *A drummer-boy's diary.* St. Cloud, Minn.: North Star Press of St. Cloud. (Original work published 1889.)

Bryan, A. (1982). *I'm going to sing: Black American spirituals.* New York: Atheneum.

Cosner, S. (1991). *The underground railroad.* New York: Franklin Watts.

Currie, S. (1992). *Music in the Civil War.* Cincinnati: Betterway.

Goldston, R. (1972). *The coming of the Civil War.* New York: Macmillan.

Hamilton, V. (1993). *Many thousand gone.* New York: Knopf.

Katz, W. L. (1974). *Slavery to Civil War 1812–1865.* New York: Franklin Watts.

Lester, J. (1968). *To be a slave.* New York: Dial Books for Young Readers.

Meltzer, M. (1989). *Voices from the Civil War.* New York: Thomas Y. Crowell.

Murphy, J. (1990). *The boys' war.* New York: Clarion.

Ray, D. (1990). *A nation torn: The story of how the Civil War began.* New York: Lodestar.

Ray, D. (1991). *Behind the blue and gray: The soldier's life in the Civil War.* New York: Lodestar.

FICTION BOOKS FOR STUDENTS

Alcott, L. M. (1880). *Little women.* Boston: Alfred Mudge & Son.

Armstrong, J. (1992). *Steal away.* New York: Orchard.

Beatty, P. (1984). *Turn homeward, Hannalee.* New York: William Morrow.

Fleischman, P. (1993). *Bull Run.* New York: HarperCollins.

Haynes, B. (1973). *Cowslip.* Nashville, Tenn.: Thomas Nelson.

Hunt, I. (1964). *Across five Aprils.* Chicago: Follett.

Lyons, M. E. (1992). *Letters from a slave girl: The story of Harriet Jacobs.* New York: Charles Scribner's Sons.

Porter, C. (1993a). *Addy learns a lesson.* Middleton, Wis.: Pleasant.

Porter, C. (1993b). *Meet Addy.* Middleton, Wis.: Pleasant.

Winter, J. (1988). *Follow the drinking gourd.* New York: Knopf.

Wisler, G. C. (1991). *Red cap.* New York: Lodestar.

chapter 11

MUSIC AND CULTURE

Picture a music store. As you enter, you notice the colorful posters of guitarists, maestros with batons poised in the air, a close-up of a female vocalist caught midsong with her eyes closed, giant fingers on a shiny saxophone. Shoppers hunt through bins upon bins of CDs displayed under labels of "Classical," "Pop," "World," "Jazz."

Consider the musical choices available to you in this store. In just one section, you can sample a variety of crystallized sounds, some recorded 20 years ago, some barely a month out of the studio. The possibilities for exploring musical styles that are new to you are expanding all the time.

Liner notes from a CD sampler of Moroccan music entice you at a listening station. You read how the musicians prepare for performance by burning incense and warming the heads of the drums. You try to imagine the sound of the bamboo flute as it mimics birdsong. Through the headphones, you hear the 99 beautiful names of Allah chanted against the galloping rhythms of the qaraqsh *and imagine the sights, smells, and sounds of this evening in Morocco.*

You realize that only a hundred years ago, it would have been difficult to hear such far-removed music. Gaining access to the beauties of Moroccan music would have necessitated either having been born there or traveling there—a once-in-a-lifetime experience. Today, through advances in communication, distribution, and recording, you have more direct access to the music of geographically distant cultures than ever before.

Music and culture share special affiliations. When we contemplate Paris, Des Moines, or Rio de Janeiro, each place name conjures up unique landscapes, foods, smells, and images. Music often bears the stamp of a place, as in Dixieland jazz, Delta blues, Russian opera, Texas swing.

Place and *culture,* however, are not necessarily the same. Place is a concept of physical location or region, whereas culture may be considered a social construct marked by memberships and affiliations. Much of the time, place connotes culture because people in a common location share social and cultural conventions. In some cases, however, the correspondence of place and culture may be less clear because several different cultures may exist within a region and people of a region or location may have more than one cultural affiliation.

The ties that bind place and culture may be loosening. As people travel and relocate, local communities begin to look like microcosms of the world. New technologies link people who are geographically distinct, thus shrinking the perceived distances between them. Cultures that were once closed and isolated have expanded dramatically because of changes in economic and political systems. These transformations in our world influence culture.

Music may hold the stamp of a place, yet it may travel, merge, and fuse. When we encounter a new musical style, we often recognize it as belonging to the culture of origin because of its particular stylistic features. The influences of other cultures may also find their way into the musical expressions of those who have visited that culture, as was the case with the jazz saxophonist Ornette Coleman and rock guitarist Jimi Hendrix, who incorporated elements of Moroccan music into their own performances. Lipsitz (1994) describes the "poetics of place" with reference to popular music, but this notion pertains to the full spectrum of musical activity as well:

> New Orleans jazz and sambas from São Paulo circulate freely throughout the world, but they never completely lose the concerns and cultural qualities that give them determinate shape in their places of origin. Through music we learn about place and about displacement.... Music that originally emerged from concrete historical experiences in places with clearly identifiable geographic boundaries now circulates as an interchangeable commodity marketed to consumers all over the globe. (p. 4)

The Plurality of Musics in Your Community

We live in our own aural bubbles, sometimes unaware of which sounds we select to hear and which ones we may vaguely sense or even ignore. It is easy for us to think of our own musical traditions as commonplace, homogeneous, and ordinary, while construing other musical traditions as rich, exotic, and foreign. But when we examine our own traditions and musical environments, we may find that they are more diverse and interesting than we imagined.

Examining Origins and Affiliations

Revisit your responses to "Examining Personal Musical Experience: The Circles Exercise" in Chapter 1, with particular attention to the musical traditions that play an essential role in the formation of your personal and cultural identity. Do your musical traditions reflect your place of birth? Your ethnicity or nationality? How do other affiliations influence the kind of music you listen to and prefer? Have your musical tastes remained the same or changed as you have moved to new locations?

Examining the Diversity of Music within a Community

In a class setting or with an interested friend, take several minutes to list all of the practicing musicians and musical venues in your community. Record as many ideas as you can in a given period of time (5 or 10 minutes, for example). Compare your lists, circling all of the common names and places. What musical styles are represented? Is there evidence of various ethnic or social affiliations? Are there common, long-standing traditions involving music? How diverse is the music in your community?

Stevens Point is a medium-sized city in the center of Wisconsin. It was settled by Poles and eastern Europeans and claims more than 30 polka bands in the Polish and distinctive Dutchmen polka style. Churchgoers regularly enjoy polka masses. One may find garage bands, an early music consort, gospel singers, a variety of Wisconsin Indian music, country singers, performers of "new music," Hmong musicians, an Elvis impersonator who regularly performs at the Holiday Dome, singer-songwriters, and a thriving school and university music life of classical performances, jazz ensembles, choirs, bands, and orchestras. Some residents cherish music from their country of origin—Ghana, Japan, Puerto Rico, and elsewhere. Some of these musics are heard over the airwaves along with rap, contemporary Christian songs, or Top 40 hits. Others are found in informal venues such as taverns, community meeting places, and homes.

As seen in the case of Stevens Point, many musical cultures may be found in one place. It may be difficult to gauge the range and diversity of ethnic, regional, and popular music found within communities, since some musical traditions and practices tend to be fostered within the home, or heard most frequently at special occasions such as weddings or celebrations within a particular community. We might consider this as "hidden" music.

The idea that local music making may be hidden from view is documented by Finnegan (1989) in her ethnography of music making in an

English city. Finnegan observed that local musicians are hidden because of lack of study and attention. She further commented that

> the system of local music-making is partially veiled not just from outsiders but even from the musicians themselves and their supporters. Of course in one sense they know it well—these are not *secret* practices. But in another it seems so natural and given to the participants that they are often unaware both of its extent and of the structured work they themselves are putting into sustaining it. (p. 4)

Roles of Music in Culture

The sheer variety and quantity of local music making suggests that this activity serves important individual and social functions. Why is music such an important force in people's lives? Why is music making so vibrant and vital? When we take any music as an object of study, it is important to analyze its reason for being. When we try to understand a culture, we may find it valuable to examine the roles that music plays in the lives of those within that culture. Table 11.1 offers an amalgamation of possible functions of music in people's lives, as seen from the perspective of scholars in ethnomusicology, anthropology, sociology, and social psychology.

Table 11.1 represents the complex ways people use music to make meaning for themselves. Sometimes music may serve several functions. For example, in Bali, temple rituals marked by special music are synchronized with the irrigation of the rice paddies. Because meticulous attention to water levels is necessary for good rice yields, the timing of the religious musical rites may be seen as an environmental adaptation as well as an enhancement of religion (Kaemmer, 1993).

The study of music's functions can reveal the multiple layers of meaning embedded in any social practice. Take the case of the Saami, indigenous Scandinavian people who live in Norway and other parts of Scandinavia, who performed at the 1994 Winter Olympics in Norway. The Saami song performed at the opening of the games served simultaneously as a conscious and positive marker of ethnicity for the Saami and as an indication of tolerance for political differences by other Norwegians, who have a history of marginalizing the Saami. Others from outside of the culture may have experienced the songs as signaling the opening of the games, teaching about Norwegian culture, or simply as entertainment.[1]

The social practice and social experience of music encompass broad and complex interactions among the musicians and listeners. A particular tune may imply different things to different listeners. For example, songs from Paul Simon's *Graceland* recording of 1986 feature a compos-

Functions of Music within a Society

Table 11.1
Functions of Music within a Society

WAYS OF KNOWING
~ communication
~ symbolic representation
~ body of knowledge
~ kinesthetic experience

GROUP IDENTITY
~ establishment and maintenance
    of group membership
~ integration of society
~ validation of social institutions
    and religious rituals
~ enforcement of conformity to
    social norms
~ contribution to continuity and
    stability of culture
~ coordination of group responses
~ marker of ethnicity
~ collective possession

EXPRESSIONS OF THE DIVINE
~ enhancement of religion
~ inducement of trances or
    altered states
~ therapy or healing
~ catharsis or release
~ moral or symbolic force

OTHER FUNCTIONS
~ signal or mark an event
~ link with the past and future
~ symbolic indicator of
    change
~ environmental adaptation
~ commodity

SELF-EXPRESSION
~ expression of emotions
~ personal experience
~ aesthetic experience
~ marker of identity
    (or identities)

POWER RELATIONS
~ symbol of political differences
~ incitement, perpetuation of
    political differences
~ control of conflict
~ indoctrination
~ subversion
~ development of nationalism
    among powerless
~ promotion of consumption

EDUCATION
~ enculturation
~ entertainment
~ body training
~ means to understand
    history and culture
~ mnemonic aid
~ aesthetic experience
~ play
~ practice for adult life

SOURCES: Gaston as cited in Hoffer, 1992;
Kaemmer, 1993; Kaplan, 1990; Kmetz,
1996; Merriam, 1964; Seeger, 1994.

ite of styles from South Africa and the United States, which may mean different things to different people within a multinational listenership.[2] Similarly, when jazz players borrow a phrase from a well-known song while improvising, the listener may hear these musical quotations as a joke, a tribute, or a comment on the passing scene. If the listener doesn't know the song being quoted, it may simply be heard as a new melodic motif in the improvisation.

Clearly, although music making may not seem utilitarian, this human activity (some would say the most human of activities) serves important needs. Certainly, music making is a part of every human society, insofar as we know. Carvings from ancient civilizations, epic poems, anthropological writings, and tonight's TV offerings confirm the ubiquitous nature of this art form. As a writer on evolution commented: "Music may be the human invention that most resembles evolution, because so many variations arose from just a few basic elements" (Willis, 1995, p. xx). But while music making is universal, meanings ascribed to music are not. The ways in which music is structured vary radically because they are rooted in the history, politics, culture, and ideals of beauty of particular peoples. As Slobin (1993) points out: "Music is at once an everyday activity, an industrial commodity, a flag of resistance, a personal world, and a deeply symbolic, emotional grounding for people in every class and cranny the superculture offers" (p. 77).

Reflecting back to the circles exercise in Chapter 1, we may ask how the music we know illustrates the functions described in Table 11.1. It is not only useful but perhaps even necessary to understand our own musical traditions in light of these functions before we start to ask questions about the music of other cultures.

Understanding the Music of Another Culture

In Chapter 4, a metaphor of location was used to describe an individual's relationship with a work of art, progressing from an initial position of detachment (removed from the work) to deep comprehension and engagement (situated within a work). How does this metaphor apply when an individual chooses to study the musical traditions of another culture? Is it possible to be "inside" a musical work if you are an "outsider" to the culture that created the work? In addition to the functions the music plays within the culture, are there other questions to ask or concepts to consider as we progress from the unfamiliar to the familiar or from superficial associations to fuller understanding and perception?

To respond to these questions, recall the music of your childhood, family, regional, or cultural traditions. Just as it may be difficult to remember how you acquired the ability to speak, understand, read, and write your primary language, it may be hard to pinpoint how years of listening to music in your environment has formed your expectations of the way music sounds. Like the acquisition of language, the syntax and structure of familiar music—its distinctive sounds, its beginnings and endings, its tensions and relaxations—seem commonplace to you. You may even judge music as beautiful, interesting, or expressive according to this syntax. Others may agree with your judgments because they hold the same membership as you in this socially constructed musical culture. From years of informal exposure through repetition, formal study inside or outside of school settings, and performance of songs, dances, and instrumental compositions, you have become an insider in one or more musical practices (see Figure 11.1).

Figure 11.1
An Insider in a Musical Culture

What happens when you are led by curiosity, interest, necessity, request, or circumstance to the task of understanding a musical tradition that is not your own? Music from unfamiliar cultural practices poses a challenge to your ears, mind, and heart. You may feel "outside" the tradition because of the characteristic ways that sounds are organized, produced, and performed (see Figure 11.2). You may perceive this music as exotic, foreign, or unusual because it is so new to you (although the style may be quite familiar to others). Your expectations about the way music moves may not transfer easily to this new tradition, as your ability to predict what comes next may not apply to this particular style. Perhaps the unfamiliar works are songs, with texts in languages you do not speak or write. The music of an unfamiliar culture is first encountered at a distance. Just as museum exhibits behind glass are also experienced at a distance, you may think about this new music as a curious artifact or novelty.

Figure 11.2
An Outsider to a Musical Culture

Fortunately for us, the work of ethnomusicologists, who traffic in the special problems and processes of understanding cultures and their musical practices, lends guidance to our efforts to move from outsider toward insider. Their insights are particularly crucial to the work of teachers, who must be sensitive to possible misrepresentations of musical traditions when presenting new musics to students in classroom settings. One of the most crucial concepts to understand is that of **authenticity,** a fidelity between the presentation of the music and the music's meaning within a cultural context. Palmer (1992) brings clarity to this notion by presenting authenticity as a continuum, ranging from complete, culturally informed and situated performance to partial representation or questionable compromise at the opposite end (see Figure 11.3).

Figure 11.3
A Continuum for Representing Cultural Authenticity[3]

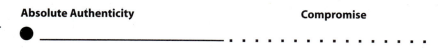

Palmer defines an absolutely authentic presentation of a musical work in a specific cultural tradition in terms of five requirements: "(a) performance by the culture's practitioners, recognized generally as artistic and representative; (b) use of instruments as specified by the composer or group creating the music; (c) use of the correct language as specified by the composer or group creating the music; (d) for an audience made up of the culture's members; and (e) in a setting normally used in the culture" (pp. 32–33). If a musical performance fulfills all of these requirements, the performance is faithful to the cultural context in full (represented in Figure 11.3 by the dot on the left). As any of the requirements are not met, the performance begins to lose fidelity to the point at which the cultural contexts are so lacking that the performance is compromised (resulting in questionable fidelity to the culture).

Compromise is unavoidable whenever music is removed from its cultural context and brought into the classroom, Palmer acknowledges, because it is not possible to fulfill all of the conditions he describes for absolutely authentic presentation of the music (particularly the fourth and fifth conditions). But the continuum helps us to think about instructional possibilities in the territory between absolute authenticity and total misrepresentation. We can reflect on Palmer's notion of authenticity, for example, to answer the question: Can we become insiders in the musical traditions of another culture? Realistically, probably not. Can we gain insight by studying the music and the cultural traditions the music embodies? Certainly. A policy statement developed by ethnomusicologists and music educators for the International Society for Music Education (1994) elaborates on this idea:

> An outsider to a culture can learn to appreciate and understand its music, and even to perform it, but there may be limits to his or her ability to gain an insider's perspective. In many cases, these limits are not sufficiently serious to inhibit students from achieving reasonable competence as listeners and even as performers or composers. (pp. 667–668)

How can teachers, who may be "outsiders" to an unfamiliar musical tradition, achieve reasonable competence as listeners or performers? We can learn, for example, about the performers and creators who are revered within the culture, and we can seek out recordings to listen to, videotapes to view, and performances to attend. Technological access allows us to be armchair listeners as never before. We can also study the way sounds are produced, including characteristic vocal and instrumental timbres. Good translations of texts can reveal literal meanings, enhancing the pairing of tune and text when returning to the original language. Outsiders to a musical culture may take an important first step by acknowledging that they can never truly become insiders but can improve their understanding of another tradition by listening widely and often, by seeking good resource materials, by asking good questions, and by remaining open to new interpretations and insights.

To return to an earlier comparison of the acquisition of language to music, think about how parents use simpler, shorter forms of language to communicate with children, while at the same time the children are surrounded by models of adult language with more sophisticated vocabulary and more complex sentence structure. As familiarity and facility with language develop, gradual changes in perception and comprehension allow children to speak in more complex sentences and to use an expanded vocabulary. Consider how this may parallel the acquisition of understanding in a new musical tradition. With immersion, study, experimentation, and guidance from others, we come to understand what was formerly incomprehensible.

Examining Musical Examples in the Context of Culture

Hilldale Elementary was still decorated with students' illustrations of folktales told by the storyteller who had been in residence the previous week. The residency had been such a success that the third- and fourth-grade teachers decided to continue the theme of folk traditions in their classrooms. The third-grade teachers chose to focus on Ireland, and the fourth-grade teachers chose South Africa. They had already selected folktales of those countries, and now were meeting in the media center to share ideas and materials for incorporating other aspects of folk culture, such as music, into their lessons.

"Well, I've got the perfect example for South African music," said Andy Jacobs. "I just saw Paul Simon's Graceland *concert on public television the other night. In one song, 'Homeless,' Paul Simon sings with a South African group called Ladysmith Black Mambazo. I really like this music and I think the fourth graders would, too."*

Crystal Connell, from the third-grade team, shared her experience of trying to find appropriate examples of Irish music. "When I first started thinking about Irish music, all I could come up with was 'My Wild Irish Rose,' 'When Irish Eyes are Smiling,' and leprechaun songs. I knew that there had to be better examples of Irish music than those. I knew I could find something more authentic, so I searched the library's online catalog and found some wonderful recordings of Irish fiddle music played by Irish fiddlers. Now I'm just trying to decide the best way to relate this music to our team's study of Irish folk culture."

"Andy, let's think again about that 'perfect' example of South African music," interjected Danielle Jackson. *"Just as we looked for the most authentic presentations of folktales we could find, I think we need to have the same criteria for music. Crystal's idea about finding really authentic examples makes me wonder about using the music from* Graceland. *'Homeless' isn't really an authentic example of South African folk music, is it? Wouldn't that confuse students?"*

"Perhaps you could try to find recordings of just South African musicians singing music representative of their folk tradition," suggested Crystal. *"I've found that liner notes on recordings can be helpful in finding out more about the music."*

"That's a good idea," Andy agreed. *"Maybe I can still use* Graceland *as an example of how musicians from different traditions can collaborate."*

The dilemmas about authenticity and cultural context of musical works posed by this scenario might be clarified by answering the questions posed by the facets model:

~ Who created it?

~ When and where was it created?

~ Why and for whom was it created?

~ What does it sound or look like?

~ What kind of structure or form does it have?

~ What is its subject?

~ What is being expressed?

~ What techniques did its creator use to help us understand what is being expressed?

In the next section, two works, "Homeless," from Paul Simon's *Graceland* recording (1986), and a set of tunes, "Sheehan's Jigs," performed by the fiddler Máire O'Keeffe (1994), will be used to explore the musical and cultural aspects of traditional and popular genres. In the case of "Homeless," from Simon's *Graceland,* the combination of American popular music styles with urban black South African styles adds to the challenge of answering the questions posed by the facets model (see Figure 11.4). Grappling with the questions, however, may lead directly to concepts and ideas for presenting the music to students. Paul Simon and

Joseph Shabalala, the leader of Ladysmith Black Mambazo (a male chorus from South Africa), created this piece as a blend of musical ideas and traditions. Although the song uses timbres, rhythms, and forms borrowed from and suggested by music from South Africa, it is not a traditional African song.

Graceland was produced at a time when apartheid was still in place in South Africa, so the collaboration between Paul Simon and Joseph Shabalala added layers of political as well as musical significance. Paul Simon contended that his motivation for this collaboration was primarily artistic: "I just fell in love with the music and wanted to play.... Essentially I come at the world from a cultural sociological point of view"

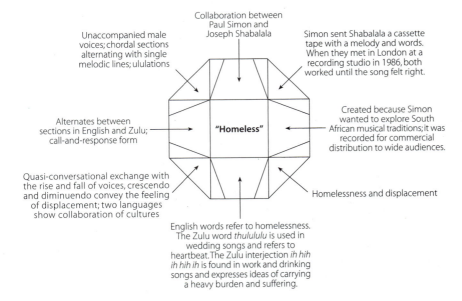

Figure 11.4
Facets of "Homeless"

(McNeil/Lehrer News Hour, Public Broadcasting Service, February 25, 1987, cited in Meintjes, 1990, p. 39).

Sometimes we want to explore the connections between music and culture in even greater depth, a task especially appropriate for music from folk traditions. To get to the heart of the processes of creation and transmission, and to situate this music firmly in its cultural context, we may need to ask additional questions, as shown in Figure 11.5.

Questions from the expanded facets model are used to examine "Sheehan's Jigs," a medley, or set, of three Irish jigs played on fiddle. Traditional music originates and travels in a way that might be different

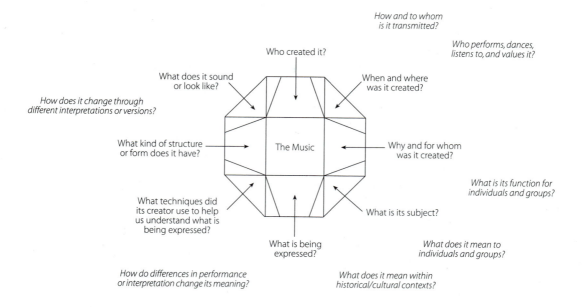

Figure 11.5
Expanded Facets Model with Focus on Culture and History

than art music or popular music. Traditional music can be described as "the product of a musical tradition that has been evolved through the process of oral transmission. The factors that shape the tradition are: (i) continuity which links the present with the past; (ii) variation which springs from the creative impulse of the individual or the group; and (iii) selection by the community, which determines the form or forms in which the music survives" (Breathnach, 1986, p.1).

To understand "Sheehan's Jigs," you must know about the fiddlers who have performed them—Máire and Pádraig O'Keeffe—and where they have been performed—County Kerry, Ireland. Máire first heard these three tunes on a recording made nearly 50 years ago by Pádraig, who, despite his surname, is no known relation. Her performance of "Sheehan's Jigs" can be heard on the CD *Cóisir House Party* (1994). In the points that follow, notice how the culture and the music are closely intertwined:

~ **How and to whom is it transmitted?**
During Pádraig O'Keeffe's lifetime, fiddlers in Sliabh Luachra, County Kerry, learned their tunes from each other, an example of oral transmission. Since this music is now widely available through recordings, people outside Sliabh Luachra can now listen to it.

~ **Who performs, dances, listens to, and values it?**
Máire O'Keeffe, the Irish fiddler who plays these jigs, is from Tralee, County Kerry, near Sliabh Luachra, a region in Ireland

known for its distinctive style of playing. In the past, people in Sliabh Luachra performed, danced, listened to, and valued these jigs. Unique styles and forms of dancing are also associated with the unique tunes.

~ **What is its function for individuals and groups?**
"Sheehan's Jigs" are played for dancing and listening.

~ **What does it mean to individuals and groups?**
Máire O'Keeffe said, "This set of tunes jumped out at me because of the melody" (personal communication, December 16, 1996). She chose to learn and record "Sheehan's Jigs" as close to Pádraig's version as she could because this medley hadn't been recorded since 1949, and because she identifies with and enjoys this way of playing. Other musicians in the area know and remember these tunes. The names of the tunes indicate the composers or the people from whom the tunes were learned.

~ **What does it mean within a**
particular historical or cultural context?
Pádraig O'Keeffe influenced the music of Sliabh Luachra through his teaching and playing. This is a unique set of jigs, which has meaning for residents of this region because these jigs may be associated with particular people, places, or things. Other Irish people who hear these jigs may also identify them with Sliabh Luachra, County Kerry.

~ **How do differences in performance or**
interpretation change its meaning?
In this case, it would be possible to compare the two recordings (of Máire and Pádraig), but because the fiddlers are from the same region, the meaning is likely to remain constant.

~ **How does it change through**
different interpretations or versions?
Because these jigs are rooted in the conventions of Kerry fiddle playing, anything outside of this tradition, such as different performance practices, would change the sound and the meaning.

Consider how closely "Sheehan's Jigs" adhere to a cultural context. As examples of Irish fiddle music, how authentic are they? The Irish jigs are played by a musician who exemplifies the Kerry style of fiddle playing, for an audience made up of Irish people (and others), and recorded in a home, where such jigs are often played. "Sheehan's Jigs" have been and will continue to be traditional tunes, played by Irish musicians. While we can't know who created these jigs or when they were composed, it is certain that they are part of a living tradition and will continue to be played, perhaps altered through the course of being taught and learned. For those reasons, if we place "Sheehan's Jigs" on Palmer's continuum, we can judge the work to represent the traditions of Irish fiddle music rather authentically.

Figure 11.6
The Cultural Authenticity of "Sheehan's Jigs" to Represent Irish Music

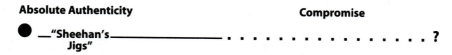

"Homeless" is a fusion of Zulu traditional styles and Western popular song. It was created by Simon and Shabalala as an expression of artistic ideas, as a piece to be performed in concert, and as a recording to be distributed commercially. Unlike folk music, we can pinpoint the date of its creation. As the facets model suggests, "Homeless" wouldn't be fully suitable as an example of a traditional song. It certainly could not serve as an *African* song because Africa is a continent in which many people live, with many musical traditions that vary by region, country, class, and group. Nor would "Homeless" qualify as a completely authentic Zulu song, because words, meanings, tone color, and other stylistic features have been altered. If the teacher's goal in the scenario above was to introduce music representative of the Zulu people, "Homeless" would obviously not be appropriate.

Figure 11.7
The Cultural Authenticity of "Homeless" to Represent South African Music

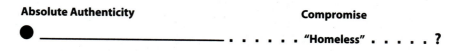

"Homeless," however, has validity as a fusion of styles achieved through musical collaboration. As you can see, the distinction between popular and traditional music is a matter of degree, not of rigid absolutes. The selection of an example for classroom use is highly dependent upon the purposes for its use. In other words, what will the example represent? As we select music for the purpose of understanding cultural groups, we need to determine the functions and cultural context of a musical work, which will illuminate both the music and the culture from which it comes. In the next section, these principles are put into practice as three teachers collaborate in curriculum generation and application using music from another culture.

Issues in Planning and Preparation

When travelers venture into unfamiliar territory, they often do so with a mixture of excitement and apprehension as they encounter new languages, social conventions, and food. Teachers sometimes experience a similar mixture of excitement and apprehension as they venture into unfamiliar worlds of music. As an example of this process, we use our own personal experience of studying a musical culture new to us and offer a description of the discoveries and insights we gained as we designed curriculum together. We were surprised at the serendipitous way that events, people, books, artwork, and recordings that could expand our understanding seemed to come our way. But the very process of collaborating with others creates its own serendipity as one person's ideas and discoveries trigger another's ideas and discoveries. The following scenario documents our processes as we developed a lesson that linked music and a place that was unfamiliar to us. During the course of curriculum generation, issues of logistics, time, and criteria for material selection arose.

Claire was preparing a lesson for graduate students taking a course on music in the interdisciplinary curriculum in which the students would interact with art in an effort to discover parallels between art and music. She went to a local museum to revisit familiar works from the permanent exhibit, thinking about instructional strategies she could design to help her students begin to see more in those works than they might through casual observation.

After viewing the permanent collection, Claire moved into the area of the museum that housed a special traveling exhibit, "Faces of Sorrow: Agony in the Former Yugoslavia." Although she suspected that the exhibit might be troubling and moving, she was unprepared for the powerful effect of seeing photographs of the Bosnian conflict in the context of an art museum rather than in a newspaper. With her hand over her mouth and tears just below the surface, she moved from one group of photos to another: faces of hostages peering through iron bars on which their clothes were hung, gaunt prisoners barely recognizable as human, Muslim women dealing with the aftermath of rape, a woman and her pet dog gunned down on the street.[4]

Claire described her experience to Janet and Kari, who were planning to collaborate with her in teaching the course. Janet asked, "Since your students will be seeing this exhibit, too, should we try to put together some kind of interdisciplinary presentation on the music of Bosnia for your class?" It sounded like a good idea, but neither Claire, Janet, nor Kari knew very much about music of the Balkan region, nor did they feel that they completely understood the current state of conflict in Bosnia and the history of ethnic rivalries in the region. They felt hindered by the fact that they had only a few days for research and planning and that they wouldn't be able to get together in person until shortly before the class. They decided, however, to see if they could find any resources that would help

Questions to Consider in Selecting and Teaching Music from Another Culture

~ Where can we find examples of music from another culture?

~ How can this music be placed in context?

~ How can we gauge representativeness and authenticity of our musical selections?

~ In what ways can students experience this music? Can this music be performed by students? Should this music be performed by students? What is the most respectful and most responsible way to use this music?

~ What is the potential of this music to promote understanding of cultures and regions unfamiliar to most students in the class?

them learn more about music of the region, then reconsider the feasibility of planning a lesson around the topic.

Claire remembered that she knew a Serbian folk dance, but wondered how a joyful dance could be used appropriately in the context of such a sobering exhibit. She also recalled a videotape from the JVC Video Anthology of World Music and Dance *(Katsumori, 1990) that included a song in which a Serbian man expresses his love for a Muslim girl. Janet consulted* World Music: The Rough Guide *(Broughton, Ellingham, Muddyman, & Trillo, 1994) for a discography of Bosnian music. She discovered* Zlata's Diary *(Filipović, 1994), a girl's account of the war similar to the* Diary of Anne Frank, *in a local bookstore, and by sheer serendipity found* I Dream of Peace: Images of War by Children of the Former Yugoslavia *(UNICEF, 1993) at her local library. She also found a book from a children's geography series on Yugoslavia that seemed rather dated and of questionable value for the project at hand. Kari, who is active in folk music circles, consulted fellow musicians she thought might have some expertise in Bosnian music. She searched local record stores for recordings that might be useful. All three began reading magazine and newspaper articles to shore up their understanding of the historical and political background of Bosnia.*

Janet and Kari listened to the entire recording Bosnia: Echoes from an Endangered World *(Levin & Petrović, 1993) and read the liner notes. They identified two intriguing contrasting selections: "Kad ja podjoh na Benbašu" [When I went to Benbašu] and "Ganga: Odkad seke nismo zapjevale" [How long we sisters haven't sung], which they later played for Claire. Someone posed the questions: "How can we make sense of these pieces, and how can we help the students make sense of them?"*

The ganga *seemed especially problematic because the women's voices move in parallel motion at the interval of a major second (e.g., C sounding simultaneously with D). The major second is considered a consonant interval in this style of Bosnian music, but it sounds dissonant to ears trained in Western music. Claire suggested an activity that she had used many times in the context of choral rehearsals: singing a scale in canon, first at the interval of a third, and then at the interval of a second. Kari recalled seeing singers from the Balkan region being physically linked, and suggested experimenting with singing the scale in seconds while standing close together, arms linked. Janet transcribed "Kad ja podjoh na Benbašu" so that the class could sing it, then discovered that this particular song was mentioned in* Zlata's Diary. *Very rapidly, the shape and flow of the lesson revealed itself.*

Before the class began, Claire took Janet and Kari to the museum to see the exhibit. Because Janet and Kari had spent some time immersing themselves in the music, art, and literature of the region before seeing the photographs, they were able to understand the context of the photographs more quickly than if they had come to them without preparation. The songs that they had been listening to that morning played over and over in their minds as they viewed and were moved by the display.

Lesson Plan
Music in the Former Republic of Yugoslavia

Rationale   At the time this lesson was written, media reports on the war in Bosnia had been so frequent and regular that we risked becoming anesthetized to the suffering and hardships of the people there and to the complex issues that had divided families and communities. To extend the impact of the class's visit to the "Faces of Sorrow: Agony in the Former Yugoslavia" exhibit, this lesson juxtaposed folk song, dance, and literature of Yugoslavia before 1991 with more contemporary examples to underscore the effects of civil war on the Balkan peoples.

Grade Level   Sixth through Twelfth

Objectives   Students will

- ~ perform a Serbian folk dance, "Sentja," adjusting movements to correspond with changes in tempo.

- ~ describe responses to a Sarajevan folk song, "Kad ja podjoh na Benbašu" [When I went to Benbašu], which will be contrasted with "Ganga: Odkad seke nismo zapjevale" [How long we sisters haven't sung].

- ~ sing "Kad ja podjoh na Benbašu" accurately.

- ~ sing a canon at the interval of a second, maintaining an independent part in order to experience the harmonic relationships in "Ganga: Odkad seke nismo zapjevale."

- ~ discuss how the arts (folk dance, songs, literature, and children's artwork) can reflect human tragedies and move "outsiders" to contemplate these difficult realities.

Materials   ~ Recording of Serbian folk dance "Setnja" (available from Worldtone Music, Seventh Avenue, New York, NY 10011)

     ~ Videotape of Serbian folk song "Beautiful Emina" from Katsumori, I. (producer) (1990), *The JVC video anthology of world music and dance* (vol. 22) [video], Tokyo: JVC

~ Books: Filipovič, Z. (1994), *Zlata's diary: A child's life in Sarajevo,* New York: Viking; UNICEF (1993), *I dream of peace: Images of war by children of the former Yugoslavia,* New York: HarperCollins. Any short travelogue or children's book to describe the people and features of Yugoslavia before the outbreak of the war, such as Lye, K. (1987), *Take a trip to Yugoslavia,* New York: Franklin Watts.

~ Recording: Levin, T., & Petrovič, A., (1993), *Bosnia: Echoes from an endangered world* [CD], Washington, DC: Smithsonian/Folkways Records.

Introducing the lesson

1) Begin by playing the music for the Serbian folk dance "Setnja." The dance is performed in an open circle formation. The leader places the left hand on the left hip; each successive dancer links his/her right arm in the left arm of the person in front of them. In the line of direction, the pattern of steps is: *step right, bend right knee; step left, bend left knee; step right, bend right knee; step left, bend left knee.* Turn 90 degrees and repeat the sequence while stepping out from the circle. When the tempo increases, replace the bend with a hop. The leader may direct the line in a "snail" maneuver throughout the dance.

2) View the videotape of the Serbian folk song "Beautiful Emina," set in Mostar. Describe how the song tells the story of a Christian poet who observes the beautiful Emina, a Muslim, as she waters her rose garden with a pitcher. She glances coldly at the poet and goes about her task. "The old poet died, and Emina drew her last breath. The garden grew quiet and overgrown, the pitcher broke, the flowers wilted. But the poem of Emina will live forever" (Tomoaki, 1990, p. 65).

3) Take turns reading selected portions of a general travel guide for Yugoslavia aloud. Discuss how the guide portrays a tranquil view of life in the area formerly known as Yugoslavia.

Developing the lesson

4) Listen to "Kad ja podjoh na Benbašu" [When I went to Benbašu] and "Ganga: Odkad seke nismo zapjevale" [How long we sisters haven't sung]. Ask students to write reactions to the music as first heard. Discuss. ("Benbašu" is a poignant melody performed in folk-song style; the ganga uses vocal timbres and harmonies that are less familiar.)

5) Establish a context for the music. Read excerpts from Zlata Filipovič's diary (pp. 6–9) as she describes the life of a rather typical child of Sarajevo anticipating a weekend of skiing and choir practice in 1991. Her choir is rehearsing "When I Went to Benbašu" for an upcoming performance. She hears of conflicts in Slovenia and Croatia and worries that the "winds of war" will blow toward Bosnia-Herzegovina.

6) Following the transcription of the melody, sing "Kad ja podjoh na Benbašu" on a neutral syllable (see Example 11.1). Read the translation and the CD liner notes, which describe the affiliation that people of Sarajevo have with this anthem. Listen again and sing with the recording. Ask the students to add to their original descriptions of the music any additional descriptions and reactions.

Example 11.1
"Kad ja podjoh na Benbašu"

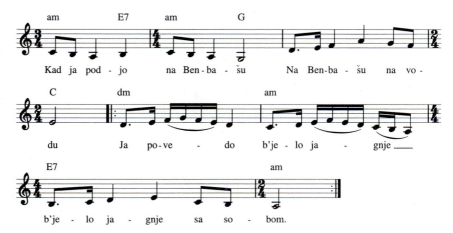

Kad ja podjoh na Benbašu	When I went to Benbašu
Na Benbašu na vodu	To Benbašu for water
Ja povedoh b'jelo jagnje,	I took a small white lamb,
B'jelo jagnje sa sobom.	A small white lamb with me.
Sve od derta i sevdaha,	Because of the suffering and passion
od tuge i žalosti	of love,
Svud sam išo svud sam gled'o	Because of sorrow and longing, I went
	and looked everywhere
Ne bil' dragu vidleo.	To try to see my darling.
Sve djevojke Benbašanke	All the girls from Benbašu
Na kapiji stajahu.	Stood in the door (of the courtyard)
Samo moja mila draga	Only my dear darling
Na demirli pendžeru.	Was at the window with the iron grill.
Ja joj nazvah dobro veče,	I told her good evening,
Dobro veče djevojče,	Good evening girl,
Ona meni doj' do večer,	She told me to come in the evening,
doj', do večer dilberče.	Come in the evening, darling.

Translated by T. Levin and A. Petrovič

7) In preparation for listening again to "Ganga: Odkad seke nismo zapjevale," sing through the A-minor scale in solfège (la ti do re mi fa sol la). Divide the

group in halves and sing the scale in canon, starting at the third. Sing again in canon at the second. Try singing the canon in seconds while linked arm-and-arm to a partner. *Can you keep steadfast to your part? How does it feel to sing such dissonant intervals while standing so close?*

8) Read the translation of the ganga and liner notes for the recording, which describe the differences in urban and rural musical traditions within the region. Listen again and ask students to describe how their perceptions changed after they learned more about the musical characteristics and context of the ganga.

Closing the lesson

9) Return to *Zlata's Diary* and read excerpts from 1992 in which Zlata expresses her confusion regarding ethnic labeling. In the entry on pp. 102–103, she describes her family and friends as a mix of Serb, Croat, and Muslim, and she expresses her dismay that politics has divided families based on these distinctions.

10) Display selections from *I Dream of Peace: Images of War by Children of the Former Yugoslavia*. The drawings, poems, and letters in this book come from UNICEF-sponsored projects to provide art therapy as a means to alleviate the psychological trauma for children caught in the midst of war.

11) Consider how people in war-torn regions use the arts to express frustration, despair, identity, determination, and hope. Identify examples of works that also educate those outside the war-torn regions to respond to the traumas of the conflict.

Assessment

~ Collect student responses to the two songs. Do their descriptions change once they understand the context for the music?

~ Do students respond to changes in tempo in the dance and adjust to the position of the leader and fellow dancers?

~ Do students accurately sing the melody of "Kad ja podjoh na Benbašu"?

~ Can students maintain an independent part, yet remain sensitive to the second part, when singing a scale in canon at the interval of a second?

~ Do students express a heightened interest in the events and outcomes of the Bosnian conflict and an appreciation for the arts as an expression of human feeling?

Extending the lesson

~ Encourage students to collect reports, images, and accounts of current events in the Balkan region for display.

~ Obtain maps that show Yugoslavia in its former configuration to contrast with maps of the political divisions at this time.

This lesson was presented first to participants in a graduate course on music in the interdisciplinary curriculum. One of the class members, an elementary music teacher, had visited Yugoslavia shortly before the breakup of the country. She described the beauty of the country and also her surprise at the depth of ethnic hatred that some Bosnians had expressed to her.

The lesson was presented again to a music methods class for elementary classroom teachers. One of the students in that class was Ruzica Jovanovič, who had been born in Yugoslavia. We were especially interested in any insights she could provide regarding the former Yugoslavia and the authenticity and accuracy of the information, materials, and experiences we had included in our lesson plan on music of the Balkan region. Kari interviewed Ruzica after the class. Here are excerpts from that interview.

Interview with Ruzica Jovanovič

Ruzica Jovanovič was born in Serbia, in a town called Kagwelitz, about an hour's journey from Belgrade. Her family moved to Racine, Wisconsin, in 1979 when she was four years old. Her mother's family was the wealthiest in her Serbian village. Her great-grandfather emigrated after World War I. Gradually he brought over all the family. Ruzica's mother's side of the family is in the United States. Ruzica's father's family is still in Serbia. Ruzica speaks Serbian fluently.

K: I noticed that when we started to do the dance, you were doing it a different way.

R: Just because there are many different ways to do it. And I figured right away when [Janet] said the name of the dance that it was a slow dance. It's easy for everybody to learn how to do it. And I figured you guys would do it the easiest way possible.

K: Absolutely. Because that would be the way that would be most successful for us. Do you notice that this happens a lot that when you hear a song or see something from back home—that it's changed a little bit?

R: Oh yeah. I went [to Serbia] this summer and a lot of things have changed. Everyone's listening to rap and disco music. No more folk music, like they used to listen to. All the youngsters are into American music. They're Americanized, like we are. And it's weird because when you go over there, you expect to see something different and you don't.

K: Besides the pop music that everybody listens to—that's global—did you notice other kinds of music that people were listening to? Did you hear any traditional musics?

K: All different music is listened to over there, mostly by the young-sters. Dancing music and stuff like that. But older people like my grandparents listen to the songs we heard today [in class]. Older songs, old fashioned songs. And when they get together, they would sing. They don't need instruments. They have their voices to express everything.

K: When they sing, do they get close together?

R: Yeah. Usually when the guys have a little bit too much to drink, they hug each other and start singing. Our whole family likes to dance and listens to music. I listen to Serbian music here at school. Instead of turning on the radio and listening to it, I turn on Serbian music and listen to it. Just because I like it so much. And I've been in a folk group ever since I was six years old.

K: Are the folk groups a lot alike? Are there certain instruments you find, or are they different, each one?

R: Most of them are alike. Some are different. You can tell they are dif-ferent by the costumes that they wear. Not every dance needs a dif-ferent costume. But certain dances tend to have a gypsy costume, the baggy pants, and the tambourine. The normal costumes are like wool skirts that my great-grandma gave me. She gave me her cos-tume that she used to wear. It's a wool skirt, pleated, really scratchy. And then a white woven blouse, woven with red roses around the collar, and then a vest. Then you tie a red bow around the arms.

K: In this lesson, we were listening to "When I went to Benbašu" and then also contrasting it with a song we don't know very much about. You were telling us something about [that song].

R: Yes. That song, "Ganga: Odkad seke nismo zapjevale"—the way they sing is the way that ladies sing at funerals if a mother were to lose a child, or a niece, or a nephew, or her husband.[5] The ladies would cry and sing like that. And that was just weird when I heard that. It sounded so sad.

K: It was hard for us to figure out what it meant because the liner notes told us some stuff but didn't tell us other things. It seemed like the words must be happy—"Too long since we sisters have sung," and now we're singing together.

R: I didn't really pay attention [to the words] because I was jotting stuff down.

K: But you could tell what the words were?

R: Yes. It's Bosnian-Serbian. It's similar because when they say, "zapje-vale" [zah-peh-vall-yeh], that's Bosnian. We say "zapjevale" [sah-peh-yall-eh]. We don't say the *j*. The two languages are very close, with differences in pronunciation.

K: So your grandmother lives next to this graveyard?

R: Yes. She lives right next door. And usually early mornings on Sundays they would go and lay out food, like the favorite food of the person that died. That's our tradition. We do that here when we go—because my grandpa died and my great-grandpa and my mom's aunt. When we go, they are all next to each other and we lay some food down. My grandpa used to smoke and we stick a cigarette in the ground for him, for his spirit, for his soul. And he used to take a shot of cognac or whiskey, so we'd put a little shot next to his place on top. It's something we always have to do. The second song that was sung ["Ganga: Odkad seke nismo zapjevale"], those are usually sung by older women. Like in their 60s and 70s.

K: This lesson is the introduction [to Bosnian music] for many people in the room. And for us, it was our first attempt at putting something together. There are many things that this lesson does not do. And it doesn't really show high culture, a lot of kinds of music. It doesn't really show the instrumental traditions. It is basically a little taste. What would you add next, or what would you change to make it closer to what you know?

R: I would let the class hear more different types of music and have them actually see how the dance is done. That's why for my presentation I'm going to bring in little excerpts from a video of my folk dancing. So they can see how it's actually done. And how you put the bounce into the steps and with the music. And how many different variations of the dance there are. That, and I'm sure that a lot of the people in the class have heard of the war in Bosnia but they don't know what it is or what's going on, or who's involved.

Reflecting upon the Bosnian Lesson

The interview with Ruzica Jovanović points out several issues that are important to our consideration of music as a reflection of culture. One is that when songs and dances are passed on from person to person, there are bound to be many different versions of those songs and dances. One does not have to go to a distant culture to see that principle in operation. For example, when you sing "All around the [fill in the words], the monkey chased the weasel," what words do you fill in? People from some parts of the United States answer, "mulberry bush," whereas people from other parts answer, "cobbler's bench." Everyone thinks that their version is the true, authentic version.

Further, as Ruzica suggests, the music and dance presented in this lesson are only a limited sample of the wealth of music found in Bosnia. Just as the well-known songs "Happy Birthday" and "Take Me Out to the Ball Game" could not possibly epitomize the variety of song possibilities in the United States, no two or three songs, however well loved, fully represent a country's music. Bosnian people, like people everywhere, interact with many styles of music in their daily lives—lullabies, work songs, popular tunes, classical compositions, hymns, and so forth.

Another issue is the danger of portraying a musical culture as monolithic or stable through time. There may be many musical traditions within in a given country or region or even generations within a region, as the interview suggests. Also, because of modern technology, traditional music competes with increasingly global popular music. The musical life of youth in other cultures may be as strongly influenced by MTV and similar popular media as that of American youth. In teaching about music from other cultures, we need to recognize the influence of global communications on local cultures and remember that in many places the traditional music is not the only type of music that is heard. In fact, in some places, some traditional musical forms may be sung and experienced widely, others much less so, while some may completely fade away.

We were fortunate that Ruzica Jovanovič, someone with connections and insights into this culture, participated in this lesson and was willing to comment on the context that is part of the music. Her perspective is naturally broader in cultural knowledge and more specific to the musical practices. She knows how the dance goes, and she can make judgments about whether variations in performance fit within the general character of the dance. Although Ruzica might not consider herself a musician or an expert, she knows how the music should sound from her lifetime of hearing the music in context.

Whenever possible, teachers should seek informed commentary from a person of the culture they are studying; a tradition bearer can verify the ways in which classroom activities align with the beliefs, values, and practices of that culture. If it is possible to have the music performed by musicians from the culture, the educational experience will be fuller, more vibrant, and more credible.

Criteria for Selection of Musical Examples from Another Culture

The previous lesson and interview illustrate how music and other arts can illuminate many aspects of culture, and that knowledge about a particular culture (or context) can illuminate music. The entry point or impetus for this study was provided by an art exhibit dealing with the then-current conflict in Bosnia. Our exploration of the music of the Balkan region was influenced by available resources, the quality of the music (quality meaning a combination of authenticity, representativeness, and musical interest inherent in the works), and the potential of this music to promote understanding of the people. While the process of finding meaningful links between music and culture is unique to each investigation, this specific lesson may suggest useful approaches. We reflected upon the issues raised through the questions posed at the beginning of this lesson.

In what ways can students experience this music? Can this music be performed by students? Should this music be performed by students? What is the most respectful and most responsible way to use this music?

We set up context for performing the music by learning the Serbian folk dance and viewing a videotape of a Serbian singer. Students first listened to "Kad ja podjoh na Benbašu," and learned it easily because of its simple folk-like tune. We chose not to try to have the class sing "Ganga: Odkad seke nismo zapjevale" because we knew that it would be difficult, if not impossible, to recreate the close harmonies and characteristic vocal timbre. Instead, we provided an approximate experience by having students listen to the recording, then sing a minor scale as a round in intervals of a second. After they sang the dissonances, they listened again, with greater appreciation for the challenging sound of the ganga.

Understanding the ganga and its role within the culture was a challenge to us. Because music can elicit a variety of personal responses, even insiders or persons very close to a culture can sometimes mislabel or misrepresent the music. A case in point is that Ruzica Jovanovič compared the ganga in the lesson to laments for the dead that she'd heard at the graveyard. The liner notes gave no indication of this practice. Upon investigation, it appears that the ganga and laments may sound similar to Ruzica, but in fact, the ganga is not a lament. The timbre of the women's voices has a quality and intensity which we could interpreted as mournful, but which would not sound sad to the people familiar with this genre.[6]

What is the potential of this music to promote understanding of cultures and regions unfamiliar to most students in the class?

For many of the teachers in the seminar and classes, as well as for us, this was the first introduction to the music of this region of the world. Singing songs and listening to the voices of the people of the former Yugoslavia lent an immediacy and a reality to our study that we could sense and feel. The music also became the impetus for us to read more about the culture and history of these peoples, and to show empathy for their current struggles.

In this chapter, we used examples from Bosnia, Ireland, and a South African/American collaboration to illustrate the synergy of music and culture. In Chapter 12, we show how the rich musical traditions of one country, Mexico, offer many possibilities for curriculum design. The role of music in celebrations, the way music reflects the blending of cultures, and the way songs are altered as they move from traditional to popular settings are some of the themes addressed in the lessons.

REFERENCES

Breathnach, B. (1986). *The use of notation in the transmission of Irish folk music.* Cork, Ireland: University College Cork Irish Traditional Music Society.

Broughton, S., Ellingham, M., Muddyman, D., & Trillo, R. (eds.). (1994). *World music: The rough guide.* London: Penguin.

Filipovič, Z. (1994). *Zlata's diary: A child's life in Sarajevo.* New York: Viking.

Finnegan, R. (1989). *The hidden musicians: Music-making in an English town.* Cambridge: Cambridge University Press.

Hoffer, C. R. (1992). Sociology and music education. In R. Colwell (ed.), *Handbook of research on music teaching and learning* (pp. 713–723). New York: Schirmer.

International Society for Music Education (1994). Policy on music of the world's cultures. *International Journal of Music Education* 24: 67–68.

Jones-Bauman, R. (1995). The *Joik* heard round the world: Mass media in Saamiland and the negotiation of ethnicity. Paper presented at the annual meeting of the Society for Ethnomusicology, Los Angeles.

Kaemmer, J. E. (1993). *Music in human life: Anthropological perspectives on music.* Austin: University of Texas Press.

Kaplan, M. (1990). *The arts: A social perspective.* Rutherford, Conn.: Fairleigh Dickinson University Press.

Katsumori, I. (producer). (1990). *The JVC video anthology of world music and dance* (vol. 22) [video]. Tokyo: JVC.

Levin, T., & Petrovič, A. (recorders and annotators). (1993). *Bosnia: Echoes from an endangered world* [CD]. Washington, D.C.: Smithsonian/Folkways Records.

Lipsitz, G. (1994). *Dangerous crossroads: Popular music, postmodernism and the poetics of place.* New York: Verso.

Lye, K. (1987). *Take a trip to Yugoslavia.* New York: Franklin Watts.

Meintjes, L. (1990). Paul Simon's *Graceland*, South Africa, and the mediation of musical meaning. *Ethnomusicology* 34 (1): 37–73.

Merriam, A. P. (1964). *The anthropology of music.* Chicago: Northwestern University Press.

O'Keeffe, M. (performer). (1994). *Cóisir house party* [CD]. Dublin: Gael-Linn.

Palmer, A. J. (1992). World musics in music education: The matter of authenticity. *International Journal of Music Education* 19: 32–40.

Seeger, A. (1994). Whoever we are today, we can sing you a song about it. In G. Béhague (ed.), *Music and black ethnicity: Carribbean and South America.* Miami, Fla.: University of Miami North South Center.

Simon, P. (performer). (1986). *Graceland* [CD]. Burbank, Calif.: Warner Brothers.

Slobin, M. (1993). *Subcultural sounds: Micromusics of the West.* Hanover, N.H.: University Press of New England.

Tomoaki, F. (ed.). (1990). *The JVC anthology of world music and dance: Book III: Europe.* Tokyo: JVC.

UNICEF (1993). *I dream of peace: Images of war by children of the former Yugoslavia.* New York: HarperCollins.

Willis, D. (1995). *The sand dollar and the slide rule.* Reading, Mass.: Wesley.

§ chapter 12 §

MUSIC AS AN EXPRESSION OF CULTURE: MEXICO

The earth could also feel that something new was coming—
something it needed
and had been secretly wishing for.
As the wind god came nearer, the earth let out a slow sigh of relief.
Its fruit began to ripen
and its flowers began to bloom with new, deeper colors.
The whole planet seemed to be waking up from a long sleep.

Finally Quetzalcoatl touched down on the earth
with the musicians and singers.
They looked around curiously at the silent, waiting planet.
Then they began to play.
Through forests
and valleys
and deserts
and oceans
they wandered,
filling the air with music.

Soon people learned to sing and play,
and so did the trees and birds,
the whales and wolves,
the running streams,
the crickets and frogs,
and every other creature.

From dawn to dusk
the melodies spread
until music covered the earth.

From *How Music Came to the World:*
An Ancient Mexican Myth (Ober, 1994, pp. 26–30)

A s this beautiful old myth illu-trates, music is an integral element of Mexican and Mexican American life. The vibrant music of street and city reverberate with the legacies of many peoples. Strands of migration, assimilation, and adaptation weave together in new aural patterns that owe much to the influence of pre-Columbian Indians, Spaniards, Africans, and others. Contemporary musical artists, heard through popular media of radio and recordings, create new songs threaded through the warp and woof of ancient, long-standing traditions. The resilience of this culture and the depth of its expression are eloquently captured in this Mexican proverb: *Out of poverty, poetry; out of suffering, song* (Herrera-Sobek, 1993).

We chose Mexico to illustrate the connections between music and culture because of its rich and diverse musical expressions and its physical proximity to the United States. Indeed, before political boundaries were redrawn in the middle of the nineteenth century, significant parcels of land in present-day Texas, New Mexico, Nevada, Utah, Colorado, Arizona, and California were part of Mexico. Today the interactions between the peoples and cultures of the United States and Mexico are more extensive than ever because people of Mexican heritage comprise the fastest growing ethnic group in the United States.

The issues of authenticity and representation of a culture's music that were raised in Chapter 11 are central to the study of Mexico's people and their music. How do we provide enough context to appreciate the complexities of culture? How does the music we choose reflect those complexities? How do we and our students approach something as intricate and sensitive as ethnicity—*other, us,* and *them*—with curiosity and understanding? Cultural stereotypes arise from overgeneralizations, simplified portrayals, insufficient information, and shallow understanding. Through the curriculum, we can move beyond picture-postcard descriptions of burros, cactus, tacos, and serapes to represent Mexico's cultural traditions with greater depth and authenticity. Music embodies nuance beyond the power of words, enabling the essence of these traditions to be heard and felt in the voices of the people.

Lesson Plan I
Introducing Mexico through the Piñata

Piñata

En la noche,
mientras dormíamos,
la piñata del cumpleaños se
cayó del árbol
como fruta demasiado madura
y tiró todos los dulces.
Nos dio mucho gusto
no tener que romperla
pues era un león amarillo
con sombrero verde.

Jennifer Clement

Piñata

In the night,
while we were asleep,
the birthday piñata
fell out of the tree
like an overripe fruit,
spilling all the candy.
We were happy
we did not have to break it
as it was a yellow lion
in a green hat.

Translated by
Consuelo de Aerenlund

From *The Tree Is Older than You Are: A Bilingual Gathering of Poems and Stories from Mexico with Paintings by Mexican Artists* (Nye, 1995, p. 28).

Rationale Holiday celebrations are festive occasions in primary classrooms, especially when they are designed to introduce children to the fascinating customs and traditions of many cultures. (See "Controversy in the Classroom: Holidays in Public School" later in this chapter.) The piñata, one of the most familiar and festive objects stemming from Mexican culture, is a natural subject for songs and stories. Two versions of a piñata lesson, one basic and one enhanced,[1] are provided to demonstrate how the contexts of music making are central to children's understanding of culture. The sequence of events in the basic version is supplemented in the enhanced version by culturally grounded stories, movement, and attention to the particular characteristics of the music and the visual elements of the piñatas. The second version is further enriched through collaboration with the art specialist: Students apply their understanding of Mexican culture to the design and creation of a piñata. The two versions illustrate how carefully selected materials and thoughtfully designed activities can improve the quality of an educational experience.

Grade Level Second and Third

Objectives   Students will

Basic Lesson	Enriched Lesson
~ learn about customs of Mexico. ~ locate Mexico on a map of the Americas. ~ sing a piñata song.	~ describe customs of Mexico after viewing a video of musicians at a Mexican festival and listening to a book, *The Piñata Maker* (El Piñatero). ~ sing a piñata song, showing changes in meter by moving and playing percussion instruments ~ describe the variety of sounds heard in a recording of a fiesta. ~ create piñatas, using designs and techniques like those of the Mexican craftsperson in the book. ~ discuss how art, music, and dance play a role in the lives of Mexican people.

Differences in versions   The objectives in the enriched version are focused more specifically on cultural understanding and describe what students will do to demonstrate that understanding. The objectives also show a range of activities such as performing, creating, describing, and valuing.

Materials

Basic Lesson	Enriched Lesson
~ Book: Ets, M. H., & Labastida, A. (1979), *Nine days to Christmas*, New York: Viking ~ Large map of the Americas ~ Music for "La Piñata" (see Example 12.1) ~ Guitar, piano, or some other instrument for accompaniment	~ Video: *Piñatas, posadas y pastorales* (Martinez & Llama, 1991) ~ Recording: "Christmas in Oaxaca" from Lewiston, D. (recorder), (1991), *Mexico: Fiestas of Chiapas and Oaxaca* [CD], New York: Elektra Nonesuch (originally released 1976) ~ Books: Ancona, G. (1994), *The Piñata maker*, San Diego, Calif: Harcourt Brace; and Pettit, F. H., & Pettit, R. M. (1978), *Mexican folk toys: Festival decorations and ritual objects*, New York: Hastings House ~ Music for "La Piñata" (Example 12.1) ~ Guitar for accompaniment ~ Art supplies

Differences in versions

Materials in the enriched lesson have been chosen to reflect scenes and sounds of real life in Mexico whenever possible. Carefully selected videotapes, audiotapes, and personal accounts of the lives of Mexican people provide more specific and authentic representations of culture.

Introducing the Lesson

Basic Lesson	Enriched Lesson
1) *Today we will begin work on a special song from Mexico for the Winter Holidays program. This year's theme is "Songs of Many Lands." Who can find Mexico on this map? Here are some maps to color while I read you a story.*	1) *Tell me about some of the special traditions and customs your family celebrates. Every culture has its own traditions. This week we're going to learn how people in Mexico celebrate one of their special holidays.*
2) Read *Nine Days to Christmas: A Story of Mexico*. This story tells about Ceci, who wanted to have her own special *posada,* or Christmas celebration. She selects a star-shaped *piñata* and is upset when it is broken by her friends. However, the piñata turns into a real star. Discuss the story with the class, prompting them to remember shapes of piñatas, what children do during *Las Posadas,* and why the piñata turned into a star.	2) View excerpts from *Piñatas, Posadas y Pastorelas*. This 25-minute video presents a collage of colorful Christmas festivities, parades, and plays from Colima, Mexico City, and Michoacán. Several sequences feature piñatas being made by hand, displayed in the market, and broken at a party. Representative music, including the piñata song from this lesson, are heard.

Differences in versions

In the basic version, the fictional story *Nine Days to Christmas: A Story of Mexico* is used to pique interest in piñatas. In contrast, the enriched version establishes cultural context by presenting scenes of real life in Mexico through a video that presents a vivid collage of parades, plays, the marketplace, and a party. References to specific people and places help students move beyond general and stereotypical notions of Mexico and its culture. The enriched version sheds light on the significance of the piñata in people's lives.

Example 12.1

La Piñata

Andale amigo, no te dilates
con la canasta de los cacahuates.
Andale amigo, sal del rincón
con la canasta de la colación.

Dale, dale, dale,
no pierdas el tino,
mide la distancia
que hay en el camino.
Dale, dale, dale,
no pierdas el tino,
porque si lo pierdes
pierdes el camino.

Bring the *piñata* with no delay,
we want to party, we want to play.
Come on my friend, please don't be tardy,
bring us the baskets with all the candy.

Hit, hit the *piñata*,
do not lose your aim,
measure well the distance
or you'll lose the way.
Hit, hit the *piñata*,
do not lose your aim,
because if you lose it
you will lose the way.

Orozco (1994)

Developing the lesson

Basic Lesson	Enriched Lesson
3) *Today we will start working on our song for the program. Let me sing it for you.* Sing the English words to "La Piñata." *What are the children doing as they sing this song? How do you know this? Sing again.*	3) Draw students' attention to the piñatas in the video *Piñatas, Posadas y Pastorelas. Have you ever seen a piñata before? Where? What did it look like? Here are some pictures of piñatas from different places in Mexico.* Show pictures from *Mexican Folk Toys: Festival Decorations and Ritual Objects.* Read description of piñata making as a family enterprise on pages 142–143. Ask students to contrast these handmade piñatas with commercial ones they may have seen. Draw attention to visual qualities and design elements by asking questions such as "What colors do the piñata makers choose?" and "What kinds of shapes and materials do they use?"
4) Display words and music for "La Piñata" on an overhead projector. *Can you find where the music changes to a new section?* Sing it again. *Right, the "hit, hit" part starts the new section. Listen again and read the words as I sing them.* Teach the song, perhaps by having the students echo phrases.	4) Read *The Piñata Maker* and share the photographs with the class. Discuss the special role of the piñata maker, the families of makers, and the kind of skills they need. Emphasize that piñata making is a way people have of expressing care for each other. Describe the significance of piñatas, using the background information ("The Significance of Piñatas in Mexican Festivals") given in this lesson. *We will be designing our own piñatas later. You'll want to think about the kind of shape you might want your piñata to have and the colors you will use.* Make books about piñata making available for reference.

Basic Lesson	Enriched Lesson
	5) *Listen to this song. Mexican children sing it while they are playing at breaking the piñata.* Sing or play "La Pinata." Show the Spanish words on an overhead. *Can you find where the music changes to a new section? Right, it changes at the "Dale, dale" part. Listen again and try to read the words as I sing them.* (If there are Spanish speakers in the classroom, invite them to demonstrate the pronunciation. You may also consult with a Spanish teacher or English as a Second Language specialist if one is available.) Have students either translate the Spanish text or read the English lyrics. Students sing the Spanish lyrics again.
	6) The rhythm changes from 6/8 meter to 2/4, a common characteristic of Mexican and some Latin American music. Invite students to show the change in rhythm by moving their bodies. Begin by swaying during the A section and switch to rocking forward and backward during the B section. In preparation for instrumental parts to be added later to the B section, tap hands right, left, right, left, in time with the eighth-note pulse.

Differences in versions

In the enriched lesson, the teacher presents several photographs of piñatas, and draws attention to their particular visual qualities. The role of the piñata maker shows the ingenuity and care with which he crafts piñatas for his local community. Although a teacher may not wish to share all of the history of the piñata with students, he or she may approach the lesson more knowledgeably as a result of research and reading. Differences in the treatment of language are also evident. In the first lesson, the song is sung only in English; in the second, it is sung in Spanish. The enriched lesson prepares students to play percussion in the next part of the lesson by drawing attention to the change in meter and asking students to move accordingly.

Closing the lesson

Basic Lesson	Enriched Lesson
5) Play a few contrasting percussion instruments with each section—for example, jingles and bongo drums on the A section, triangles during the B section. Keep it simple so that students can hear how their instrument fits with the song. Rotate the instruments so that students have a chance to play during both sections.	7) Add percussion instruments to the performance of the song. Because the character of the A section is very lyrical, perform with voices only. In the B section, emphasize the duple meter by assigning one student to play maracas on the eighth-note pulse and another to play claves on the first beat of every measure. Finish by singing, moving, and playing instruments.

Differences in versions

In the enriched lesson, culturally appropriate instruments are chosen to accompany the song in a way that suits the character of the music. The lesson ends with a satisfying musical performance that closes this introduction to the music and culture of Mexico. To provide a more comprehensive view than just one day's experience can provide, a second experience, which builds on information and ideas presented in the first, has been planned. In the second lesson, students begin the process of creating a piñata with the guidance of the art teacher, who helps students focus on design elements.

Continuing the lesson

8) *Let's listen to a recording of a festival in the Mexican city of Oaxaca. This fiesta takes place during the day with many people singing, playing musical instruments, and enjoying the sights.* Read this selection or have a student read it:

> The Christmas season is celebrated in Oaxaca (wah-HA-kah) with a fiesta, culminating in a parade on Christmas Eve in the main plaza. Brass bands from nearby villages march with floats depicting holiday themes in the boisterous parade; merry-

Enhancing the Understanding of Context:
The Significance of Piñatas in Mexican Festivals

At Christmastime in Mexico, piñatas of all colors (lime green, hot pink, iridescent silver, and wild combinations of colors) and shapes (stars, Batman, airplanes, donkeys, parrots, etc.) hang in the marketplace, from lampposts, under trees, and in homes. The whimsical vessels are filled with treats, small plastic toys, candy, nuts, and fruit. They are displayed throughout *Las Posadas,* a nine-day reenactment of the biblical Christmas story. At the end of the celebration, after days of high anticipation, children are finally allowed to break the piñata and eagerly scoop up its contents.

The piñata originated in Italy, where it was called *pignatta* (Italian for "fragile pot"). The pignatta was a pineapple-shaped pottery vessel hung from the ceiling. This pignatta, filled with sweets, was broken at masquerade balls during the Renaissance period. The game traveled to Spain, where it was adapted for dances and masquerades and was called the *piñata.* In Spain, the container was called an *olla.* It was at first unadorned, like the Italian pignatta, but soon became more colorful.

When this custom was brought to Mexico by sixteenth-century missionaries, it was soon accepted by the Aztec Indians, who had a similar tradition. At the end of the year, Aztec priests prepared a clay pot decorated with bright feathers and filled with treasures as an offering for their god of war. On the anniversary of the god's birth, the pot was placed on a pole in the temple and broken with a club. The treasures spilled out beneath the idol's altar as a tribute.

As Mexicans gradually converted to Catholicism, piñatas took on a new religious meaning. Brilliantly decorated, they became metaphors for the Devil, who entices unsuspecting souls. Sweets hidden inside the piñata symbolized temptations that lead people into evil. The blindfolded child was thought to represent blind faith, using a stick that symbolized virtue. The smashing of the piñata was a representation of the power of faith to triumph over evil; the resulting shower of treats and candies was the reward for courageous and faithful souls. For Mexican Catholics, then, this child's game held and may still hold deep religious significance in its message that all things come through faith.

SOURCES: Elmer, Beall, & Robertson, 1993; Holmes, personal communication, May 2, 1996; Perl, 1983; Ross, 1991; Silverthorne, 1992.

making spectators cheer and students sing carols. There are over 500 brass bands in the state of Oaxaca, and many of them perform during this festive season (Lewiston, 1991).

9) Listen to "Christmas in Oaxaca." Because this selection is five minutes long, you may decide to limit the first listening to a small section of the recording. Discuss the variety of sounds such as brass bands and carolers, which enter and exit as they parade by.

10) Review the piñata song learned previously with reference to the meaning of this holiday custom. Invite students to design their own piñatas.[2] Return to the books on piñata making to review the *piñatero's* process and to examine the design elements of the piñatas in the photographs.

Closing the lesson

11) Over the course of several days students work to complete their piñatas. Display the finished piñatas and discuss the design elements that students chose, raising specific questions about color, texture, and shape. You may wish to question students about how learning about celebrations in Mexico influenced the design of their piñatas. As a culminating activity, sing "La Piñata" while playing the game with a piñata the teacher has made for the occasion.

Emphasis for the continuation of the lesson

The second day extends the study of culture with the use of a recording that captures the ambient sounds of a Christmas parade in Oaxaca. The process and techniques for creating the piñata, based on the traditional practices of the Mexican piñatero, are guided by the art teacher. Bringing art and music together in the classroom provides students with a more complete experience of this festive celebration in Mexican culture.

Basic Lesson	Enriched Lesson
~ How easily and enthusiastically do students learn the song?	~ Can students show changes in form and meter in "La Piñata" through movement?
~ Are instrumental accompaniments rhythmic?	~ Can students accurately sing the song and pronounce the Spanish text?

Assessment

continues

Basic Lesson	Enriched Lesson
~ Can students identify the location of Mexico on a map?	~ Are instrumental accompaniments accurate and stylistically appropriate?
	~ Do students show care in the design and construction of their piñatas?
	~ Do they incorporate elements of design derived from authentic piñatas?
	~ Do students ask questions and volunteer ideas that reflect growing awareness of the role of holiday celebrations in other cultures?

Differences in versions

The assessment questions in the enriched lesson reflect more depth in musical and cultural content.

Extending the lesson

~ Watch dances of Mexico's national folklore dance troupe in the color video *Ballet Folclorico Nacional de México* (1990). This hour-long video presents many different regional dances. Note differences in costumes, musical ensembles, and dance steps.

~ There are many Mexican fiestas that celebrate religious, patriotic, and local events. One of the most colorful is *Los Días de los Muertos* [Days of the Dead], celebrated from October 31 through November 2. This fiesta honors the spirits of the dead and combines solemn personal rituals with lively parades of "skeletons" and mariachi bands. Marigolds adorn the freshly washed gravestones; the orange color of this spicy scented "flower of the dead" has been associated with death since pre-Columbian times. Bakeries sell *pan de los muertos,* special cakes for the occasion, and children happily munch small colored sugar skulls with their names written on them. The video *Day of the Dead: A Living Tradition* (Llama, 1989), offers an accessible introduction to the celebration that includes music. Recent children's books that document this colorful event include *Pablo Remembers: The Fiesta of the Day of the Dead* (Ancona, 1993), *Day of the Dead: A Mexican American Celebration* (Hoyt-Goldsmith, 1994), and *Days of the Dead* (Lasky, 1994).

~ Students may wish to hear sounds of other festivals in Mexico, such as "Son Sventa N'ahual San Lorenzo," from *Mexico: Fiestas of Chiapas and Oaxaca* (Lewiston,1991). This is a recording of the Fiesta of Guadelupe, held in December.

~ Other piñata songs may be found in *Amigo Cantando* (Merman, 1960). For other Christmas carols, see *Las Navidades: Popular Christmas Songs from Latin America* (Delacre, 1990).

CONTROVERSY IN CURRICULUM

Holidays in Public School

Some educators say that children deserve to learn about and celebrate holidays in school. They argue that religious and secular symbols such as the cross, Christmas tree, piñata, menorah, shamrocks, rabbits, eggs, and so forth are significant cultural symbols, and that understanding the meanings of traditions should be a part of a child's education. They feel that holidays offer opportunities to focus on different cultures. Music and the other arts naturally play a vital role in these customs, as seen in the piñata lesson.

Others feel that the holiday approach both trivializes and stereotypes cultures. Still others are concerned that celebrating any aspect of holidays in schools can reinforce or promote the views of one group over another. For example, some Christian groups oppose having their children participate in school holiday celebrations, a posi-

tion based on their interpretation of the Bible. Based on teachings of the Koran, Muslims avoid images except for geometric abstractions. In both instances, parents may object to a reenactment of a Mexican piñata party on religious grounds, but for different reasons.

Teachers need to consider their local school culture and community when mediating issues of tolerance and religious freedom in education. The study of a culture is inextricably bound to the practices and beliefs of that culture, including religion. While it is perfectly appropriate for schools to teach *about* religions, they may not promote any particular religion or practice. When cultural studies touch upon religious issues, it is vital that teachers communicate the broad educational purposes of those studies to parents.

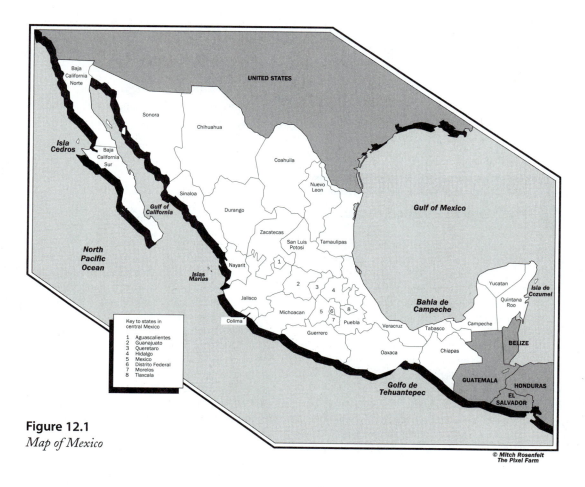

Key to states in
central Mexico

1 Aguascalientes
2 Guanajuato
3 Queretaro
4 Hidalgo
5 Mexico
6 Distrito Federal
7 Morelos
8 Tlaxcala

© Mitch Rosenfelt
The Pixel Farm

Figure 12.1
Map of Mexico

Mexico's Music: A Mix of Cultures

Many musical traditions thrive in Mexico, reflecting this culture's unique
blending of indigenous, colonial, and contemporary influences. The people of Mexico are extremely diverse because of overlapping and continuous waves of immigration. From at least 1000 B.C. to the present day,
Mexican and Mesoamerican[3] populations have been in a state of continual flux and migration. Sixty percent of the Mexican population is mestizo, that is, having a mixture of Spanish and Indian blood. The mestizo
population, however, is not homogeneous: There are more than 50 iden-
tifiable Indian groups in Mexico, whose members speak 200 dialects.
Each region, city, and village has its own identity and traditions. In fact,
these more localized units and language groups tend to confer stronger
collective identity than political or nation-state affiliations. Mestizos
continue to celebrate folk expressions, which draw upon the roots of the
combined cultures.

The colonial influence on Mexico's music began with the arrival of Spanish fortune hunters led by Hernando Cortez in 1519. "We came here," wrote Bernal Diaz Castillo, a soldier-author, "to serve God and also to become rich" (Marrin, 1986, p. 63). The clash between the European colonizers and the sophisticated Aztec Empire was bitter.[4] An Aztec poem written in the 1520s records the distress of the defeated peoples.[5]

> Our walls are keening,
> Our tears fall down like rain.
> Weep, weep, our people,
> For we have lost México.

Marrin, 1986, frontispiece

As the Spanish began to colonize Mexico, their culture dominated. There they re-created a two-tiered class system, similar to the medieval society in Spain and Portugal. Spanish-born people occupied the highest social class, with the lower classes stratified according to racial mix (Constable, 1985). Indigenous religion, music, and culture were discouraged. Spanish monks established the first music schools in the New World as a way of Christianizing indigenous people. The musics started to blend as European scales, triadic harmony, and the sounds of new instruments were fused into mestizo music.

As people travel, so, too, do musical instruments. One way of examining cultural influences is to trace the path of instruments from one culture to another. When the Spanish arrived in Mexico, what kinds of musical practices did they find? Ancient Mexican murals depict musicians with small drums, footed drums, and rattles. Early musicians played a variety of wind instruments—such as flutes, whistles, and ocarinas—as well as rattles and drums, but no stringed instruments (Diagram Group, 1976).

Stringed instruments, primarily the guitar, were originally introduced to Mexico by the Spanish. Over time, other guitar-like instruments evolved to become prominent in Mexican folk music. One such instrument, the *vihuela,* is smaller than a guitar, and has five strings and a convex back. Another is the *huapanguera,* which is slightly wider and deeper than a guitar and has eight strings in five courses. The largest of the three guitar derivatives is the *guitarrón,* a large, six-stringed bass guitar with a convex, spined back. The Iberian violin and diatonic harp[6] were also transplanted to the New World.

For a brief time in the early 1600s, the Spaniards imported some 150,000 slaves from West Africa to work in the fields (Constable, 1985). The African influence in Mexican music is heard in the rhythms and

Figure 12.2
Mariachi Ensemble (Two Trumpets, Two Violins, Guitarrón, and Vihuela) Performing in Plaza Garibaldi, Mexico City. Photo by Daniel Sheehy.

buzzing timbres of the wooden marimba, which evolved from the West African xylophone (Olson, Sheehy, & Perrone, 1987).

Bringing the Music of Mexico into the Classroom

We often have to rely on indirect experiences of reading books or listening to lectures to learn about other cultures and their interactions. Through the sounds of music, however, we can hear direct evidence of cultural assimilation. In Lesson Plan II, students will discover the influence of African musical traditions on Mexican music by comparing the sound of a marimba from Mexico with the sound of one from Ghana.

Lesson Plan II
Mexican Marimbas

Rationale   The fluid and dynamic nature of musical traditions is strikingly apparent in the music of Mexico. As populations migrate, interactions of persons from various cultures cause cultural practices and traditions to be influenced and modified. One way to trace these processes of acculturation is to study how the introduction of new instruments into a culture parallels the infusion of new cultural groups and musical ideas. In the following lesson, students learn about the migration of an African instrument to Mexico and play a children's game song from Mexico on Orff xylophones. Because this lesson features the processes of music performance and perception, it would most likely be taught by the music specialist. The activities in the lesson also draw upon related content in science, language arts, and social studies, however, suggesting possibilities for collaboration with other teachers or connections to other settings.

Suggested grade level   Fourth through Sixth

Objectives   Students will

- ~ discover how the acoustical properties of vibration and resonance operate in xylophones and marimbas.
- ~ compare the sound of a Mexican marimba with the sound of a West African xylophone.
- ~ trace the influences of African music on the music of Mexico.
- ~ sing a Mexican children's song, "Víbora de la mar," and play the song on xylophones.

Materials

- ~ Song: "Víbora de la mar" (see Example 12.2, page 293)
- ~ Recordings of Mexican marimba music such as Marimba Yajalón (performers), (1994), *¡Chiapas!* [CD], Kansas City, Mo.: Heart of Wood Project; or Lewiston, D. (recorder), (1991), *Mexico: Fiestas of Chiapas and Oaxaca* [CD], New York: Elektra Nonesuch (originally released 1976)
- ~ Recordings of xylophone music from Ghana, such as Jay, S. (recorder), (1991), *Ghana: Ancient ceremonies, song and dance music* [CD], New York: Elektra Nonesuch, and Kobom, J. (1992), *Xylophone music from Ghana* [audio cassette], Crown Point, Ind.: White Cliffs Media
- ~ World map
- ~ Pictures of marimbas. Consult Hart, M., and Lieberman, F. (1991), *Planet drum: A celebration of percussion and rhythm*, San Francisco: HarperCollins, or Diagram Group (1976), *Musical instruments of the world*, New York: Paddington Press, for picture sources
- ~ Orff xylophones and a marimba, if available; various mallets (hard rubber, felt, yarn-wrapped)
- ~ Combs and waxed paper for each student

Introducing the lesson

1) Play a scale on an Orff xylophone. *What is the name of this instrument?* Write *xylophone* on the board. *If we divide the word in two, we have* xylo *and* phone. *What other words can you think of that have the letters* p-h-o-n *in*

them? Responses may include *telephone, phonograph,* and *phonics. What do these words have in common with a xylophone? They both have something to do with sound. The xylo part of the word comes from the Greek word meaning wood. So the xylophone is "wood that makes sound." All sounds are caused by vibration. What makes a xylophone vibrate? When we strike the xylophone with a mallet, the wooden bars vibrate. We can change the sound of the xylophone by striking it with different types of mallets.* Have students write down words that describe the difference in the sound of a xylophone when it is played with a hard rubber mallet, a felt mallet, and a yarn-wrapped mallet.

2) *Today we're going to listen to recordings of relatives of our Orff xylophones from different parts of the world. Let's keep track of places where xylophones are played by placing pins in the map.* Have a student put a pin on the map to mark your school's location and then find the state of Chiapas in Mexico and mark its location with a pin. *The marimba is a type of xylophone that is very popular in Chiapas. As you listen to this recording of a Mexican marimba, write down some words that describe how its sound is different from our Orff xylophone.* Play "Chiapas" from the recording by Marimba Yajalón (1994), "El Chinito" from *Mexico: Fiestas of Chiapas and Oaxaca* (Lewiston, 1991), or any other available recording of a Mexican marimba.

    What words did you use to describe the sound of the Mexican marimba? Students may observe that the Mexican marimbas have a buzzing quality not heard in the Orff xylophones.

Figure 12.3
Marimba Yajalón

Figure 12.4
*Central American
Marimba. Photo
by Shawn Kolles.*

3) Show a picture of a marimba.

*In what ways does the marimba look the same as the Orff xylophones? In what
ways does it look different?* Both instruments have wooden bars that are sus-
pended on a frame. The bars on the Mexican marimba are laid out in two
rows, similar to the rows of white and black keys on the piano. *What could
possibly create the buzzing sound in the Mexican marimba?* You may wish to
summarize or have a student read "The Marimbas of Mexico and Central
America," below.

Enhancing the Understanding of Context:
The Marimbas of Mexico and Central America

Any percussion instrument with vibrating wooden keys or bars can be
called a **xylophone;** a **marimba** is a special type of xylophone because it
uses hollow resonators made of metal, gourds, wood, or bamboo to ampli-
fy the vibration of the bars. Mexican marimbas, with their distinctive sound,
are especially popular in the state of Chiapas, as well as in the states of
Oaxaca, Veracruz, and Tabasco. The instrument itself, the musicians who
play it, and the music they play are respected as cultural treasures. Kaptain
(1995) explains that "the marimba is often described as having human
qualities in both conversation and in literature, and the people of Chiapas
often refer to the marimba as *las maderas que cantan* (the wood that

sings)" (p. 250). The residents of nearby Guatemala are also proud of the marimba, honoring it as the national instrument.

The source of the distinctive buzzing sound in Mexican marimbas can be found at the end of the wooden resonating chambers. A piece of wax at the bottom of the column supports a thin membrane of pig intestine, which is stretched over a small hole. When the musicians set the bar into motion by striking it with a mallet, the air in the chamber vibrates; so does the membrane at the bottom of the chamber. This produces the kazoo-like buzz that is so characteristic of marimbas in this region.

Figure 12.5
Pig Intestines Used in Mexican Marimba Resonators. Photo by Shawn Kolles.

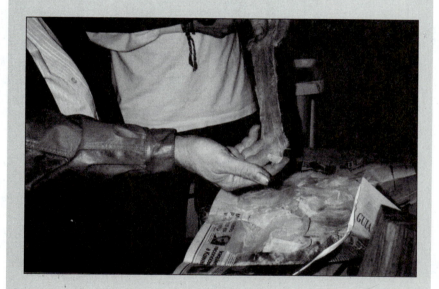

In Chiapas, it is common for several musicians to perform on the same marimba, standing side by side as each person plays in a certain register of the instrument. Chromatic marimbas (with two rows of pitches like the black and white keys of the piano) can include as many as six octaves. Performers play with three or four mallets, alternating them rapidly for a smooth, sustained sound.

Sources: Chenoweth, 1961/1984; Kaptain, 1992, 1995; O'Brien, 1982

4) *You may be trying to imagine what pig intestine membranes look like. When you go to the grocery, take a look at the thin film that covers a chorizo, bratwurst, or Italian sausage. That's the kind of material that makes the buzzing*

sound in Mexican marimbas. Let's experiment to see how those membranes could create that buzzing sound. Provide a plastic comb and rectangle of waxed paper approximately the size of the comb for every student, if possible, or at least one for demonstration. Allow the student a chance to experiment with producing a sound by humming into the comb covered with waxed paper. Not only will they hear the buzzing sound produced by the waxed paper, but they will feel the vibration on their lips.

Developing the lesson

5) *The marimba is not originally from Mexico. For almost 300 years, the Spanish who settled Mexico and Central America imported slaves to work in the fields, just as plantation owners in the United States did. Many of these slaves came from the west coast of Africa.* Locate the west coast of Africa and the modern country of Ghana on a map. Ask a student to mark it with a pin. Then wrap a piece of yarn around the pin in Ghana and connect it to the pin in Chiapas to show the distance and direction between them. *The slaves brought their culture, their language, and their music with them. It is thought that the basic concept for a marimba-like instrument (and ideas for its design) was carried by slaves to Mexico from Africa.*

6) *Listen to this music from Ghana. Does the sound of the xylophone from Ghana sound more like the Mexican marimba or more like our Orff xylophones?* Play "Dzil Duet" from *Ghana: Ancient Ceremonies, Song and Dance Music* (Jay, 1991) or any recording from the Kobom (1992) tape. Students may recognize that both the African and Mexican instruments have a buzzing quality that the Orff instruments do not. Summarize or have a student read "The Marimbas of West and Central Africa," below.

**Enhancing the Understanding of Context:
The Marimbas of West and Central Africa**

The first reference to xylophone-type instruments in Africa can be traced to oral and written records from the thirteenth- and fourteenth-century kingdom of Mali. Scholars who study the origins of musical instruments attribute the name *marimba* to the Bantu of Malawi and Mozambique, who call a single bar sticking out a *rimba* and many bars a *marimba*. An African xylophone of particular interest is the **dzil** (or **gyil)** of Ghana, which may include bars of mahogany or other wood that sit on a frame. Underneath each bar, gourds are used as resonating chambers. A hole is drilled in each gourd and is covered with a spider's egg case (with a texture like a wasp's nest). These egg cases buzz when the bar is struck, in the same way that the pig intestines vibrate in the Mexican marimba.

Figure 12.6
Xylophone from Ghana

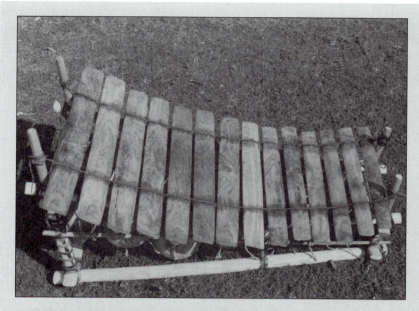

Figure 12.7
Resonating Gourds with Spider's Egg Cases

The dzil can be played as a solo instrument or by two players at once. The performers sit facing each other, holding thick beaters; one player plays the melody, and the other provides repetitive accompaniment patterns. Wiggins and Kobom (1992) describe how playing the xylophone is considered to be spiritually dangerous, an undertaking only appropriate for men, according to the regional Dagaare myths and legends.

Three important clues seem to suggest the African marimba as the direct ancestor of the Mexican marimba: (a) the common name of the instrument, (b) the lack of any archaeological evidence for xylophone-type instruments in pre-Columbian Central America before the Spanish began importing Africans to work as slaves, and (c) the buzz produced by a membrane over the resonators.

SOURCES: Anderson, Blades, List, & O'Brien, 1984; Jay, 1991; Kaptain, 1995; Kubik, Blades, & Roberts, 1984; O'Brien, 1982; Wiggins & Kobom, 1992

Closing the lesson

7) Teach "Víbora de la mar," a traditional game song similar to "London Bridge" that is played by children in Mexico.[7] To highlight the eighth-note triplets in the song and to promote their smooth, even performance, have students lightly pat the beat on their thighs as they sing, using a small vertical rebound for beats with quarter or eighth notes and a circular rebound for beats with triplets.

Example 12.2
Notation for "Víbora de la mar"

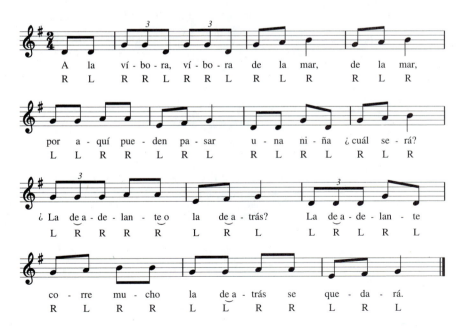

A la víbora, víbora, de la mar,	Serpent, serpent from the sea
por aquí pueden pasar una niña, ¿cuál será?	One girl can pass your way. Which one will it be?
¿La de adelante o la de atrás?	One in front or one in back?
La de adelante corre mucho la de atrás se quedará	One runs, one stays.

8) Students may want to try playing the melody of "Víbora de la mar" on Orff xylophones, following the sticking patterns as suggested.

Assessment

~ Can students identify the source of vibration in xylophones and marimbas and explain the purpose of resonators in Mexican marimbas and xylophones from Ghana?

~ Can students identify the similarity of timbre between the Mexican marimba and the West African xylophone music?

~ Can students sing and play "Víbora de la mar" accurately?

Extending the lesson

~ Students may wish to play the game for "Víbora de la mar." Two children form an arch (as in "London Bridge"). Children pass under the upraised arms of the head couple. On the final cadence of the song, the head couple lower their arms to catch the child who is passing through.

~ West African percussion ensemble music has been transcribed in several sources. Wiggins and Kobom (1992) include transcriptions of Ghanaian xylophone pieces that may be accessible to students, such as "Simple Kpanlogo" or "Simple Tomeyielu" (play Kobom's [1992] recording for students to introduce the rhythmic feel of the pieces). Although they are based on various drums—*gankogui* and *axatse*—rather than xylophones, the ensembles found in *All Hands On! An Introduction to West African Percussion Ensembles* (Jessup, 1996) may also be used to extend the study of cultural music and percussion instruments.

~ Contrast the music from the Chiapas region with other regional musics. In the Mexican state of Veracruz, a distinctive ensemble called a *conjunto jarocho* features vocals and harp, a small melody guitar *(requinto),* and rhythm guitars *(jarana).* An example of this style may be found on the recording *Music of Veracruz: The Sones Jarochos of Los Pregoneros del Puerto* (Los Pregoneros del Puerto, 1990). See Olson et al. (1987) for lesson plans using jarocho music of Veracruz and other Latin American musical forms.

Spanish and African musical traditions were not the only influences on the evolving music of Mexico. In the 1900s, German immigrants brought the button accordion to the music of the northern borderlands, along with dances such as the polka, waltz, and schottische. Thus, the new style called *norteño, conjunto,* and later Tex-Mex, was forged of old and new along the Rio Grande between 1928 and 1960 (Peña, 1985).

Contemporary Mexican music covers an impressive range of styles and traditions, including classical, folk, jazz, and popular. In these musics, listeners can hear the influences of other Latin American countries and the United States. Big band sounds and the 1940s swing style from the United States were taken up by Mexican dance bands. Mexican listeners enjoy pan-Latin styles such as *salsa,* the Cuban *bolero* and *danzón,* and Colombia's *cumbia* (Farquharson, 1994; Manuel, 1988). Other forms and styles, such as the *balada, bomba, bossa nova, habañera, lambada, merengue, rumba, samba, tropical, tropicalismo,* and waltz are popular in Mexico, as they are throughout the American continents.

Lesson Plan III charts the transformation of a traditional Veracruz song to a 1950s rock-and-roll hit so resilient that it resurfaced in the 1980s. In the lesson, students identify the ways a traditional version differs from a popular version. By noting which elements of the music remain stable and which change, students analyze how music preserves and transmits culture while it also adapts to changes in economic, social, and geographical context. They are also encouraged to form critical opinions about the effects of the changes. This lesson is appropriate for a Spanish, geography, general music, or music performance class.

Lesson Plan III
Travels of "La Bamba" from Veracruz to Los Angeles

Rationale   Several years ago I heard a fascinating talk that followed the Mexican folk song "La Bamba" through multiple permutations (Solomon, 1989). During its journey, this song moved from a traditional tune rooted in a region in Mexico to a commercial product with global distribution, simultaneously transforming and transcending connections with a geographic location. I was left wondering about the song. Was the song itself enduring? Or did it become enduring through being interpreted by many singers? At what point did "La Bamba" become a product and not part of a process? Who "owned" "La Bamba"? These questions and others may engage middle school students who are often keenly aware of ever-changing commercial "youth music," but who may be unaware of the ways in which music travels from place to place and the ways in which people make meaning for themselves through music.

Example 12.3
"La Bamba"

La Bamba

Para bailar la Bamba,	In order to dance the Bamba,
Para bailar la Bamba,	In order to dance the Bamba,
Se necesita una poca de gracia,	It is necessary to have a little grace,
Una poca de gracia para mi, para ti,	A little bit of grace for me, for you,
Y arriba y arriba	And upward and upward
Y arriba y arriba	And upward and upward
Por ti seré!	For you I will be!
Por ti seré! Por ti seré!	For you I will be, for you I will be!
Yo no soy marinero,	I am not a sailor,
Yo no soy marinero,	I am not a sailor,
Soy capitán,	I am a captain,
Soy capitán, soy capitán.	I am a captain, I am a captain.
Bamba, Bamba,	Bamba, Bamba,
Bamba, Bamba,	Bamba, Bamba,
Bamba, Bamba, Bamba!	Bamba, Bamba, Bamba!

Suggested Grade Level   Seventh through Twelfth

Objectives   Students will

- ~ explore traditional and contemporary music, ensembles, and styles of Mexico and the United States by comparing different versions of "La Bamba."
- ~ sing a traditional Mexican/Mexican American song in Spanish.
- ~ explain why a musical example sounds "traditional" or "popular."
- ~ describe differences between two performances of the same song and make judgments about their aesthetic value.

Materials   Many versions of "La Bamba" are available. For this lesson, the teacher should collect recordings from two categories: the more traditional Veracruz style of performance and popularized versions.

- ~ Recordings in the Veracruz style: Los Pregoneros del Puerto (performers), (1990), *Music of Veracruz: The sones jarochos of Los Pregoneros del Puerto* [CD], Cambridge, Mass.: Rounder Records; Conjunto Alma Jarocha (performers), (1994), *Sones jarochos* [CD], El Cerrito, Calif.: Arhoolie Productions (original recording 1979); Llerenas, E. (producer), (1996), *La iguana: Sones jarochos from Veracruz, Mexico* [CD], Cambridge, Mass.: Rounder Records.

~ Recordings in the popular style: Los Lobos, (1987), *La Bamba: Original motion picture soundtrack* [LP], Los Angeles: Slash/Warner Brothers; Valens, R. (1958), *The best of Ritchie Valens* [LP], Los Angeles: Del-Fi; Los Lobos (1995), *Papa's dream* [CD], Redway, Calif.: Music for Little People

~ Valdez, L. (producer), (1987), *La Bamba* [video], Burbank, Calif.: RCA/Columbia Pictures Home Video

~ Music for "La Bamba" (see Example 12.3)

Introducing the lesson

1) *Sometimes a song travels from place to place and changes as it is sung by new people. Listen to this recording and tell me if you recognize this song.* Play one of the Veracruz recordings of "La Bamba." *This is a well-known song originally from the state of Veracruz in Mexico.* Have students locate Veracruz on the map.

Developing the lesson

2) Set up a listening lesson in which students will listen to several versions of "La Bamba," including representative examples from the Veracruz style and popular versions. On the board, construct a chart similar to the one in Table 12.1. Play a recording from each style, asking students to fill in the chart with descriptions of the musical elements used in each.

Table 12.1

	"La Bamba" Version 1	"La Bamba" Version 2
Instruments		
Rhythmic character		
Melodic character		
Tone color		

3) If additional recordings from either style are available, extend the chart by adding more columns, labeled "Version 3," "Version 4," and so on. After listening to the recordings, students can decide which examples more closely resemble version 1 or version 2. Supplement student responses with information from the chart in Table 12.2 and label the two styles as "Veracruz" and "Popular."

4) *Have you ever thought a current hit was original only to find out that it was a remake of a previous recording? Musicians often "cover" previously recorded tunes, giving them a musical spin to appeal to contemporary listeners. For example, a current cover of a 1960s song would most likely include synthesized and electronic sounds that weren't available in the sixties. "La Bamba," as*

Table 12.2

	Veracruz Style	Popular Style
Instruments	Acoustic instruments: guitars of various sizes *jarana, requinto* harps in many examples	Acoustic and electrified instruments including guitar, drum set, and bass
Rhythmic character	Fast, consistent rhythm Accents on beats 1 and 3	Tempo varies with version Accents on beats 2 and 4
Melodic character	Narrow range in higher register of singer's voice	Wider range that uses singer's lower register
Tone color	Bright and brittle vocal sound "Conversational" style	Deeper, resonant vocal sound Song-like style

recorded by Ritchie Valens, a rock-and-roll star of the 1950s, is an example of a cover, but in this case, traditional or "folk" music was the original source. Show video clip of *La Bamba* in which Valens wows a critical New York crowd with his gold lamé outfit and electric guitar.

5) *We've heard several versions of "La Bamba" today. Which of the versions do you think is the original one?* (Have the class vote and tally the responses.) *It may not be possible to identify an original version of a tune, but the versions from Veracruz sound "original" to us because they reflect the traditional practices of the culture. What is "traditional" music? What is "popular" music?*[8] *As other musicians borrow tunes and texts, they change aspects and elements of the music to transform the work and make it "new." We can sometimes trace the history of a tune by examining various versions and the changes.* Summarize the travels of this song, using a map of Mexico to point out Veracruz and its proximity to Los Angeles. Invite students to speculate how the song spread to other places. For example, the version of "La Bamba" provided in Example 12.3 was contributed by Carla Moreno, a university student from Texas. What are some of the ways that she could have learned the song?

Distribute or display notation and text for "La Bamba." Practice the Spanish words, asking students who have studied Spanish for help with pronunciation. Then sing the song. Enlist students who play the guitar to accompany the singing, using strumming patterns heard on the recordings.

Closing the lesson Challenge the students to find examples of songs recorded in several versions, sometimes referred to as "covers." Some examples include "Cotton-Eyed Joe," as recorded by the Rednex and by traditional fiddlers; "Hound Dog" as recorded by Big Mama Thornton and later by Elvis Presley; and the second movement of the

Pathétique Sonata by Beethoven as transformed into "This Night" by Billy Joel. Ask students to write a paper that includes (a) a description of the changes in the more recent versions or that reflect the different backgrounds of the musicians who performed them, (b) judgments about whether the cover is an improvement or corruption of the earlier version, and (c) reasons to support those judgments.

Assessment

~ Can students recognize the use of musical elements in Veracruz and popular versions of "La Bamba"?

~ Can students define the differences between traditional and popular music?

~ Do students give full and accurate descriptions of the musical differences between two performances of the same music and do they justify their judgments about the aesthetic value of the two versions?

Extending the lesson

~ "La Bamba" is often arranged for performance by school bands. The instrumental music educator may ask students to compare the arrangement with versions of "La Bamba" from Veracruz to see how the arrangement differs from traditional performances.

~ Extend the discussion of how music is transmitted by viewing *Chulas Fronteras* (1976). This documentary of norteño styles focuses on the way traditions are passed from generation to generation. One particularly effective sequence begins with Flaco Jimenez playing accordion in a club, continues with Jimenez's son teasing out a melody on the accordion, and is followed by a cut of Flaco accompanying his father, also a renowned player.

~ Have students make a taped collage of popular Mexican American music, noting the diversity of styles and traditions.

~ Raise issues of ownership and copyright of music by citing the case of "La Bamba." If a version of "La Bamba" makes a lot of money through sales of recordings, who does the money belong to? Did Ritchie Valens own this song? Does it belong to the people of Veracruz? Can students describe other instances where ownership is unclear?

Exploring Other Styles of Mexican Music

The diversity of musical styles within Mexico is echoed within Mexican American communities in the United States. Steven Loza comments on the many Mexican and Chicano musical genres:

> In Mexico alone, there is a wide diversity of regional cultures. There are many regions: Chiapas, Chihuahua, Jalisco, Oaxaca, Veracruz, for example. Music in Mexico includes the popular *banda* music, but also *mariachi* music, *tropical* music, *norteño* music, *ranchera* music (especially among the working class), *salsa* music, *jarocho* music, and *huapango* music. All of these are Mexican music, and all of it can be found in the United States. (Loza, as cited in Campbell, 1995, pp. 52–53)

The rich heritage of Mexican folk music exists alongside more modern musical developments. Popular music industries in Mexico and the United States target communities throughout the Americas. Like folk music of Mexico, much popular music is based on imported style features that combine with indigenous musics. Enduring Spanish influences in contemporary musics may be heard in such details as harmonies in thirds, triple meter, dance forms, and timbres. As illustrated in Lesson Plan II, the buzzing timbres produced by gourd resonators in the marimba trace back to African influences from slaves in the seventeenth and eighteenth centuries.

Some of the traditional and popular music of Mexico is described in Table 12.3.

Banda [BAHN-dah]	Village bands that play brass instruments and drums. *Bandas* play a variety of dance music such as polkas and waltzes as well as songs such as *rancheras* and *corridos* in *norteño* style.	**Table 12.3** *Mexican and Mexican American Music*
Canción [cahn-see-OHN]	Literally "song," especially a through-composed, sentimental, slow song, not associated with dance. A *canción romantica* is a love song.	
Conjunto [cohn-HUHN-to]	Accordion, guitar, and vocal music of northern Mexico; another term for *norteño* or Tex-Mex.	
Corrido [coh-REE-do]	Mexican ballads of true events, often about the revolution, villains, and heroes. *Corridos* that chronicle current events are often heard over the airwaves.	
Danzón [dahn-ZOHN]	Popular Mexican dance derived from European dances and a Cuban salon dance popular from the late nineteenth to early twentieth century.	

continues

Table 12.3 *Mexican and Mexican American Music, continued*	**Huapango** [wah-PAHN-go]	Instrumental dance music and a generic term for music from central and eastern Mexico. *Huapango* music is played on violin, small guitar (*jarana*), rhythm guitar, and sometimes percussion.
	Jarocho [hah-ROH-cho]	Traditional ensemble in Veracruz (eastern Mexico) that features *requinto* (small guitar-like lute), *jarana*, and harp.
	Mariachi [mah-ree-AH-chee]	Mexican band associated with west Mexico and Jalisco, derived from *mestizo* music of the 1800s; popular in urban areas for parties, weddings, and dining. *Mariachi* bands play trumpets, violins, rhythm guitars (*vihuelas*), other guitars, and bass guitar (*guitarrón*). They perform dance music such as *son,* polka, and waltz, and songs such as *rancheras, boleros, corridos, huapangos,* and other popular musics.
	Mestizo [mes-TEE-zo]	"Mixed" music, a term for a new music formed in about 1775 from a combination of Indian, European, and African musics. *Mestizo* music was often performed on harp, one or two violins, some form of guitar, and voices. *Mariachi* music evolved from this style.
	Norteño [nor-TAY-nyo]	Accordion, guitar, and vocal music from the north of Mexico, also known as *conjunto* and as Tex-Mex in its U.S. incarnation. *Corrido* ballads may be included in this style.
	Ranchera [rahn-CHAY-rah]	Mexican urban song, often nostalgic for rural lifestyles, frequently melodramatic and sentimental. Refrains often include *"ay, ay, ay, ay."*
	Son [SOHN]	Generic term for various Mexican styles, of which there are several regional variants such as *son jarocho, huasteco, jaliscience,* and *abajeño.* Instrumental genres, such as *son marimba,* are also included.
	Tex-Mex	Accordion-led music originally from northern Mexico where it is known as *norteño* or *conjunto.* The term "Tex-Mex" is used by or for cultural outsiders almost exclusively.

Sources: Apel, 1977; Béhague, 1986; Broughton, Ellingham, Muddyman, and Trillo, 1994; Campbell, 1995; Harpole and Fagelquist, 1989; Manuel, 1988, 1955; Myers, 1993; Sheehy (personal communication, June, 1996).

Embedded in the history and transmission of musical practices are the musical element of style, which encompasses melody, rhythm, harmony, tone color, and form, and the social studies themes (National Council for the Social Studies, 1994) of (a) culture; (b) time, continuity, and change; (c) people, places and environments; (d) individual development and identity; (e) power, authority, and governance; and (f) global connections. The following are some ideas for integrating the study of music, history, culture, and Spanish language.

Ranchera or *ranchera romántica* is a popular song form from the borderlands between Mexico and Texas. These songs are slow ballads with verses and a refrain that are usually rendered in a heartfelt manner by a male singer. Rancheras are often nostalgic for an idealized rural life, or a lost love, and are expressive of passion and machismo. Guadalupe Betancourt, a popular vocalist who performs on both sides of the border, sings "Volver, volver" ([I will] Come back, come back) on *The JVC/Smithsonian/Folkways Video Anthology of Music and Dance of the Americas,* Volume 6, *Central and South America II* (McArthur & Yoshida, 1995).

Corridos are narrative ballads that record historical events or comment on current issues through Mexican eyes. One prolific body of corridos from the Texas-Mexican border region relates tales of migration and the hardships of migrant workers. Other popular corridos include songs about the Mexican revolution, historical heroes such as Gregorio Cortez, and contemporary figures such as John F. Kennedy. These songs may be sung by one person, but are more typically sung by at least two singers who harmonize in thirds, accompanied by guitars.

~ Historic recordings and documentation of corridos from 1928 to 1937 may be sampled on the newly issued CD *Corridos and Tragedias de la Fronteras* (Strachwitz, 1994). Compare these with the dust-bowl ballads of Woody Guthrie and other traditional American ballads.

~ Maria Herrera-Sobek's meticulous *Northward Bound* (1993) explores immigrant corridos. Supplement these songs of longing for the homeland with other voices of immigrants. Varied experiences of Mexican Americans may be explored in Santoli's (1988) *New Americans, an Oral History: Immigrants and Refugees in the U.S. Today,* a collection of interviews and profiles of recent immigrants from Afghanistan, Poland, Ethiopia, Laos, and other countries. The experiences of those who straddle the borderlands of the Southwest are eloquently portrayed in Martínez's (1994) *Border People: Life and Society in the U.S.-Mexico Borderlands* and Davis's (1990) *Mexican Voices, American Dreams: An Oral History of Mexican Immigration to the United States.*

~ Encourage students to create corridos that have political implications, modeled on historical and modern corridos.

Canciones or *canciones románticas* are love songs favored by Mexican and Mexican American singers.

~ Change and stability in this song form can be illustrated by comparing older and new versions. View a video clip of Lydia Mendoza, the "Nightingale of the Border" who recorded from the 1930s on. Contrast Mendoza with modern singers. Mendoza sings "Tango Negro" on two videos: *The JVC/Smithsonian/Folkways Video Anthology of Music and Dance of the Americas,* Volume 6, *Central and South America II* (McArthur & Yoshida, 1995) and *Tex-Mex: The Music of the Texas-Mexican Borderlands* (Marre, 1980).

~ Recent recordings of popular singers that offer distinct contrasts include Tish Hinojosa (1995) singing "Sólo Tus Ojos" (Only Your Eyes) with Peter Rowan on *Frontéjas* and Linda Ronstadt (1991) performing "Mi Ranchito" (My Little Ranch) with her two brothers on *Mas canciones.*

Norteño, Tex-Mex, or *conjunto* music ensembles consist of accordion and *banjo sexto* (12-string guitar) and the *contrabass,* which in the 1950s was replaced with electric bass. At that time, the dance band drum set was added. The big band sounds of Glenn Miller and Tommy Dorsey were echoed in the Mexican American *orquestas.* Two films that document *norteño* music are *Chulas Fronteras* (1976) and the more controversial *Tex-Mex: Music of the Texas-Mexican Borderlands* (Marre, 1980). The second film, from the "Beats of the Heart" video series, films music in the contexts of commercial and private venues. Shots of scavengers in a junkyard, confrontations between police and border crossers, and other scenes of real life are woven throughout.

Mariachi bands, associated with the state of Jalisco and west Mexico and now popular in many Mexican and Mexican American communities, play for weddings, fiestas, and other joyful occasions. See Campbell (1995) and Harpole & Fogelquist (1989) for lesson plans using guitar and voices to augment listening lessons based on mariachi music.

Extending the Study of Mexico Across the Curriculum

Music and the arts open unique windows on the ways different people know and express their understanding of the world. As Charles Fowler (1994) writes:

In America, our sense of community depends on our establishing linkages across our many ethnic and racial differences. Music is one of the splendid connectors between different peoples and cultures. It is a way for America to speak to itself in all its different guises. It is a way for Americans to attain a feeling of unity and cohesiveness—of oneness. (p. 527)

In addition to the music-focused curriculum ideas presented in this chapter, you may wish to explore how other art forms can illuminate the study of Mexico.

~ Students may wish to read poems to augment their understanding of Hispanic and Mexican American lives. Recent Hispanic poetry may be sampled in *Cool Salsa: Bilingual Poems on Growing up Latino in the United States* (Carlson, 1994) and *Unsettling America: An Anthology of Contemporary Multicultural Poetry* (Gillan & Gillan, 1995). *Here is My Kingdom: Hispanic-American Literature and Arts for Young People* (Sullivan, 1994) is a beautiful book with artwork and poems.

~ Photo documentaries offer a valuable perspective. *Material World: A Global Family Portrait* (Menzel, 1994) offers a remarkable geography lesson about material culture. Photographers visited 30 countries, living for a week with a family that is statistically average for that nation. Each visit was commemorated by a portrait of the family posed outside of their home with all of their possessions. Details of a family from Guadalajara, Mexico, capture a mother and four children in spotless white dresses and shirts going to church, kids on the bus, window shopping, and working on the job. Pictures of a Texas family are of a similar nature but reveal striking differences in lifestyle.

References

Ancona, G. (1993). *Pablo remembers: The fiesta of the Day of the Dead.* New York: Lothrop, Lee & Shepard.

Ancona, G. (1994). *The piñata maker.* San Diego, Calif.: Harcourt Brace.

Anderson, L. A., Blades, J., List, G., & O'Brien, L. L. (1984). Xylophone. In S. Sadie (ed.), *The new Grove dictionary of musical instruments* (pp. 869–879). London: Macmillan.

Apel, W. (1977). *Harvard dictionary of music.* Cambridge, Mass.: Belknap.

Ballet Folclorico Nacional de México. (1990) [video]. New York: Gessler.

Banks, J. A. (1991). *Teaching strategies for ethnic studies.* Boston: Allyn & Bacon.

Béhague, G. (1986). Hispanic-American music. In H. W. Hitchcock & S. Sadie (eds.), *The new Grove dictionary of American music* (vol. 2, pp. 501–508). London: Macmillan.

Broughton, S., Ellingham, M., Muddyman, D., & Trillo, R. (eds.). (1994). *World music: The rough guide*. London: Penguin.

Campbell, P. S. (1995). Steven Loza on Latino music. *Music Educators Journal* 82 (2): 45–52.

Carlson, L. M. (ed.). (1994). *Cool salsa: Bilingual poems on growing up Latino in the United States*. New York: Henry Holt.

Carmack, R. M., Gasco, J., & Gossen, G. H. (1996). *The legacy of Mesoamerica: History and culture of a Native American civilization*. Upper Saddle River, N.J.: Prentice-Hall.

Chenoweth, V. (1984). The differences among xylophone-marimba-vibraphone. In *Percussion Anthology* (p. 186). Evanston, Ill.: The Instrumentalist Company. (Article originally published 1961.)

Chrisp, P. (1993). *The Spanish conquests in the new world*. New York: Thomson.

Chulas fronteras (1976) [video]. El Cerrito, Calif.: Brazos Films.

Conjunto Alma Jarocha (performers). (1994). *Sones jarochos* [CD]. El Cerrito, Calif.: Arhoolie Productions. (Original recording 1979.)

Constable, G. (ed.). (1985). *Mexico*. Amsterdam: Time-Life.

Davis, M. (1990). *Mexican voices, American dreams: An oral history of Mexican immigration to the United States*. New York: Henry Holt.

Delacre, L. (1990). *Las Navidades: Popular Christmas songs from Latin America*. New York: Scholastic.

Diagram Group. (1976). *Musical instruments of the world*. New York: Paddington Press.

Elmer, M., Beall, C., & Robertson, S. (1993). *Festivals of light*. Seattle, Wash.: The Children's Museum.

Ets, M. H., & Labastida, A. (1979). *Nine days to Christmas*. New York: Viking.

Farquharson, M. (1994). Over the border: Mexico is a whole lot more than mariachi. In S. Broughton, M. Ellingham, D. Muddyman, & R. Trillo (eds.), *World music: The rough guide*. London: Penguin.

Fowler, C. (1994). *Music! Its role and importance in our lives*. New York: Glencoe.

Gillan, M., & Gillan, J. (eds.). (1995). *Unsettling America: An anthology of contemporary multicultural poetry*. New York: Penguin.

Grant, C. A., & Sleeter, C. (1989). *Turning on learning: Five approaches for multicultural teaching plans for race, class, gender and disability*. Columbus, Ohio: Merrill.

Harpole, P., & Fogelquist, M. (1989). *Los mariachis! An introduction to mariachi music*. Danbury, Conn.: World Music Press.

Hart, M., & Lieberman, F. (1991). *Planet drum: A celebration of percussion and rhythm*. San Francisco: HarperCollins.

Herrera-Sobek, M. (1993). *Northward bound: The Mexican immigrant experience in ballad and song*. Bloomington: Indiana University Press.

Hinojosa, T. (1995). *Frontéjas* [CD]. Cambridge, Mass.: Rounder Records.

Hoyt-Goldsmith, D. (1994). *Day of the Dead: A Mexican American celebration*. New York: Holiday House.

Jay, S. (1991). Liner notes to *Ghana: Ancient ceremonies, song and dance music* [CD]. New York: Elektra Nonesuch. (Originally released 1979.)

Jessup, L. (1996). *All hands on! An introduction to West African percussion ensembles*. Danbury, Conn.: World Music.

Kaptain, L. D. (1992). *The wood that sings: The marimba in Chiapas, Mexico*. Everett, Pa.: HoneyRock.

Kaptain, L. D. (1995). The marimba in Mexico and related areas. In J. H. Beck (ed.), *Encyclopedia of percussion* (pp. 239–256). New York: Garland.

Kobom, J. (1992). *Xylophone music from Ghana* [audiocassette]. Crown Point, Ind.: White Cliffs Media.

Kubik, G., Blades, J., & Roberts, R. (1984). Marimba. In S. Sadie (ed.), *The new Grove dictionary of musical instruments* (pp. 614–617). London: Macmillan.

Lasky, K. (1994). *Days of the Dead*. New York: Hyperion.

Lewiston, D. (recorder). (1991). *Mexico: Fiestas of Chiapas and Oaxaca* [CD]. New York: Elektra Nonesuch. (Originally released 1976.)

Llama, M. A. (producer). (1989). *Day of the Dead: A living tradition* [video]. New York: Gessler.

Llerenas, E. (producer). (1996). *La iguana: Sones jarochos from Veracruz, Mexico* [CD]. Cambridge, Mass.: Rounder Records.

Los Lobos. (1987). *La Bamba: Original motion picture soundtrack* [LP]. Los Angeles: Slash/Warner Brothers.

Los Lobos & Guerrero, L. (1995). *Papa's dream* [CD]. Redway, Calif.: Music for Little People.

Los Pregoneros del Puerto (performers). (1990). *Music of Veracruz: The sones jarochos of Los Pregoneros del Puerto* [CD]. Cambridge, Mass.: Rounder Records.

Manuel, P. (1988). *Popular music of the non-Western world: An introductory survey.* New York: Oxford University Press.

Manuel, P. (1995). *Caribbean currents: Caribbean music from rumba to reggae.* Philadelphia: Temple University Press.

Marimba Yajalón (performers). (1994). *¡Chiapas!* [CD]. Kansas City, Mo.: Heart of Wood Project.

Marre, J. (producer). (1980). *Tex-Mex: The music of the Texas-Mexican borderlands* [video]. Newton, N.J.: Harcourt Films.

Marrin, A. (1986). *Aztecs and Spaniards: Cortes and the conquest of Mexico.* New York: Atheneum.

Martinez, L. A., & Llama, M. A. (producers). (1991). *Piñatas, posadas y pastorelas* [video]. New York: Gessler.

Martínez, O. (1994). *Border people: Life and society in the U.S.-Mexico borderlands.* Tucson: University of Arizona Press.

McArthur, S., & Yoshida, H. (producers). (1995). *The JVC/Smithsonian/Folkways video anthology of music and dance of the Americas.* Vol. 6, *Central and South America II* [video]. Tokyo: JVC.

Menzel, P. (1994). *Material world: A global family portrait.* San Francisco: Sierra Club.

Merman, J. (1960). *Amigo cantando.* Delaware Water Gap, Pa.: Wide World Music.

Myers, H. (ed.) (1993). *Ethnomusicology historical and regional studies.* New York: W. W. Norton.

National Council for the Social Studies. (1994). *Expectations of excellence: Curriculum standards for social studies.* Washington, D.C.: Author.

Nye, N. S. (1995). *The tree is older than you are: A bilingual gathering of poems and stories from Mexico with paintings by Mexican artists.* New York: Simon & Schuster.

Ober, H. (1994). *How music came to the world: An ancient Mexican myth.* Boston: Houghton Mifflin.

O'Brien, L. L. (1982). Marimbas of Guatemala: The African connection. *The World of Music* 25 (2): 99–103.

Olson, D., Sheehy, D., & Perrone, C. (eds.). (1987). *Music of Latin America: Mexico, Ecuador, Brazil* (study guide for *Sounds of the World* series). Reston, Va.: Music Educators National Conference.

Orozco, J. (1994). *De Colores and other Latin-American folk songs for children.* New York: Dutton Children's Books.

Peña, M. (1985). *The Texas-Mexican conjunto: History of a working-class music.* Austin: University of Texas.

Perl, I. (1983). *Piñatas and paper flowers.* New York: Clarion.

Pettit, F. H., & Pettit, R. M. (1978). *Mexican folk toys: Festival decorations and ritual objects.* New York: Hastings House.

Reilly, M. (1992). *Mexico.* New York: Marshall Cavendish.

Ronstadt, L. (1991). *Mas canciones* [CD]. New York: Elektra/Warner Brothers.

Ross, C. (1991). *Christmas in Mexico.* Lincolnwood, Ill.: Passport.

Santoli, A. (1988). *New Americans, an oral history: Immigrants and refugees in the U.S. today.* New York: Viking Penguin.

Silverthorne, E. (1992). *Fiesta! Mexico's great celebrations.* Brookfield, Conn.: Millbrook.

Solomon, T. (1989). "La Bamba": Mass mediation and the political economy of a Mexican "folk song." Paper presented at the annual meeting of the Society for Ethnomusicology, Cambridge, Mass.

Stein, R. C. (1984). *Mexico: Enchantment of the world.* Chicago: Children's Press.

Strachwitz, C. (producer). (1994). *Corridos and tragedias de las fronteras* [CD]. El Cerrito, Calif.: Arhoolie Productions.

Sullivan, C. (ed.). (1994). *Here is my kingdom: Hispanic-American literature and arts for young people.* New York: Harry N. Abrams.

Tapia, O. M., & Los Mecateros (1994). *Songs of Mexico II* [CD]. Los Angeles: JVC.

Valdez, L. (producer). (1987). *La Bamba* [video]. Burbank, Calif.: RCA/Columbia Pictures Home Video.

Valens, R. (1958). *The best of Ritchie Valens* [LP]. Los Angeles: Del-Fi.

Wiggins, T., & Kobom, J. (1992). *Xylophone music from Ghana.* Crown Point, Ind.: White Cliffs Media.

Resources for Teachers and Students
~~

AUDIO RECORDINGS

Conjunto Alma Jarocha (performers). (1994). *Sones jarochos* [CD]. El Cerrito, Calif.: Arhoolie Productions. (Original recording 1979.)

Hinojosa, T. (1995). *Frontéjas* [CD]. Cambridge, Mass.: Rounder Records.

Jay, S. (recorder). (1991). *Ghana: Ancient ceremonies, song and dance music* [CD]. New York: Electra Nonesuch. (Originally released 1979.)

Kobom, J. (1992). *Xylophone music from Ghana* [audiocassette]. Crown Point, Ind.: White Cliffs Media.

Lewiston, D. (recorder). (1991). *Mexico: Fiestas of Chiapas and Oaxaca* [CD]. New York: Elektra Nonesuch. (Originally released 1976.)

Llerenas, E. (producer). (1996). *La iguana: Sones jarochos from Veracruz, Mexico* [CD]. Cambridge, Mass.: Rounder Records.

Los Lobos. (1987). *La Bamba: Original motion picture soundtrack* [LP]. Los Angeles: Slash/Warner Brothers.

Los Lobos. (1988). *La pistola y el corazón* [CD]. Los Angeles: Slash/Warner Brothers.

Los Lobos & Guerrero, L. (1995). *Papa's dream* [CD]. Redway, Calif.: Music for Little People.

Los Pregoneros del Puerto (performers). (1990). *Music of Veracruz: The sones jarochos of Los Pregoneros del Puerto* [CD]. Cambridge, Mass.: Rounder Records.

Marimba Yajalón (performers). (1994). *¡Chiapas!* [CD]. Kansas City, Mo.: Heart of Wood Project.

Ronstadt, L. (1991). *Mas canciones* [CD]. New York: Elektra/Warner Brothers.

Strachwitz, C. (producer). (1994). *Corridos and tragedias de las fronteras* [CD]. El Cerrito, Calif.: Arhoolie Productions.

Tapia, O. M., & Los Mecateros. (1994). *Songs of Mexico II* [CD]. Los Angeles: JVC.

Valens, R. (1958). *The best of Ritchie Valens* [LP]. Los Angeles: Del-Fi.

VIDEO RECORDINGS

Ballet Folclorico Nacional de México. (1990). New York: Gessler.

Chulas fronteras. (1976). El Cerrito, Calif.: Brazos Films.

Llama, M. A. (producer). (1989). *Day of the Dead: A living tradition.* New York: Gessler.

Marre, J. (producer). (1980). *Tex-Mex: The music of the Texas-Mexican borderlands.* Newton, N.J.: Harcourt Films.

Martinez, L. A., & Llama, M. A. (producers). (1991). *Piñatas, posadas y pastorelas.* New York: Gessler.

McArthur, S., & Yoshida, H. (producers). (1995). *The JVC/Smithsonian/Folkways video anthology of music and dance of the Americas.* Vol. 6, *Central and South America II.* Tokyo: JVC.

Valdez, L. (producer). (1987). *La Bamba.* Burbank, Calif.: RCA/Columbia Pictures Home Video.

MUSIC SOURCES

Campbell, P. S. (1995). Steven Loza on Latino music. *Music Educators Journal* 82 (2): 45–52.

Delacre, L. (1990). *Las Navidades: Popular Christmas songs from Latin America.* New York: Scholastic.

George, L. (1987). *Teaching the music of six different cultures.* Danbury, Conn.: World Music.

Harpole, P., & Fogelquist, M. (1989). *Los Mariachis! An introduction to mariachi music.* Danbury, Conn.: World Music.

Merman, J. (1960). *Amigo cantando.* Delaware Water Gap, Pa.: Wide World Music.

Olson, D., Sheehy, D., & Perrone, C. (eds.). (1987). *Music of Latin America: Mexico, Ecuador, Brazil* (study guide for *Sounds of the World* series). Reston, Va.: Music Educators National Conference.

Orozco, J. (1994). *De Colores and other Latin-American folk songs for children.* New York: Dutton Children's Books.

Yurchenco, H. (1967). *A fiesta of folk songs from Spain and Latin America.* New York: G. P. Putnam's Sons.

NONFICTION BOOKS FOR STUDENTS

Ancona, G. (1993). *Pablo remembers: The fiesta of the Day of the Dead.* New York: Lothrop, Lee & Shepard.

Ancona, G. (1994). *The piñata maker.* San Diego, Calif.: Harcourt Brace.

Arnold, H. (1996). *Mexico.* Austin, Tex.: Raintree Steck-Vaughn.

Chrisp, P. (1993). *The Spanish conquests in the new world.* New York: Thomson.

Hoyt-Goldsmith, D. (1994). *Day of the Dead: A Mexican American celebration.* New York: Holiday House.

Irizarry, C. (1987). *Passport to Mexico.* New York: Franklin Watts.

James, I. (1989). *Inside Mexico.* New York: Franklin Watts.

Katz, W. L. (1993). *A history of multicultural America: Minorities today.* Austin, Tex.: Raintree Steck-Vaughn.

Lankford, M. (1994). *Quinceañera: A Latina's journey to womanhood.* Brookfield, Conn.: Millbrook.

Lasky, K. (1994). *Days of the Dead.* New York: Hyperion.

Reilly, M. (1992). *Mexico.* New York: Marshall Cavendish.

Silverthorne, E. (1992). *Fiesta! Mexico's great celebrations.* Brookfield, Conn.: Millbrook.

Stein, R. C. (1984). *Mexico: Enchantment of the world.* Chicago: Children's Press.

FICTION BOOKS FOR STUDENTS

Bernhard, E., & Bernhard, D. (1994). *The tree that rains: The flood myth of the Huichol Indians of Mexico.* New York: Holiday House.

Ets, M. H., & Labastida, A. (1979). *Nine days to Christmas.* New York: Viking.

Fisher, L. (ed.). (1988). *Pyramid of the sun, pyramid of the moon.* New York: Macmillan.

Haskins, J. (1989). *Count your way through Mexico.* Minneapolis: Carolrhoda.

Ober, H. (1994). *How music came to the world: An ancient Mexican myth.* Boston: Houghton Mifflin.

{ chapter 13 }

MUSIC AND THE CURRICULAR IMAGINATION

One of the long-standing traditions in Beth's urban middle school was the annual trip to the Youth Symphony concert. Although she looked forward to the performance, she sensed that her students felt differently about it because the music was so far removed from their daily experience. "In the past, the students have enjoyed getting out of school, but they have not developed a love of the music they were hearing," she admitted. One semester, Beth set out to make a change in the way she prepared students for the concert, hoping to make the experience more meaningful and perhaps more lasting than just a day's excursion.

Fortunately, Beth learned of the program for the concert several months in advance, giving her time to plan and to gather resources. Among the compositions the orchestra would perform was Elgar's Enigma Variations. She remembered hearing them once before but didn't know too much about them.

Beth began to listen to and study this work, finding out how Elgar had paid tribute to his family and friends through a set of variations, each bearing the honoree's initials or nickname. The music of each variation reflected something about the honoree's personality or relationship to Elgar. Once Beth knew what to listen for, she could recognize what Elgar did to portray the chapel organist's bulldog running down the hill to paddle in the water, or the way the abrupt violin figures referred to the young musician, Dorabella, who stuttered and loved to ride her bike. Beth was certain that her students would enjoy hearing the stories behind the music, but she also wanted to interest them in the musical techniques Elgar used to show the endearing quirks and traits of his family and friends. As she kept searching for ideas, Beth decided to include paintings and poems in her lessons, feeling that students might understand the notion of "tribute" more fully if she used several art forms.

Beth planned questions and activities that would lead students to realize that writers, musicians, and artists can characterize the individuality and influence of significant people through words, sounds, and images. Over several days, as students listened to and learned about the Enigma Variations, Beth encouraged them to think of influential people in their lives, and the ways they might create a poem, drawing, or piece of music to represent those individuals. The students eagerly took up the challenge, some choosing famous celebrities, others selecting close friends or family members. One student devoted lunch and recess time to work on his project. With the aid of a software program, he creat-

ed a tribute to a famous basketball player in the form of a musical work with four movements to parallel the four quarters of a basketball game. All in all, the students' tributes were funny, imaginative, revealing, and moving.

When the sixth graders finally attended the Youth Symphony performance, Beth was gratified to see how engaged and absorbed the students were during the performance, watching their smiles of recognition as they heard the variations they had studied. Because they had grappled with the challenges of creating their own tributes, they understood the performance in a deeper, more immediate way. As Beth reflected on what she had learned about her students and the music, she felt satisfied and eager to move on to another new project.

The curricular imagination is at work whenever teachers consider what is possible and turn those possibilities into the realities of classroom experience. When this imagination is lacking, curriculum work feels like a technical exercise—dull, impersonal, and mundane. When a teacher or group of teachers give rein to the possible, curriculum work feels engaging and challenging. At its best, curriculum planning is a form of artistry involving essential elements of passion, craftsmanship, and caring.

Passion is at the heart of the teacher's creative impulse. Teachers are frequently passionate about the subjects and students they teach, particularly as a result of years of study and commitment to their fields. Strong convictions about the content of the curriculum and the quality of schooling are expressed through innovative interdisciplinary projects and plans. Invention may also spring from a deep-seated desire to communicate ideas to students or to enable students to communicate their own ideas through music, creative writing, drawing, or other expressive forms. Individual interests often fuel the imagination as teachers "embellish their teaching with the kind of originality, flair, and panache that artists bring to their projects" (Rubin, 1991, p. 56). Passion is crucial in collaborative work to convince others of the potential and integrity of an interdisciplinary idea; passion is also needed to sustain the momentum of teachers' ideas through the inevitable ebbs and flows of a new project.

Kristin, a preservice teacher in both elementary and Spanish education, speaks about the importance of originality in her search for curricular ideas and materials:

> Usually dead ends inspire me the most. Then, I think, no one else has really thought of this before, in this way. Thus my work is truly valuable. I dislike ideas that seem overused or trite. I don't want to do something that anyone could easily do in the same way.

Craftsmanship in curriculum design involves a potent blend of knowledge and skill. Teachers draw upon a base of disciplinary knowledge to generate new ideas and test valid connections among themes and subject areas. Yet, especially in interdisciplinary work, this base of knowledge is continually being modified, reorganized, and enlarged as we confront what we know and what we don't know. Hodgkin (1976) writes: "We learn best as teachers; we teach best as learners. The effort to communicate strengthens knowledge and to be an authority is to know how to doubt" (p. 3). There is a certain humility in acknowledging that you cannot be an expert in all things, yet there is also a freedom to inquire that comes with that acknowledgment.

A well-stocked storehouse of metaphors, images, and examples is invaluable for interdisciplinary connections. The psychologist Keith Simonton describes a theory of scientific genius by using a metaphor of the playroom (Ramo & Rosenberg, 1993). He compares a genius who solves perplexing problems in a discipline through the innovative combination of the discipline's elements to a child with many sets of Legos. The child with many Legos has a far greater chance of creating a masterpiece by combining the pieces in novel ways than does a child with a basic set of just a few pieces. We are reminded of this "Lego theory" every time we come across music and materials that are compelling and full of possibility. In staying on the lookout for new works and materials and remaining open to their potential, teachers find inspiration and exercise their creativity.

Craftsmanship is also shown through the ways teachers combine elements of the educational experience to make a satisfying whole, which is parallel to artistic processes. For example, teachers may use a broad theme or essential questions as unifying devices to show relationships throughout a series of lessons. Within the project, they may attend to elements of variety and contrast so that the educational experience will sustain student interest and enthusiasm. A balance among elements is achieved when teachers attend to the ways subjects complement each other and the ways essential content and processes of various disciplines are emphasized. There is also a sense of artistry in the way transitions from one element of the lesson to the next allow the lesson to unfold naturally and inevitably. Another way that artistry is expressed is through the improvisatory give-and-take that results from honoring unexpected events in the classroom and responding flexibly to those teachable moments.

Joanna, whose journal in Chapter 4 showed her depth of preparation to teach Zwilich's *Concerto Grosso 1985*, describes how the process of designing interdisciplinary lessons serves as an exercise of artistic craftsmanship for her:

An arts metaphor says it best for me—how I choreograph a lesson. This seems really important, maybe more so when designing interdisciplinary lessons. The dance we do through a lesson—the bridges, hinges, transitions, connections, pace, order, etc.—has a powerful role to play in how successfully students are engaged and learning. If conscious connections are made from music to poetry, art, movement, culture, geography, and back again, the lesson could take on more "gem-like" qualities.

Care in curriculum work involves consideration of the ultimate aims and goals of education and evaluation of the way those goals are attained in school practice. Eisner (1990) challenges teachers by stating that "the purpose of education in the broadest sense, and particularly given the characteristics of our world today, is to succeed at the paradoxical activity of helping children become what we are not" (p. 62). What qualities, traits, and dispositions are important for students to acquire and how does the school community and the curriculum foster the development of students as individuals? What habits of mind and heart are acquired in classroom settings? In creative curriculum design, teachers model intellectual curiosity by asking good questions and sharing insights they have gained from listening to new works, reading widely and deeply, conversing with colleagues, and seeking out new opportunities to learn. Teachers model intellectual flexibility by showing a willingness to seek new information and to modify old ideas when they no longer hold true. They also show intellectual maturity when they see complex problems and issues from many perspectives.

The Facets Model and the Interdisciplinary Curriculum

A central premise of this book is that intense engagement *with* a work and deep comprehension *of* a work come from efforts to describe its structure, to consider its contextual content, and to contemplate its expressive meaning. These essential processes led to the development of the facets model. As we have experimented with the use of this model in our own classrooms, we have noticed how often engagement with a work has led us outward to related areas of the curriculum as natural and necessary extensions of our musical study. In turn, understanding gained from study in related areas has augmented our perception and performance of the work. These insights have led us to believe that teachers can use the facets model as a starting point and as a helpful strategy in designing curriculum projects that are balanced, valid, and comprehensive.

Creative teachers who take pride in the originality of their plans and derive satisfaction from knowing that their personal and professional talents have been put to good use are inspiring models of the curricular imagination. Although the demands of time and energy are considerable whenever teachers invent curriculum from scratch, the corresponding benefits are just as significant. Teachers who are considering interdisciplinary work for the first time may wish to begin with projects of small and manageable scope before taking on more ambitious initiatives, such as all-school projects or collaborations across many areas of the curriculum.

The process for designing an interdisciplinary curriculum cannot be described adequately as a linear series of steps, insomuch as the playful exploration of possibilities and the serendipitous discovery of connections may move teachers and students in productive but unpredictable directions. As a new curricular initiative takes shape, however, the questions provided in Figure 13.1 can help teachers define the purpose for the project, identify the participants who will be involved, and clarify the relationships of content to be emphasized.

Figure 13.1
Facets of the Interdisciplinary Curriculum

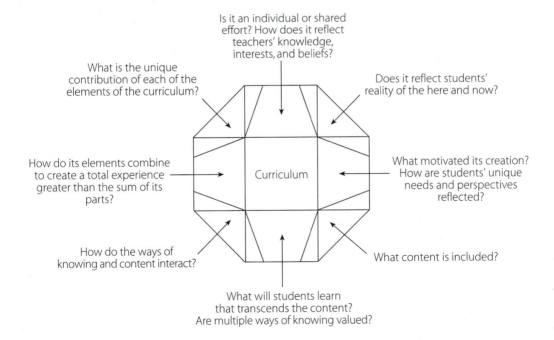

The questions—Is it an individual or shared effort? How does it reflect teachers' knowledge, interests, and beliefs? Does it reflect students' reality of the here and now? What motivated its creation? How are students' unique needs and perspectives reflected?—clarify who the curriculum designers are, and for whom they are designing. Individual teachers often take the initiative to make the curriculum in their own classrooms more interdisciplinary in nature by emphasizing how ideas and concepts connect. Collaborations among colleagues are also powerful, because complementary areas of expertise are widely distributed within a school community. Music teachers develop expertise in music, of course, but also possess expertise in teaching music to students of many ages and levels. Classroom teachers, who hold many areas of expertise and content knowledge, have a well-developed understanding of student development particular to the students they teach. This is why it is essential, whenever possible, to bring music specialists and classroom teachers together to work on interdisciplinary curriculum planning in a mutually satisfying and intellectually stimulating way.

Teachers' knowledge, interests, and beliefs often provide the impetus for curriculum planning. In Chapter 1, we recommended that teachers survey their musical idiocultures and those of their students to find common areas of interest or unique areas of knowledge or expertise as starting points. Nothing is more real and immediate to students than their musical worlds; music is a part of the way they make sense of their experience. Students' knowledge, interests, and beliefs also motivate the creation of curriculum. Teachers design with these interests in mind, as well as consideration of the developmental fit of the lesson and its appropriateness for the school community.

The questions—What content is included? What is the unique contribution of each of the elements of the curriculum? How do its elements combine to create a total experience greater than the sum of its parts?—are essential for teachers to address. Music is an expressive form of human experience; through music and the arts, we intensify and deepen thoughts and feelings. Through the arts, the achievements and aspirations of individuals and groups are represented through culture and history. The way these ideas are manifested in the curricular goals of school subjects—music, art, dance, theater, literature, and social studies—demonstrates how intertwined and complementary they are. As school subjects, these disciplines offer students the opportunity to experience the world through many forms—through sound, image, gesture, narrative, and symbol.

The integrity of content is of primary importance in the interdisciplinary curriculum. Teachers must attend to the integrity of each form of study for students to acquire a thorough and sequential grounding in the knowledge and ways of thinking central to the disciplines. But as the lessons in this book have demonstrated, it is also possible to attend to the integrity of combined disciplines and the way they overlap without compromising their validity or trivializing the importance of particular subject areas. Sensitive, artistic, and imaginative correlations encourage the development of concepts and perspectives that transcend separate disciplines. As one workshop participant put it, "The right equation for putting two subjects together must be 1 + 1 = 3."

The questions—What will students learn that transcends the content? Are multiple ways of knowing valued? How do the ways of knowing and content interact?—are central to the design of an interdisciplinary curriculum. Teachers are committed to the challenge of assisting students to realize their potential as competent, curious, and caring individuals. Music and the arts cultivate students' perception of and aesthetic response to the sensory qualities of experience. The impression of an aesthetic experience lingers with us long after the encounter of a work; we preserve and cherish those works that have profound impact on our thoughts and feelings. We study the works that others who are separated from us by time or place have valued, and we empathize with them as fellow human beings. When students work with the forms and materials of a discipline to produce and create new works, they question, interpret, and represent meaning from their own sense of the world.

The ways the subject is explored are as important as the subject itself. To know music, for example, students must perceive, produce, and reflect upon qualities of sound. Certainly, we can learn *about* music through other types of experience, but without an emphasis on sound and thinking *in* music, the fullness of the encounter will be diminished. The ways we learn about art, literature, dance, or the social world must also honor ways of knowing in those disciplines as well. To design interdisciplinary projects that are comprehensive and engaging, teachers must not only select the content to be taught but also consider how that content will be experienced.

In the preface to this book, we explained how the title, *Sound Ways of Knowing*, is a wordplay on the double meaning of *sound*. Through music, we explore who we are and how we relate to others, particularly through the realms of expression, history, and culture. The strength, validity, and substance of the students' educational experiences are influenced and made possible by the artistry of teachers. This artistry is reflected in the care they take in designing curriculum and their imagination, craftsmanship, and passion.

References

Eisner, E. W. (1990). A developmental agenda: Creative curriculum development and practice. *Journal of Curriculum and Supervision* 6 (1): 62–73.

Hodgkin, R. A. (1976). *Born curious: New perspectives in educational theory.* London: John Wiley & Sons.

Ramo, J. C., & Rosenberg, D. (June 28, 1993). The puzzle of genius. *Newsweek,* pp. 46–51.

Rubin, L. (1991). The arts and an artistic curriculum. In G. Willis & W. H. Schubert (eds.), *Reflections from the heart of educational inquiry: Understanding curriculum and teaching through the arts* (pp. 49–59). Albany: State University of New York Press.

Notes

Chapter 2

1. We use the term "work" or "artwork" broadly as a reference to any example or process involving music, art, poetry, literature, dance, or theater. For an engaging critique of the concept of an aesthetic "work" as an object that distances the perceiver from full representations of meaning and understanding, see *Music Matters: A new philosophy of music education* (Elliott, 1995).

Chapter 4

1. The stages of interaction with a musical work in Table 4.1 are based very loosely on a model for use of innovations described in Hall, Loucks, Rutherford, and Newlove (1975).

Chapter 5

1. For example, Haack (1970) found that junior high school wind instrumentalists who were taught to recognize the stylistic characteristics of classicism and romanticism in both art and music were more successful at classifying the style of music exemplars than were similar students taught to recognize style characteristics in music only.

2. Some museums provide opportunities for visually impaired people to experience paintings by touching them.

3. A lesson plan that explores multiple facets of "Simple Gifts" and its use in *Appalachian Spring* can be found in Ch. 7.

Chapter 6

1. From "Song of the Train" by David McCord (Cole, 1984, pp. 34–35).

2. From "Slowly" by James Reeves (Blishen, 1984, p. 138).

3. The times indicated in Table 6.5 correspond to the recording of "Farandole" from *L'Arlésienne* performed by the New York Philharmonic, Leonard Bernstein conducting. This is the same recording used in the set of CDs that accompany the *Music and You* textbook series (Davidson, Ferguson, Staton, & Staton, 1990).

4. Variations on "Simple Gifts" is recorded in several versions: the version from the full ballet and the version from *Appalachian Spring Suite*. Some performances utilize a full orchestra; others use the original chamber instrumentation. The listening chart in this lesson is based on *Appalachian Spring Suite* for full orchestra. If you intend to use the listening guide with another version of Variations on "Simple Gifts" you will need to make some minor changes in the descriptors.

Chapter 8

1. The complete list of content standards is provided in Ch. 3.

2. See "Controversy in the Curriculum: Should You Sing Dixie?" and "Controversy in the Curriculum: The Use of Dialect" in Ch. 10 for further discussion of the way changes in text compromise the authenticity of songs.

3. These texts are taken from *Songs of the Civil War* (Silber and Silverman, 1995).

Chapter 9

1. Brueghel's name can be found variously written as *Brueghel, Bruegel, Breughel,* or *Breugel.*

2. The performance of the dance is discussed in *Orchesography* (Arbeau 1588/1967). The "Gesture of the first passage," as described on pp. 187–189, has relatively easy steps and sword gestures.

3. The exact dates for the Renaissance are debated. Some scholars contend the Renaissance continued outside Italy until as late as 1750. Others argue that there was no Renaissance at all, but that what happened in Italy was an extension of developments that had been occurring throughout the Middle Ages. This chapter takes the starting point of the Italian Renaissance as the beginning of the fourteenth century and the end as 1633, when Galileo was forced to deny his discoveries in astronomy (Wood, 1993, p. 46). Musicologists usually date the Renaissance period in Western art music from 1430 to 1600 (Lockwood, 1980, p. 736).

4. The bubonic plague, initially spread by fleas from infected rats, has mutated to pneumonic plague, which is spread through the air. An epidemic, which claimed several lives, began in India in August 1994 (Richardson, 1995).

5. Literally, "The Feast of the Vow."

6. This retelling of the feast is derived from accounts given in Cartellieri (1929), Chamberlin (1969), Fallows (1991), Lafortune-Martel (1984), Vaughn (1970), and Wright (1979, 1980) based on primary sources of Mathieu D'Escouchy (1858–1864) and Olivier De La Marche (1883–1888), among others.

Chapter 10

1. Recordings of these bugle calls can be found in *The Civil War: Its Music and Its Sounds* (Eastman Wind Ensemble, 1990).

2. These essential questions for interdisciplinary study of the Civil War period come from Glascock & Mitchell (1990).

3. National Council for the Social Studies (1994, p. 82).

4. The list on page 206 is drawn from the Consortium of National Arts Education Associations (1994, pp. 42, 44–45).

5. The chart on page 234 was inspired by Lovell (1972).

6. It will be important to clarify with students how their perceptions are formed. Perceptions may differ based on their own ethnic backgrounds, the ethnic and socioeconomic characteristics of their community, and their exposure to either broad information or narrow stereotypes via the media. Discuss the role of individual perceptions and generalizations. How can they sometimes be helpful? How can they sometimes be misleading or dangerous?

Chapter 11

1. Inspiration for this example came from a paper by Richard Jones-Bauman (1995).

2. See Meintjes (1990) for an intriguing discussion of this recording.

3. This continuum was adapted from Palmer (1992).

4. At the time of publication, the Faces of Sorrow exhibit could be accessed on the World Wide Web. It can be found at this address:

   http://www.i3tele.com/photoperspectives/facesofsorrow/html/exhibition.html

or by searching for the words *faces of sorrow* with a search engine.

5. Although "Ganga: Odkad seke nismo zapjevale" reminded Ruzica of a funeral lament, it is not.

6. Thanks to Dane Kusic for clarifying the meaning of *ganga*.

Chapter 12

1. This format is adapted from Grant and Sleeter (1989).

2. For further directions on piñata making, see *Fiesta! Mexico's Great Celebrations* (Silverthorne, 1992), *Piñatas and Paper Flowers* (Perl, 1983), or *Christmas in Mexico* (Ross, 1991).

3. This definition of Mesoamerica is drawn from Carmack, Gasco, & Gossen (1996). It means "Middle America," referring to all the indigenous peoples of Central America before and after Spanish contact.

4. In 1519, the Spaniards journeyed to Tenochtitlán. With two million people, this Aztec capital may have been the biggest city in the world. Montezuma welcomed Cortes and his men with wreaths of flowers. Soon after, the Spaniards betrayed their hosts, murdering Montezuma and driving the Aztecs from the city. As bloody as the conflicts were, the real villain was smallpox, brought to the New World by the conquerors. Smallpox decimated the Aztecs and many other native peoples of America. When Cortes arrived in Mexico, there were more than 20 million Indians; by 1620, there were not even 1 million left. Spaniards continued domination of the Aztecs, Mayans, and Incas in their colonization of the Americas (Chrisp, 1993; Marrin, 1986; Menzel, 1994; Stein, 1984).

5. Mesoamericans accept that they were invaded and defeated in wars by the Spanish but insist that they were never conquered (Carmack, Gasco, & Gossen, 1996).

6. The diatonic harp is limited to the pitches of a single scale, or key, in contrast to the orchestral harp, which can play all the pitches of the chromatic scale.

7. The version of "Víbora de la mar" in Example 12.2 was recorded by David Tovey in an Indian village outside of Oaxaca, Mexico.

8. See Ch. 11 for a discussion of traditional and popular music.

PERMISSIONS AND CREDITS

49 "Sometimes Running," from *In Fact* by John Ciardi. Used by permission of the Ciardi Family.

61 Photograph of Ellen Taaffe Zwilich by Andrew Sacks. Courtesy of Andrew Sacks and the *New York Times*. Reproduced by permission of Music Associates of America.

62 Excerpts from *Concerto Grosso 1985* by Ellen Taaffe Zwilich. Copyright © 1985 by Mobart Music Publications. Reprinted by permission.

71 *The Sleeping Gypsy* by Henri Rousseau. The Museum of Modern Art, New York. Gift of Mrs. Simon Guggenheim. Photograph copyright © 1997 The Museum of Modern Art, New York.

80 "I Am Growing a Glorious Garden" from *Something Big Has Been Here* by Jack Prelutsky. Copyright © 1990. Used by permission of Greenwillow Books, a division of William Morrow and Company, Inc.

97 *Back I, Back II, Back III, Back IV* by Henri Matisse. Photograph by Lee Stalsworth. Used by permission of Hirshhorn Museum and Sculpture Garden, Smithsonian Institution. Gift of Joseph H. Hirshhorn, 1966.

113 "Jump or Jiggle" from *Another Here and Now Story Book* by Lucy Sprague Mitchell. Copyright © 1937 by E. P. Dutton, renewed © 1965 by Lucy Sprague Mitchell. Used by permission of Dutton Children's Books, a division of Penguin Books USA, Inc.

119 "Whirligig Beetles" from *Joyful Noise*. Text copyright © 1988 by Paul Fleischman, illustration copyright © 1988 by Eric Beddows. Used by permission of HarperCollins Publishers.

124 Shakers' Slat Back Chairs, with Rockers. Reprinted from *Illustrated Catalogue and Price List of Shakers' Chairs* (Washington, D.C.: Smithsonian Institution Press), page 22, by permission of the publisher. Copyright © 1972.

135–56 Portions of Chapter 8 were first published as K. K. Veblen, J. R. Barrett, & C. W. McCoy. "Where did you come from? Where do you go? Searching for context in the music curriculum." *Quarterly Journal of Music Teaching and Learning* 6 (3) 1995: 46–56. We are grateful to the editors, who have granted permission for use of this material.

151 "Dixie" reproduced from the Americana Collection, Mills Music Library, University of Wisconsin–Madison. Reproduced with permission.

163 *Children's Games* by Pieter Brueghel the Elder. Used by permission of Kunsthistorisches Museum, Vienna.

177 *The Garden of Love at the Court of Philip the Good* (1432). Photograph copyright © Réunion des Musées Nationaux.

198   Copy of a composite tintype of the 1st Brigade, 3rd Division, 15th Army Corps Band, Wis., Civil War. Reprinted with the permission of the State Historical Society of Wisconsin, negative number (X3) 35083, lot 2947.

216   *News from the War* from *Harper's Weekly*, June 14, 1862. Wood engraving by Winslow Homer. The Metropolitan Museum of Art, Harris Brisbane Dick Fund, 1929. All rights reserved, The Metropolitan Museum of Art.

232   "All God's Chillun Got Wings" from *The Books of American Negro Spirituals* by James Weldon Johnson and J. Rosamond Johnson. Copyright © 1925, 1926 by the Viking Press, Inc., renewed 1953 by Lawrence Brown, 1953, © 1954 by Grace Nail Johnson and J. Rosamond Johnson. Used by permission of Viking Penguin, a division of Penguin Books USA, Inc.

261   "Kad ja podjoh na Benbašu" courtesy of Smithsonian Folkways Recordings (SF 40407). Translation by T. Levin and A. Petrović.

271   Excerpt from *How Music Came to the World* by Hal Ober. Text copyright © 1994 by Hal Ober. Reprinted by permission of Houghton Mifflin Co. All rights reserved.

273   The poem "Piñata" reprinted by permission of Jennifer Clement. Translation by Consuelo de Aerenlund.

276   "La Piñata/The Piñata," from *"De Colores" and Other Latin American Folk Songs for Children* by José-Luis Orozco. Copyright © 1994 by José-Luis Orozco. Used by permission of Dutton Children's Books, a division of Penguin Books USA, Inc.

285   "Our Walls Are Keening." Reprinted with the permission of Atheneum Books for Young Readers, an imprint of Simon & Schuster Children's Publishing Division, from *Aztecs and Spaniards* by Albert Marrin. Copyright © 1986 Albert Marrin.

292   Photographs of Ghanaian xylophone from *Xylophone Music from Ghana* by Trevor Wiggins and Joseph Kobom, page 6. Reproduced by permission of White Cliffs Media, Inc.

Name Index

SUBJECT INDEX

Page numbers in boldface indicate works actually provided in the book,
for example, reproductions of paintings, songs, poems, etc.